D1603227

STUDIES IN ORIENTAL CULTURE

NUMBER 1

THE ŌNIN WAR
History of Its Origins and Background
With a Selective Translation of *The Chronicle of Ōnin*

Provinces of Premodern Japan

OCEAN

Scale of Miles

SEA OF JAPAN

PACIFIC

MUTSU

DEWA

IWAKI

IWASHIRO

SHIMOTSUKE

HITACHI

SHIMŌSA

KAZUSA

AWA

ECHIGO

KŌZUKE

MUSASHI

SAGAMI

IZU

SADO

SHINANO

KAI

SURUGA

TŌTOMI

NOTO

ETCHŪ

HIDA

MINO

OWARI

MIKAWA

SHIMA

KAGA

ECHIZEN

L. Biwa

ŌMI

IGA

ISE

WAKASA

TANGO

TAMBA

YAMASHIRO

YAMATO

TAJIMA

INABA

SETTSU

IZUMI

KAWACHI

KII

OKI

HŌKI

MIMASAKA

BIZEN

HARIMA

AWAJI

IZUMO

BITCHŪ

SANUKI

AWA

IWAMI

BINGO

Inland Sea

IYO

TOSA

AKI

SUWŌ

NAGATO

TSUSHIMA

IKI

CHIKUZEN

BUZEN

BUNGO

HIZEN

CHIKUGO

HIGO

HYŪGA

SATSUMA

ŌSUMI

THE ŌNIN WAR

BY H. PAUL VARLEY

History of Its Origins and Background
With a Selective Translation of
The Chronicle of Ōnin

1967

COLUMBIA UNIVERSITY PRESS

NEW YORK & LONDON

H. Paul Varley is Assistant Professor of Japanese History
at Columbia University.

To My Mother

AND

To My Wife Betty Jane

STUDIES IN ORIENTAL CULTURE

Edited at Columbia University

Preface

In contrast to the intensive study now being made by Western scholars of Japanese history from approximately the seventeenth century on, very little specialized research has been undertaken in recent years on pre-Tokugawa affairs. Professor Ivan Morris's *The World of the Shining Prince* is a valuable contribution to our understanding of Heian cultural history and Professor John Hall's *Government and Local Power in Japan, 500 to 1700,* published this year, has established a new level of sophistication in the interpretation of Japanese institutional developments in the premodern era. Since I completed the present study before the publication of Professor Hall's book, I did not have the opportunity to consider his ideas when formulating my own interpretations of the nature of Kamakura and Muromachi institutions. I would be enormously gratified if my efforts were regarded as a useful supplement to the work he has begun. Finally, I would like to call attention to Professor Minoru Shinoda's *The Founding of the Kamakura Shogunate, 1180–1185,* a monograph on the origins of military rule in Japan which treats in detail the events immediately preceding the narrative undertaken here.

Acknowledgments

My first expression of appreciation must go to Columbia University and the United States Government, whose financial support made possible the undertaking of this work. In 1962 and 1963 I studied in Tokyo under a Columbia Traveling Fellowship in Chinese and Japanese; thereafter I was able to complete my research and writing in New York with the aid of a National Defense Foreign Language Fellowship.

Professor Donald Keene has supported me at each stage of my studies. It was he, in fact, who originally suggested *The Chronicle of Ōnin* as a translation project. He also provided invaluable linguistic assistance that made possible completion of the translation as it now stands.

During my stay in Japan I was counseled by Professor Fujiki Kunihiko and Mr. Kuwayama Kōnen, both of Tokyo University. Mr. Kuwayama tutored me over a period of many months in the intricacies of Muromachi language. He also directed and largely shaped my approach to the study of medieval Japan.

To Professor Ivan Morris I owe particular thanks. It would be impossible to calculate accurately the number of hours he spent guiding me through the final stages of translation and writing. Suffice it to say that we met constantly over a period of some seven or eight months and that our relationship, so far as I am concerned, was an ideal one for the completion of a work such as this.

Professor Herschel Webb made a number of valuable suggestions concerning the expository portions of the work and I have tried to incorporate them in the final draft. Thanks are also due to Professors Hans Bielenstein, Yoshito Hakeda, and Marius Jansen for reading and commenting on the original manuscript. Finally, may I express my appreciation to Miss Miwa Kai and Professor Philip Yampolsky of the East Asian Library of Columbia University for their help with materials.

Columbia University, 1966   H. Paul Varley

Contents

x *Contents*

PART TWO

Illustrations

The drawings on pages 139, 168, 181, and 191, by Warren Infield, are based on the Mongol Scroll, painted *ca.* 1293.

PART ONE

Introduction

Japan's age of rule by military government (Bakufu)
extended from approximately 1185 until 1868. During this span
of nearly seven centuries we can distinguish three broad periods:
1) the first attempt at central control under the Bakufu from its
founding in 1185 until the Ōnin War (1467–77); 2) a century
of near anarchy and intermittent warfare in the provinces until
reunification in 1568; 3) three centuries of effective central government under Nobunaga (1534–82), Hideyoshi (1536–98) and
the Tokugawa (to 1868).

This study deals with the first period, and is an examination
both of the institutional development of military government from
its inception until the mid-fifteenth century and of the Ōnin War,
which marked the end of this initial attempt at central control.
One of the chief aims will be to demonstrate the institutional continuity from pre-Kamakura days through the first centuries of
Bakufu rule. Both the founding of the Kamakura Bakufu in 1185
and the transition to the Ashikaga Bakufu[1] in the early fourteenth

[1] The Ashikaga Bakufu was established in 1336 by Ashikaga Takauji (1305–
58). It is also known as the Muromachi Bakufu after the location in north-

century are thus shown, not as revolutionary breaks with the past,
but as evolutionary stages in the history of these years.

(Perhaps the most distinctive characteristic of the first three centuries of military rule was the Bakufu's attempt to use the estate
(*shōen*) system, an institution of former times related to the imperial court, as a means of extending its influence throughout the
land. The pattern of estate-holding was in fundamental opposition
to the growth of a warrior society; yet Bakufu leaders felt impelled
to rely upon the relative stability of the estates to manage areas outside their direct control. In fact it is possible to trace the history of
the Kamakura and early Ashikaga periods in terms of Bakufu-
estate relations. Much of the success of the Kamakura Bakufu was
due to the orderly arrangement of estates in distant provinces.
Once these estates began to weaken in the late thirteenth and early
fourteenth centuries, the Bakufu itself was obliged to move its center of operations westward.

The Bakufu was also forced to expand its regional structure
when it could no longer rely fully upon the estates. By the mid-
fourteenth century Ashikaga leaders had reluctantly granted extensive powers to a group of vassals or provincial officers, known as
constable-daimyo (*shugo-daimyō*), who ruled their domains in a
nearly autonomous manner. It was the balance of power between
these constable-daimyo and the Bakufu that dominated the years
leading to the Ōnin War. Failure of this balance was as disastrous
to the constable-daimyo as it was to the Bakufu; for the constable,
who had imposed his rule over a wide area in a short space of time,
was unable to dispense with Bakufu support despite his own
strongly decentralist tendencies.

The Ōnin War, which marked the end of the Bakufu-constable
balance, was a long and costly conflict centered for more than a
decade in the capital city of Kyoto. While the great constable-
daimyo families attempted to settle their differences here, a more
vigorous class of deputy or lower grade warriors took *de facto* control in the provinces. The first period of military government had

---

eastern Kyoto where the third Ashikaga shogun, Yoshimitsu (1358–1408), erected
his shogunal palace.

come to an end, owing, it would appear, to a lack of local institutions needed to replace the outmoded estate system. Institutional development at the upper and intermediate levels had been impressive, but it remained for these successors to the fragmented domains of the constable-daimyo to establish a firmer base for the next attempt at central military rule.

A study of the Ōnin War, therefore, need not be simply a chronicle of the dismal collapse of central government in medieval Japan. The Ōnin War was the end of one period, but it was also the beginning of another. The Ashikaga Bakufu was not just a futile attempt to revive power that had vanished with the fall of Kamakura; and the later Bakufu-constable balance was not just a device to postpone political disintegration of the country. Both the Bakufu and the constable played real roles in the development of Japanese feudalism, and it will be important to see what they accomplished and to suggest what course they opened for the future.

Let us begin with the founding of the first Bakufu at Kamakura by Minamoto Yoritomo (1147–99).

I

The Kamakura Constable

In 1185 Minamoto Yoritomo, after emerging victorious over the forces of the Taira, received permission from the imperial court to post constables and stewards (*jitō*)[1] to provinces and estates throughout the land. This is most frequently regarded as the date of the founding of the Kamakura Bakufu.[2] In fact, Yoritomo's mandate to assign these officials, although epoch-making, was not entirely revolutionary. The Taira had used stewards to manage their extensive holdings in the west, while the court had for years commissioned constabulary officers (*sō-tsuibushi*)[3] to

[1] A generic term originally used to designate land, but later extended to mean the "holder" of that land. Discussed in Yasuda Motohisa, *Nihon Zenshi*, IV, 88–89.

[2] The date of the founding of the Kamakura Bakufu is a disputed point. Two other dates suggested are 1183, when Yoritomo received acknowledgment of his right to enforce discipline in the east (in the provinces of the Tōkaidō and the Tōsandō), and 1190, when he first received high rank (*Ukon'e-taishō*) at court. For a discussion of materials on this question see Tōyama Shigeki and Satō Shin'ichi, *Nihon-shi Kenkyū Nyūmon*, II, 84–90.

[3] The relationship between the constable and the *sō-tsuibushi* is another subject of controversy. Yasuda Motohisa has outlined it and has given a list of relevant articles in *Nihon Zenshi*, IV, 94–95, *n.* 4.

quell disturbances in the provinces. Nevertheless, it was under Yoritomo that the steward and the constable first became part of a nationwide network of military appointees.[4]

Much of the country at that time was still divided into peaceful and fairly well-managed estates. Yoritomo did not make any attempt to destroy these estates. Through the commendation of certain lands and the confiscation of others,[5] he became one of the largest estate holders (*shōen ryōshu*) in the land. The estate system became the basis of his financial and economic power, and he was as vitally interested in its maintenance as were the nobles and great religious institutions. With his personal vassals posted as stewards in various estates, Yoritomo could exercise direct control over a large part of the system. Furthermore, he was in a position to influence, either directly or indirectly, the entire economic foundation of his rivals at court, since the nobles also relied almost exclusively on income from their landed holdings.

Thus Yoritomo, far from destroying the established pattern of land tenure, simply grafted his network of officers onto it. Indeed, appointment as steward meant in many cases nothing more than confirmation of estate managers and functionaries occupying positions they were thenceforth to hold as officials of the Bakufu.[6] Other stewards received appointment, often in distant provinces, as reward for service in the war against the Taira.[7] In either case the steward, backed by his own rights (*shiki*) in some part of the land or its produce, was in a strong position to gain control of the estate by infringing upon or arrogating the rights of the estate holder. Many of these holders were absentee landlords and, although they took what legal action they could, they were often unable to mount effective resistance to steward incursions. As the

---

[4] Yoritomo met considerable resistance to his policy in the central and western provinces, where great landholding nobles and religious institutions were particularly strong, and was forced to cancel a number of his original steward appointments. It was only after the defeat of imperial forces in the Jōkyū Incident (1221) that the Bakufu was able to employ these local officers on a wide scale.

[5] Yoritomo had his own broad estates in the east as well as the entire lot of confiscated Taira lands in the west.

[6] *Honryō ando jitō* ("steward confirmed in his holding").

[7] *Shin'on jitō* ("steward receiving new benefice").

years passed the steward cut ever more deeply into the interests and rights of the estate holder.

In attempting to sustain the estate system under his own control, Yoritomo faced a fundamental problem. For the steward, by the very nature of his authority, was in a position to commit depredations within the estate that would eventually lead to a weakening of the entire system. While the Bakufu was naturally anxious to help and to strengthen its local officialdom, it could not afford to sanction a complete breakdown of the very system in which it had its own financial base.[8]

Thrown into an ambivalent course of action, the Bakufu tried first to aid the steward, then to check him. The trend of the times, however, was on the side of the steward. The estate as a self-sufficient economic and political unit could not contain the emerging warrior of medieval Japan. Yoritomo was able to establish power in the east with relative speed and efficiency by grafting his rule onto this prevailing system of landholding. But in so doing he created an economic base that his successors were to have difficulty in maintaining against the onslaught of their own retainers.

Yoritomo appointed constables to the various provinces to maintain law and to provide leadership for the stewards. The powers of the early constable were three:[9] 1) to chastise rebels; 2) to pursue and apprehend murderers; 3) to enforce guard duty. The first and second powers clearly reflected the constable's heritage from the *sō-tsuibushi*. In the event of rebellion or serious crime the constable was empowered to take the necessary steps to deal with offend-

---

[8] In fact, the Bakufu sought to compromise. When the estate owner petitioned against the steward's illegal actions, the Bakufu sanctioned a division of the estate between the two (*shitaji chūbun*).

[9] These powers are known collectively as the *taihon sankajō*, and were officially codified in the Jōei Code (*Go-seibai shikimoku*). In addition, the constable came to perform two other functions: 1) intermediary for all correspondence between the shogun and his direct vassals (*go-kenin*). In theory this was enormously important because it suggested that the constable's position as middleman between shogun and houseman (e.g., steward) was complete. In fact it is not certain that the constable did act as sole intermediary; 2) repair of temples and shrines and upkeep of roads and post stations. These were duties formerly performed by the provincial governor (*kokushi*), and their transfer to the constable revealed the extent to which the offices of the old order had fallen into disuse.

ers and to restore order in the province. He was also free, while in the course of duty, to enter domains not normally open to his surveillance. This police function gave the constable considerable authority in time of emergency; but it was an irregular authority, especially in those areas where the steward was able to deal with most trouble before it spread beyond the boundaries of the estate. In fact, it was the third power that gave the constable his special status and that presaged his development as a great feudal baron in later centuries.

Enforcement of guard duty, while seemingly a routine function, had important implications for the Kamakura constable. In the early years of his rise to power Yoritomo had maintained an intensely personal relationship with his direct vassals, or shogunal housemen (*go-kenin*). Even after the extension of Bakufu rule to other parts of the country and after it had become impossible to retain such close ties, the fiction was still maintained that each houseman, no matter how distant his post, was a "direct" vassal of the shogun. To demonstrate his loyalty, the shogunal houseman was obliged to fight in case of war and to mount guard in time of peace. Actually, guard duty during the Kamakura age consisted largely of symbolic service in the Capital.[10] It was nevertheless a most important service, since faithful performance was the houseman's only way of reaffirming his readiness to serve the shogun as a fighting man.

It was the constable's job to draw up guard rosters and to make sure that the stewards of his province, all of whom were housemen of the shogun, met their obligations regularly. This meant that the constable was not simply a police official available in times of emergency but, in effect, leader of the housemen in his prov-

---

[10] The most important duty was at the imperial palace (known as Kyoto *ōban yaku*); but there were also levies for the protection of Kamakura (Kamakura *ōban yaku*), the shogunal palace (shogun *gosho naiban yaku*), and the streets of the capital (*kagariya banyaku*). The term of duty was not fixed. After the Jōkyū Incident it was six months; later it was shortened to three months and, at the end of the Kamakura period, was reextended to six months. In some cases it was assigned to certain families several times in one generation; other families received duty every second generation, etc. For a discussion of this subject see Nitta Eiji, "Kamakura Bakufu no Go-kenin Seido" in Tōkyō Daigaku Shuppan Kai, *Nihon Rekishi Kōza*, II, 241–44.

ince. In the event of war he would be the logical man to assume command of the Bakufu's regional armies.

Despite these powers, the constable was not able to realize his full potential during the Kamakura period. For one thing, the province was not an important political unit. So long as nearly autonomous estates continued to fill the land, provincial boundaries would hold little significance; the course of events would center on the steward in the estate and not on the constable in the province. The constable would have to await a further relaxation of barriers to intercommunication among the estates before he could hope to assert full command on the provincial level.[11]

Second, the constable was hampered by Bakufu policy. Most of the men assigned to this post were eastern warriors who held stewardships and other rights as housemen of the shogun. Since there was no profit directly attached to his office, the constable was forced to rely on his own sources of income. At the same time he enjoyed little security of office. Although injunctions were issued to the contrary, the Bakufu made frequent replacements during the early years and further complicated the constable's attempts to establish a base of power in the province.

This "disruptive" policy stemmed in part from a basic attitude toward the constable shared by both the Kamakura and the Muromachi Bakufu. What Bakufu leaders really wanted was a representative to do their bidding. They were well aware of the danger they would face if the constable were allowed to gather too much power into his own hands. At the same time they could not weaken the constable's position too greatly or make him too dependent on central support through fear that he might lose control altogether. The problem was to find the mid-point that would insure stable relations.

This thinking led to two general aims: 1) that no constable be assigned to his native province; 2) that, although it might be difficult to prevent hereditary transmission of the office, the Bakufu

---

[11] Japanese scholars speak of the breakdown of the estate (*shōen*) and the development of the village (*gōson*) in the transition from Kamakura to Muromachi. This new and more flexible politico-economic unit, coupled with improved transportation and communication, made province-wide control a far more feasible goal.

should attempt, at all costs, to reserve the right of summary dismissal and reappointment. Otherwise, Bakufu leaders tried simply to extend or restrict the constable's powers according to the conditions of the times. As we shall see, these leaders, especially during the Muromachi period, had little success in "restricting" the constable. At best they were able to limit the extent of his gains.

In one respect they did achieve their aim. By appointing men from other provinces, Bakufu rulers made certain that their representative was a newcomer to his post and not a local magnate who might use the office to become too powerful too rapidly. Faced with the task of establishing jurisdiction as quickly as possible over unfamiliar territory and without a local power base of his own, the constable was forced to rely heavily on Bakufu support. At the same time he had no alternative but to compromise and to deal with conditions as he found them. The early Kamakura constable in the west had a particularly difficult job. Not only was he a newcomer without connections in the province; he had no substantial warrior class from which to recruit his armies, since the still powerful estate system inhibited the growth of such a class.[12]

The policy of the Bakufu, then, served to emphasize the essentially bureaucratic nature of the constable. He was forever an official of the central government who imposed his control from above, and not a regional chieftain who had established firm feudal relations with those below. No matter how widely the constable might extend his influence, his foundation remained weak; no matter how actively he might seek autonomy, he was never able to dispense fully with Bakufu support. This was the most significant characteristic of the constable, and the one that marked him as a

---

[12] One of the reasons that a military class arose in the Kantō before it appeared in the home provinces was the relative strength of the estate system in the two areas. In the east the estate system was relatively weak; men were able to cross boundaries and to form military alliances with warriors in other estates, and eventually a vast network of warrior units covered the provinces of the Kantō. In the home provinces, on the other hand, where estates were still firm, autonomous bodies, the estate dweller did not have this opportunity: while he might take up arms on behalf of the estate owner or under levy from families such as the Taira, he did not have horizontal relations with potential warriors in other estates. See Ishii Susumu, "Kamakura Bakufu Ron" in Iwanami Shoten, *Iwanami Kōza Nihon Rekishi*, V, 91–92.

transitional figure in the development of Japanese feudalism. When the central government upon which he relied finally collapsed during the Ōnin War, the constable was obliged to make way for a more vigorous class of local warriors who were in firm command of their landed bases.

There is one further subject that must be considered before we go on to the Muromachi Bakufu. It concerns the matter of family headship within the military class and has became the central point of recent theories on the nature of the transition from Kamakura to Muromachi. Unfortunately it is also a subject that has not yet been fully studied. There are many points of regional variation and of relationships within the family that must be left to future research. Nevertheless, the conclusions thus far advanced by Japanese scholars are impressive.[13]

During early Kamakura, divided inheritance was the common practice among military families. But, even though a man might distribute his estate to several offspring (including females), his principal successor was able to retain residual control over the entire family through his position as family head (*sōryō*). By means of the family head's authority, the family or clan remained a tightly knit unit despite the centrifugal effects of divided inheritance. Any official contact with the outside was handled through the family head, while, conversely, outsiders who wished to deal with members of the family were obliged to see the head first.

The family headship system, which was especially strong in the east, is generally regarded as a primitive carry-over from former tribal customs. In any event, it provided the Kamakura Bakufu with a useful tool for political organization. Those men who became housemen, or direct vassals, of the shogun were heads of their respective families. When they entered into this relationship of vassalage, not only they but their families and branch families as

---

[13] The theme of the following discussion (decentralization at the end of the Kamakura period based on the weakening of blood ties and the growing involvement of the Bakufu's representatives in local and regional affairs) is treated by Satō Shin'ichi, "Bakufu Ron," in Chūō Kōron Sha, *Shin Nihon-shi Kōza*.

well came under the jurisdiction of the Bakufu. Thus a sturdy and broad foundation was placed under the Bakufu's system of direct vassalage, which proved particularly valuable for the posting of stewards in distant areas.

Many of those appointed as stewards in the western provinces, for example, were important shogunal housemen already holding stewardships and other posts in the east. It was obviously impossible for them to fill their new assignments personally without neglecting their home bases. Instead they adopted the practice of sending members of their branch families to represent them in the field. With their authority as family heads, the shogunal housemen were able to command firm allegiance from these branch members (*shoshi*), although the latter might be separated from home by a considerable distance. Even the constable had to go through the family head when he wished to present guard rosters to those under his command.[14] In this manner the family headship system provided cohesion to the whole network of vassalage during the Kamakura period.

The eventual breakdown of the family headship system was only one of several fundamental reasons for the collapse of the whole houseman structure (and, with it, the Bakufu) at the end of Kamakura. Yet the fate of the family head typified a far-reaching political transition that was to usher in and to characterize the Muromachi period.

The strength of the family headship system lay in the blood ties that held its members together. Like the relationship between vassal and lord, it worked best on the local level. Therefore, although the family headship system was one of the means which made possible the stationing of shogunal housemen, or representatives from their branch families, in distant provinces, this very test of its strength inevitably brought about its collapse. When the new family representative went forth to his assignment, he was heavily dependent on the family head for support in an unfamiliar territory. But with the passing generations he became more and more involved in regional affairs and his need for the family head decreased proportionately. Blood ties hardly seemed real or important

[14] Nitta, "Kamakura Bakufu no Go-kenin Seido," p. 241.

at such a distance. Furthermore, although the branch member had originally been sent to manage the new land on behalf of his family, he increasingly came to regard the holdings he occupied as his own possession. His interests had become local and he saw no need for interference from relatives in a far-off province.

As the bond between the family head and the branch representative weakened, a leadership gap was created, which the constable was in a position to fill. The constable's powers, as we have seen, qualified him to be military leader in the province in the first place. But, so long as the family head's authority remained forceful and the constable was obliged to deal through him, the constable's own command over local warriors could not be complete. With a new feeling of independence the constable himself was undergoing a process of localization. His interests were turning from Kamakura to the purely local affairs of his own domain. Thus the branch representative and the constable came together as their reliance on Bakufu support waned and as their blood ties with the eastern warrior were replaced by strong local and regional loyalties.[15]

By the end of the thirteenth century the Kamakura Bakufu was crumbling. In a sense this can be viewed as a fairly natural and inevitable stage in the development of Japanese feudalism. The Bakufu was an eastern power. It was able to extend its influence to distant areas within a relatively short period of time, not by means of its own revolutionary character, but through use of existing institutions characteristic of an earlier period: the estate system of landholding and the sōryō system of family headship. As stated above, the Bakufu, which had imposed its network of officials on far-off estates and had controlled these officials through the strength of vassalage and blood ties, was involved in a basic contradiction. In order to protect its own structure, the Bakufu was obliged to support the stewards in their struggle against the estate owner. By backing steward incursions on estate rights, the Bakufu

---

[15] This merging of the local warrior and the constable must not be oversimplified. In the absence of strong central control during the final decades of the Kamakura period, these warriors sought to achieve their aims through the activities of "bands" (akutō). Then, with the reappointment of constables by the Muromachi Bakufu, many became vassals of the constable of their own province.

was, at the same time, indirectly encouraging the collapse of the very system in which its own economic base was located. Furthermore, the stronger these local representatives became, the more they could assert their independence of Bakufu control.

II

The Muromachi Bakufu

The outward similarity in organization between the first two Bakufu reflects the continuity from Kamakura to Muromachi. Ashikaga Takauji, who was neither a revolutionary nor an innovator, turned to the models of the government he had helped destroy for the means with which to meet the challenges of his time. But governmental institutions in Japanese history can be most deceptive if one seeks to evaluate them solely on surface organization. The locus of power is ever-changing, and one must look carefully beyond the title to determine the function.

It is not sufficient, then, to say that the leaders of the Muromachi Bakufu inherited and maintained in large part the offices and institutions of the Kamakura Bakufu; for the nature of these offices and institutions may have varied considerably during the century and a half of Kamakura rule. There was a vast difference, obviously, between the shogunacy during Yoritòmo's lifetime and during the incumbency of the imperial princes. While it is beyond the scope of this study to examine in detail the institutional growth of the Kamakura Bakufu, it is nevertheless important to note certain broad developments in order to understand the type of governmental structure that the Ashikaga inherited.

The Kamakura Bakufu can be divided into three main administrative periods: 1) the shogunal authoritarianism[1] of Yoritomo and his Kyoto officials; 2) assembly rule under the early Hōjō regents (*shikken*); 3) Hōjō (Tokusō) authoritarianism following the Mongol invasions (1274 and 1281).

The aristocratic court at Kyoto was ill equipped physically, ideologically, and geographically to meet the demands of the dynamic warrior society that emerged in the eastern provinces during the later Heian period. Yet paradoxically it was Yoritomo's own aristocratic background (Seiwa Genji) that enabled him to bring together the feuding chieftains of this region into a unified military and political power under his own authoritarian rule. In class-conscious Japan even the burgeoning warrior of the Kantō turned for leadership to the man of high birth.

Although he sought constantly to identify himself with the aims of the Kantō warrior, Yoritomo was both unwilling and unable to discard entirely the duality of his heritage. He championed the martial virtues, yet turned for authority to a thoroughly civilian court; he retained near-dictatorial powers in his own hands as military leader (*tōryō*), yet relied heavily on the advice and support of officials summoned from Kyoto. He even went so far as to appoint the aristocrats, Ōe Hiromoto (1148–1225) and Miyoshi Yasunobu (1140–1221), as heads, respectively, of the administrative board (*mandokoro*) and the board of inquiry (*monchūjo*), two of the three main administrative posts below the shogun. Only to headship of the board of retainers (*samurai-dokoro*) did he assign an eastern warrior, Wada Yoshimori (1147–1213).

Ōe, Miyoshi, and the other Kyoto officials supported shogunal authoritarianism. Lacking a landed base of power in the east, they were dependent on the rule of a strong shogun for the preservation of their own positions. At the peak of Yoritomo's rule they stood as his closest advisers above the great shogunal housemen who had made possible the Minamoto rise to power. This was

[1] Authoritarianism (*sensei taisei*) in this context means complete control of the central organs of the Bakufu.

bound to prove frustrating to chieftains such as Chiba and Miura, who wanted a greater voice in Bakufu affairs yet found themselves completely subordinate to shogunal command and even outranked by newcomers from Kyoto. It is not surprising, therefore, that the principle of shogunal authoritarianism, which characterized the first period of Kamakura rule, was challenged and finally destroyed after the death of Yoritomo in 1199. Although the Kyoto officials retained a degree of power during the next two decades and even continued on in the government, it was the eastern houseman faction headed by Hōjō Yoshitoki (1163–1224) that finally emerged supreme in Bakufu councils.

Early Hōjō rule is often cited as a rare example of good government in medieval Japan. Through the establishment of a council of state (*hyōjōshū*) and the issuance of the Jōei Code (1232), the Hōjō regents instituted and codified government by joint deliberation and thereby met shogunal houseman demands for a greater voice in Bakufu affairs. While Yoritomo's achievements were of course outstanding, Hōjō rule proved far more compatible with the times than shogunal authoritarianism once the Kamakura government had been established. Yoritomo had attached great personal prestige and power to the office of shogun. Following his death, Japanese leaders left shogunal prestige with a puppet officeholder but transferred shogunal power to other hands (that is, to those of the Hōjō regent).

Yet even during the years of greatest Hōjō achievement through assembly rule the seeds were sown for a reversion to authoritarianism—not of the shogun, but of the Hōjō family. Yoritomo's claim to power had been based on direct authority from the throne plus his own noble background and the support of aristocratic officials. Like so many other aspects of his rule, shogunal authoritarianism during the first years of the Kamakura Bakufu reflected Yoritomo's fundamental conservatism and attachment to the old order. Hōjō authoritarianism after the Mongol invasions, on the other hand, while also based on a carry-over from prefeudal times—the family headship system—was much more a product of eastern warrior society.

When the Hōjō regents took power and began to broaden the

base of Kamakura rule, they made extensive use of clan members for the new positions they created, such as Kyoto *tandai* (deputy), *rensho* ("cosigner"), and vacancies on the council of state. This was a radical departure from the practice of Yoritomo, who had been inordinately suspicious of relatives and had in fact liquidated most of his. The key to Hōjō success in utilizing relatives lay in the strength of family blood ties centered on the family head (who, in the case of the Hōjō, bore the special title Tokusō, adapted from an alternate name of Hōjō Yoshitoki). It became a cardinal rule that the regency be occupied by the Hōjō Tokusō. Even in the cases of Nagatoki (1230–64) and Masamura (1205–73) this principle was not really abandoned, for they were merely caretakers in the regency during the minority of the young Tokusō, Tokimune (1251–84).[2] In this manner the Hōjō were able to concentrate the power of both the leader of the Bakufu and the leader of their family in the hands of one man. During the years of assembly rule before the Mongol invasions the position of regent was the more important of the two, the regent's role as Tokusō serving only as a check against family quarrels.

After the invasions a unique transition in power from regent to Tokusō took place. The rigors of mounting a defense against the Mongols plus the gradual weakening of the shogunal houseman system placed a heavy strain on the Bakufu. The reaction of the Hōjō was to gather the powers of the realm ever more firmly to themselves. Backed by the large cadre of Hōjō officials already occupying important positions, the Hōjō leaders, Tokimune and Sadatoki (1270–1311), weakened and eliminated certain branches of the Bakufu and finally succeeded in transferring the decision-making process from the office of regent and from the council of state to the private sanctum of the Hōjō family council (*yoriai*). Thus we see the curious phenomenon of the Hōjō regent rendering himself a figurehead and assuming authoritarian powers as leader of the Hōjō family.[3]

[2] Nagatoki and Masamura, the fifth and sixth Hōjō regents, ruled from 1256 to 1268. They were members of branch lines of the family. When Tokimune came of age, Masamori stepped aside in his favor.

[3] For a discussion of Hōjō authoritarianism under the Tokusō, see Satō Shin'ichi

In addition to maintaining complete control of the government at Kamakura, the Hōjō also attempted to extend family rule as far afield as possible through the monopolization of constable appointments. By the fourteenth century, Hōjō relatives or direct vassals (*miuchi*) occupied the post of constable in thirty provinces, or nearly half the national total of sixty-six. Thus, as the weakening of blood ties and the growth of regional loyalties undermined the Bakufu's houseman system, Hōjō (Tokusō) authoritarianism emerged to dominate the final years of the Kamakura period.

We can draw several general conclusions from these transitions in Bakufu administration. First of all, the shogunate established by Yoritomo was basically dualistic, partaking of both the military and the aristocratic. Yoritomo, as shogun, was at once a private military leader with personal ties to his vassals and a public official of the court deriving authority directly from the emperor. In Yoritomo's case the more important of these two roles, once the Bakufu had been established, was the latter. This statement may seem surprising in view of the care with which the Minamoto chieftain built his country's first military government. Nevertheless, the extent of Yoritomo's leaning toward the aristocratic side of his character is shown not only in his insistence on direct imperial authority to justify his every move and in his reliance on Kyoto officials in the Bakufu, but also in his failure to utilize the warrior's pattern of family control. Far from establishing a firm warrior dynasty based on the family headship system of his housemen, Yoritomo centered his authoritarianism entirely upon himself and attempted to form what one scholar has termed a new "kingly order." [4]

Shogunal, or Bakufu, dualism was not an accidental phenomenon resulting from the unique background of Minamoto Yoritomo. Rather it would be accurate to say that this dualism was,

---

"Kamakura Bakufu Seiji no Sensei-ka ni tsuite" in Takeuchi Rizō, ed., *Nihon Hōken-sei Seiritsu no Kenkyū*, pp. 95–136. Professor Satō explains the manner in which Sadatoki abolished organs like the board of coadjutors (*hikitsuke-shū*) and then weakened the council of state by appointing an excessive number of young and inexperienced Hōjō to its membership. The Hōjō family council, meetings of which were held in the private homes of the Tokusō, gradually became formalized above the council of state. See *ibid.*, pp. 105–8.

[4] Ishii, "Kamakura Bakufu Ron," p. 96.

an inevitable development under the conditions of twelfth-century Japan, and that Yoritomo was the one specially equipped to implement it. Burgeoning warrior society in the east was based on such intimate relationships as those between lord and vassal, and between family head and branch relative—relationships that worked best on the local level. Paradoxically the strength of these local warrior relationships made possible the extension of Kamakura rule to other parts of the country. But extension of rule would not have been possible on the basis of these relationships alone. There had to be public, court recognition of the *right* to extend. And the dualism that Yoritomo created in obtaining this right became a fundamental and even necessary characteristic of all future Bakufu. From that time the extent to which one aspect or the other of this dualism was stressed by Bakufu leaders helped to determine Bakufu policy.

In contrast to Yoritomo, for example, early Hōjō rulers emphasized the private, military side of Bakufu dualism. Regent authority could still be traced, of course, to the emperor; but the ties between sovereign and subject had become indirect. While maintaining the fiction of shogunal supremacy, the Hōjō regents turned more to family development and warrior rule through assembly than to the subtleties of Bakufu-court relations.

The second stage of Hōjō rule—Tokusō authoritarianism—went one step further and became almost entirely military, at least so far as the Hōjō leaders and their personal vassals were concerned. Relations between Tokusō and emperor were remote. Yet the basic Bakufu dualism still existed, for the shogun, although powerless, remained the emperor's first military leader and the object of houseman allegiance. Thus, although the Hōjō were in a sense able to set up a truly military rule under the Tokusō, they did so at the expense of alienating many of the warriors who constituted the shogunal houseman structure. Granted this structure was considerably weakened, it was still the foundation of the Kamakura Bakufu. By overemphasizing the private-military above the public-aristocratic side of the Bakufu, the Hōjō created an imbalance that contributed to their own downfall.

The Kamakura Bakufu, which declined sharply during the early years of the fourteenth century, was finally destroyed in 1333 by the forces of the Emperor Go-Daigo (1288–1339). Apart from a common desire to be rid of Hōjō rule, however, those who joined Go-Daigo were a diverse group, with both class and personal animosities that were to make later unity impossible.

One of the principal reasons for the collapse of the Kamakura system was, as we have seen, the weakening of blood ties between the eastern warriors and their provincial representatives (the steward class), and the growth of local loyalties and attachments among the latter. Whereas the east had taken the lead in military developments during the Heian period, a new class of independent warriors had now emerged in the central and western provinces and had become a key force in the overthrow of the Bakufu. And, although these two warrior types (east and west) had joined in temporary alliance against Hōjō tyranny, their fundamental differences and conflicts were to have an important effect in shaping the course of the new Bakufu.

The great warriors of the east were direct descendants of those chieftains whom Yoritomo had united a century and a half before. Little hindered by the estate system, which had never been fully established in the Kantō, these men for generations had controlled large holdings and had commanded sizable followings of kinsmen and vassals. In the economically and socially backward provinces where they held sway, older forms such as the family headship system and the practice of slave labor were still strong. When these eastern warriors turned westward in search of conquest they found it to their advantage not to destroy the powerful estate system of the west but to compromise with its great holders and to impose their own rule from above. By placing stewards in estates throughout the country, Yoritomo became a national leader for the first time. He also created a contradictory situation in which his own officials helped weaken the very system upon which Yoritomo relied for stability and for economic support. This was unavoidable. If the eastern warrior exploited the old order long enough, he would eventually cause its collapse. A more revolutionary and thorough policy would have been to sweep away the entire pattern of estates and to construct a new system of rural landholding. Yet this would have been to risk disorder and even anarchy—a risk the medieval chieftain was unwilling to take. Thus the attitude of the eastern warrior remained the same in Muromachi as in Kamakura—to establish rule as quickly as possible over the west through the use of existing institutions.

The two most important eastern warriors, apart from the Hōjō themselves, were Nitta Yoshisada (1301–38) and Ashikaga Takauji, both high-ranking descendants of the Seiwa Genji clan. Although the Nitta were technically above the Ashikaga,[5] Nitta leaders had incurred the displeasure of Yoritomo around the time of the founding of the Kamakura shogunate and had occupied a position inferior to the Ashikaga during ensuing generations. Yoshisada as a result was intensely jealous of the Ashikaga and was ever-watchful for the opportunity to assert Nitta superiority. The personal animosity between these two men contributed heavily to the failure of Go-Daigo's attempt at restoration of imperial rule.

Though both Ashikaga and Nitta were powerful eastern families, Ashikaga Takauji possessed a distinct geographical advantage that proved a vital factor in his ultimate victory. The family seats of the Ashikaga and the Nitta were in Shimotsuke and Kōzuke, respectively. In addition, Takauji held the post of constable over the provinces of Kazusa and Mikawa. The Ashikaga had been particularly successful in founding a base in Mikawa, where they established a number of collateral lines—Niki, Hosokawa, Hatakeyama, Imagawa, Isshiki, and Kira. Possession of this province midway between Kyoto and Kamakura placed the Ashikaga within strategic range of the central regions. While the Nitta were exclusively an eastern family, the Ashikaga were able to partake of both east and west, once the barrier of Hōjō authoritarianism had been removed.

Conditions in the western provinces were far different from those in the east. The strength of the estate system had inhibited the growth of a warrior class and the average holding of the emerg-

[5] Both Nitta and Ashikaga were descended from Minamoto Yoshikuni (d. 1155) through his sons Yoshishige (Nitta) and Yoshiyasu (Ashikaga). Since Yoshishige was the older brother, his line was senior to the Ashikaga.

GENEALOGICAL TABLE OF THE
ASHIKAGA FAMILY

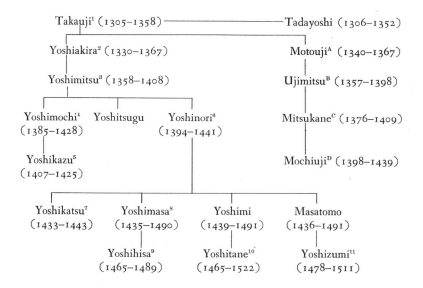

The successive Ashikaga Shoguns are numbered. The letters indicate the four branch family members who held the office of Kantō kanrei (later, Kantō kubō).

ing landowner-warrior in the highly developed and fragmented regions west of the Kantō was much smaller than that of the great eastern chieftains. Yet this smaller steward, or local samurai (*kokujin*)[6] class warrior as he came to be called during Muromachi, had a strong potential for feudal growth, through development of landlord-peasant relations based on feudal rent (*jidai*) and through ties of vassalage and military alliance based, not on blood relationships, but on local power realities.[7]

[6] Another term for local samurai is *ji-samurai*. Professor Nagahara Keiji suggests that the more frequently used term, *kokujin*, reflects the desire of this type of warrior to extend his power to the provincial (*koku*, or *kuni*) level. "Shugo Ryōkoku-sei no Tenkai," in *Nihon Hōkensei Seiritsu Katei no Kenkyū*, p. 347.

[7] During the days of eastern family headship control the family head had been the principal party and had controlled the extended family organization from the top down. In this new relationship, however, individual families were the prin-

Unlike the eastern warrior, the local samurai was first and foremost an enemy of the estate system and of those who supported it. Thus he was fundamentally opposed also to court rule, since the latter was inseparably bound with the whole structure of estate holding. Although the local samurai might join the court temporarily in order to throw off the onus of Hōjō oppression, he nevertheless remained an implacable foe of the old order. The eastern warrior might choose to compromise, but the local samurai would not relax his relentless assaults on the estate as an independent economic unit.

The local samurai was also in need of leadership. The country was in a state of ferment and change, and the tasks facing him were enormous: not only the continuing struggle against the estate holder, but the problems of establishing firm relations with his peasant base as well as furnishing protection against the incursions of other aggressive samurai. It was this need for leadership that simplified the constable's job of organization in the early years of Ashikaga rule. But, as we shall see, the local samurai was always the opportunist. He joined the constable only so long as it suited his needs. When his constable lord showed signs of weakening, the local samurai was the first to turn elsewhere.

Typical of the local samurai of the central and western provinces were Kusunoki Masashige (d. 1336) and Kō no Moronao (d. 1351). Masashige is traditionally revered as the most loyal of Go-Daigo's supporters and as the man who sacrificed most for the throne. Yet he too was involved in a basic contradiction born of the times. As a landowner of middling estates in the province of Kawachi, Masashige belonged to that class most antagonistic toward the estate system. While he may have remained personally loyal to the court, most of the other members of this class could not long have supported the kind of return to a golden past envisioned by Go-Daigo. Temporary alignment did not alter their fundamental role as destroyers of the old order. Kō no Moronao, a

---

cipals and the ties were formed from the bottom up. They might place a family head at the top, but only out of necessity for general supervision. Satō Shin'ichi, "Shugo Ryōkoku-sei no Tenkai," in Toyoda Takeshi, ed., *Chūsei Shakai*, in *Shin-Nihon Shi Taikei*, pp. 102–3.

man of considerably less personal attachment to the throne who entered the service of Ashikaga Takauji, was also unalterably opposed to the outmoded system of estate holdings. Unlike Masashige, he was not distracted by feelings of loyalty or self-sacrifice. A leader of local samurai from the central provinces, Moronao was prepared to launch an open assault upon all barriers to warrior growth. His role in the new Bakufu and his relationship to the eastern leaders will be important in our examination of the early years of the Muromachi Bakufu.

These divergent warriors from east and west—Nitta, Ashikaga, Kusunoki—turned against their Hōjō overlords, overthrew the Kamakura Bakufu and joined in the so-called Kemmu Restoration.[8] Before three years had elapsed, however, their uneasy alliance disintegrated. Nitta Yoshisada induced the court to move against Takauji, who responded by driving Go-Daigo and his followers to sanctuary in the mountains of Yoshino. Thus began the period of war between the courts, which continued from 1336 until 1392.

Ashikaga Takauji, the most powerful of the eastern warriors, wished to establish his Bakufu at Kamakura like Yoritomo before him; but conditions compelled him to settle instead in Kyoto.[9] Faced with problems of wartime emergency, Takauji proceeded in almost *ad hoc* fashion, attempting to gain control rapidly over as wide an area as possible. Takauji was a soldier, not a statesman. The organs of central government that he instituted did not become fully established or regularized until the rule of Yoshimitsu several decades later.[10] In general it may be said that Takauji sought to model his Bakufu on the pattern set by Yoritomo. He

[8] This was the attempted restoration of imperial rule under Go-Daigo, which lasted from 1333 until 1336.

[9] In the Kemmu Code (1336), which was little more than a reaffirmation of the Jōei Code, Takauji rationalized his inability to establish the Bakufu in Kamakura by stating: "While Kamakura is an auspicious place for the conduct of military affairs, the success or failure of government is not dependent upon location, but upon virtue."

[10] The central organs of the Bakufu will be discussed in Chapter IV, "The Bakufu–Constable Balance of Power."

returned power to the hands of the shogun, eliminated the office of shogunal regent, and outwardly copied the forms of the Kamakura government. But many years had passed since the founding of the first shogunate, and Takauji was as much influenced by the accretions of Hōjō rule as he was by the models of Yoritomo. In particular he attempted to use the techniques of Tokusō authoritarianism by appointing to the office of constable in the various provinces as many members of the Ashikaga clan (*ichimon*) as possible. Ostensibly Takauji had considerable success with this policy. He was faced, however, with one fundamental problem: the Ashikaga simply did not have a strong family headship structure, and were unable to utilize the strength of blood relationships as effectively as had the Hōjō.[11] From the outset it was apparent that Ashikaga clansmen and relatives formed an exceedingly loose group.

Takauji's first task, then, was not so much the establishment of administrative organs in the Capital as it was the appointment of officers to command those provinces in the central and western regions that were most important from a military standpoint. In provinces near the Capital, many of which had been controlled by the Hōjō, it was a relatively easy matter to assign constables from the Ashikaga clan—e.g., the Hosokawa to Awaji, Kawachi, Izumi, and the Shikoku provinces of Sanuki and Awa; the Shiba to Wakasa and Echizen; the Hatakeyama to Kii; the Niki to Iga, Ise, Tamba, Tango and Tajima.[12] In other areas Takauji was faced with demands for recognition from powerful local families that could not be ignored. This was particularly true of the provinces of the San'yōdō. Takauji's policy in these cases was to acknowledge the local magnate as constable, and to place an Ashikaga collateral in the capacity of general (*taishō*) over the province. This proved to be a clever tactical maneuver; for within a few years the Ashikaga general, backed by the power of the Bakufu, usually succeeded in usurping the constable status for himself.[13]

---

[11] Professor Satō stresses the weakness of family headship control in the Ashikaga family. "Bakufu Ron," p. 33.

[12] Satō, "Shugo Ryōkoku-sei no Tenkai," p. 109.

[13] Professor Satō lists the three policies that Takauji adopted in regard to ap-

Examples are Bizen, where Hosokawa replaced Matsuda, and Nagato, where Shiba took over from Kōtō. Only in a few cases, such as those of the Akamatsu of Harima and the Sasaki (Kyōgoku)[14] of Ōmi, were locally powerful warriors able to retain their positions as constables counter to Takauji's policy of favoring Ashikaga clansmen.

Since the records are incomplete and fragmentary, it is exceedingly difficult, if not impossible, to trace with complete accuracy the appointment and dismissal of constables during the chaotic early years of the Muromachi Bakufu. We do know that in some provinces the turnover was extremely high. Between 1336 and 1363, for example, Wakasa witnessed twelve changes, Iga ten, and Izumi eight.[15] The general trend in the central and western provinces was clear. While the number of outside (tozama) warriors holding constable rank (as compared to Ashikaga collaterals) may have been relatively high in the early years, these outsiders were gradually replaced by warriors subject, theoretically, to Takauji's family headship control.

In the eastern provinces, Kyushu, and the north, Takauji had less success in establishing his control. He dispatched representatives (Ōshū tandai) of the Shiba, Ishidō, and Kira to the northern provinces of Mutsu and Dewa, while to Kyushu he sent the first of a long line of deputies, which included Isshiki, Shiba, Shibukawa, and Imagawa, in an attempt to subdue the warriors of that independent island. Only through the efforts of Imagawa Sadayo (Ryōshun) at the end of the century, however, were the Ashikaga able to establish even temporary control in Kyushu.

---

pointment of constables: 1) accede to the demands of the local warrior (gōzoku) and appoint him; 2) reject his demands and appoint a member of the Ashikaga clan; 3) appoint the local warrior as constable and assign a general above him. "Muromachi Bakufu Ron," in Iwanami Shoten, Iwanami Kōza Nihon Rekishi, VII, 17.

[14] The Sasaki family was Uda Genji and had joined Yoritomo in 1180. At one point five Sasaki brothers held the post of constable in five different provinces. But around the time of the Jōkyū Incident the family split into two branches, the Kyōgoku and the Rokkaku. During the Ōnin War the Kyōgoku generally sided with the eastern army, while the Rokkaku joined the west.

[15] Satō, "Muromachi Bakufu Ron," p. 18.

The Kantō presented a special problem. Takauji sought to maintain in Kamakura a governmental structure similar in organization to the Kyoto Bakufu. He appointed as head (Kantō *kanrei*)[16] first his son Yoshiakira (1329–67) and then Yoshiakira's younger brother, Motouji (1340–67), who began a line that was to continue until the next century. From the beginning, relations between Kamakura and Kyoto were none too cordial, creating the impression at times that Kamakura was a separate government rather than a branch of the Bakufu.

Other constables who were able to protect their holdings and to continue into the Muromachi period were Takeda of Kai, Chiba of Shimōsa, Oyama of Shimotsuke, Shōni of Chikuzen, Ōtomo of Bungo, and Shimazu of Satsuma. Without exception they were men from the east or from Kyushu.[17] This meant that, aside from the Akamatsu and the Sasaki (Kyōgoku), all constables from the central and western provinces were new appointees from the time of Takauji. These were the men who comprised Takauji's real regional organization and from whose ranks the constable-daimyo were to emerge after the middle of the century. In areas remote from the Capital, on the other hand, constable status meant little. Chieftains there ruled in their own right with a minimum of aid or interference from the Bakufu.

The years that witnessed the war between the courts can be divided into three major periods:[18] 1) active struggle from 1336 until the return of Kitabatake Chikafusa (1293–1354) from Hitachi in 1342, during which time the effective power of the southern court was destroyed; 2) discord in the Bakufu terminating with the assassination of Takauji's brother, Tadayoshi (1306–52), in 1352; 3) development of the constable-daimyo and reassembly of Bakufu power under Yoshimitsu.

It must be understood from the outset that the question of who

---

[16] This office was later styled Kantō *kubō* and the title Kantō *kanrei* went to the Uesugi family.

[17] Nagahara, "Shugo Ryōkoku-sei no Tenkai," p. 340.

[18] Professor Nagahara subdivides the third period listed here into: 1) scattering of power and its reassembly; 2) strengthening of shogunal territory and unification under Yoshimitsu. "Nanboku Chō no Nairan," in Tōkyō Daigaku Shuppan Kai, *Nihon Rekishi Kōza*, III.

was to rule the country as emperor was not the only issue at stake in the war between the courts. In the beginning, to be sure, the court did have a degree of power in its ties with the old order of great estate-holding nobles and religious institutions. But most of the real power of the land had passed into military hands several generations earlier, and this war, although complicated by a dispute over succession to the throne, was really the result of conflict among members of the military classes, especially those in the central and western provinces, who were in a period of rapid growth and expansion. The main issue was not the throne, but the redistribution of land and military power.

The last vestiges of court power, in fact, vanished within a few years after the commencement of fighting. Although most of the nobles stayed with the northern court and attempted to retain their separate identity, they were soon submerged by the authority of the Bakufu. This in turn forced the great estate holders, who had relied on court support, to strike out on their own and to deal with the Bakufu and the warriors as best they could.[19] The southern court and its supporters fought stoutly for a few years and even continued their forays into the second half of the century, but their last serious attempt to mount a full offensive failed in 1342 when Kitabatake Chikafusa was obliged to abandon his position in Hitachi.

It might be well asked how the southern court was able to persist for another fifty years despite the destruction of its offensive powers in the early years of the war. For one thing, the court had an excellent strategical location in the mountain fastness of Yoshino, near great temples from which aid could be solicited, and accessible to good lines of communication. Secondly, the strategy of the northern court did not call for a show-down struggle with the south.[20] Finally, and most important, the southern court was an excellent rallying point for all elements discontented with the Bakufu.

Discord in the Bakufu had been brewing for several years. It

[19] Nagahara Keiji, "Nanboku Chō Nairan," in Iwanami Shoten, *Iwanami Kōza Nihon Rekishi*, VI, 76.
[20] *Ibid.*, p. 74.

centered around Takauji, his brother Tadayoshi, and the Kō brothers, Moronao and Moroyasu. Tadayoshi and Kō no Moronao were particularly antagonistic toward each other. In 1350 Tadayoshi, who had rendered valuable administrative service to the Bakufu, was forced to abandon his duties and to take the tonsure as a result of pressure placed on the shogun by Kō. Shortly thereafter Tadayoshi went over to the southern court and in 1351 encompassed the murder of the Kō brothers. With the Kō gone, Takauji and Tadayoshi came to terms and the latter returned to his administrative posts. But there was great distrust between the two, possibly stemming from Takauji's determination to have his sons, and not Tadayoshi, inherit the Bakufu. Finally, in November, 1351, Takauji himself "surrendered" to the southern court, obtained a commission to chastise Tadayoshi, and moved northward to attack his brother in Izu Province. By March of the following year Tadayoshi had been captured, removed to Kamakura, and there poisoned. This series of events is known after the year period as the Kannō Incident.

Modern scholars tend to discount the personal antagonisms and ambitions that were undoubtedly involved in this running dispute, which witnessed the death of three of the Bakufu's leading generals; instead they interpret this period in terms of fundamental ideological differences in Bakufu councils. The representative figures in this interpretation are Ashikaga Tadayoshi and Kō no Moronao. While part of the success of the Ashikaga in seizing power after the fall of Kamakura was, as we have seen, attributable to the strategic advantage they enjoyed through control of the province of Mikawa, the family was still basically an eastern power. Tadayoshi in particular had his roots in the Kantō and was supported by other great chieftains of that region. His aim was to establish a strong shogunate by a policy of moderation toward the estate system and firm bureaucratic control of the constables (in other words, by a continuation of a Kamakura-type Bakufu). Moronao, by contrast, was a revolutionary. As a representative of the dynamic class of local samurai of the central and western provinces, Moronao favored complete destruction of the old order and was opposed to all restrictions placed on the warrior in his struggle against the estate holder. His aim was warrior control in the separate provinces with a figurehead shogun above.[21]

While it is dangerous to carry this distinction of warrior classes and their conflicting aims too far, we can draw certain tentative conclusions from this period of discord within the Bakufu that will aid our analysis of the third period, reassembly of power. First, Takauji's assassination of Tadayoshi brought to an end direct interference and the imposition of sectional views by the eastern warrior in Bakufu affairs. Takauji himself was an eastern chieftain and he did, so to speak, inherit Tadayoshi's position of shogunal authoritarianism and moderation toward the estate system. But Takauji was a pragmatist and took what measures he saw fit to sustain power. Upon his death the west and the east, under his sons Yoshiakira and Motouji, began to drift apart. From this time the practical sphere of the Bakufu, despite the temporary successes of Imagawa Sadayo in Kyushu and occasional *rapprochements* with Kamakura, was limited to the central and western provinces.

Second, during the confusion of these years of struggle, shifting loyalties, and opportunism, many members of the constable class fell—Kō, Ishibashi, Momonoi, Ishidō, Niki. By the time of Yoshimitsu the number of families holding constable status (excluding those in Kyushu, the Kantō, and the Mutsu-Dewa region) had narrowed to eleven. Of these, six were Ashikaga collaterals—Hosokawa, Shiba, Hatakeyama, Isshiki, Yamana, and Imagawa—and five were outside constables—Sasaki, Akamatsu, Toki, Ōuchi, and Togashi.[22]

---

[21] *Ibid.*, p. 80. Also "Muromachi Seiken e no Gimon," in Yūzankaku, *Shinsetsu Nihon Rekishi*, V, 157.

[22] Satō, "Shugo Ryōkoku-sei no Tenkai," p. 113.

The Muromachi Constable

The growth of the constable-daimyo was one of the most important institutional developments of the early Ashikaga period. Within a short span of years a small group of great feudal barons emerged from the chaos of strife-torn central and western Japan to dominate the affairs of the Muromachi Bakufu until the Ōnin War. Their growth was all the more remarkable in view of the fact that nearly all were newcomers with no economic or military foothold in their provinces prior to the rise of the Ashikaga. By utilizing their positions as officers of the Bakufu, these men were able to extend control over territories encompassing, in some cases, three or more provinces. Their development to daimyo[1] status

---

[1] The term *daimyō* came originally from estate usage and referred to a man with many rice-lands, in contrast to one with few (*shōmyō*). It was later loosely and commonly applied to great warrior chieftains; but, although the term appears frequently in works such as *The Chronicle of Ōnin,* it was not officially codified until the time of Toyotomi Hideyoshi (1536–98), and then was written *taishin.* See Miura Hiroyuki, "Shugo to Daimyō," in *Zoku Hōsei-shi no Kenkyū,* pp. 1191–93. Professor Miura analyses the course of constable development to daimyo status as a process of taking over the functions of the former provincial governor

was largely decentralist and extralegal, through the steady arroga-
tion of rights and powers not at first envisioned by the Bakufu
and through the acquisition of local warriors as vassals. Yet the
very term applied to these chieftains—constable-daimyo—implies
that their attempts to establish independent domains were not
wholly successful. While striving to consolidate their holdings,
they could never dispense with their role as constables of the
Bakufu; and, while seeking independence, they remained dependent on central support.

This dual character of the constable has already been discussed.
Here I shall attempt to trace the growth of the constable both as
successor to the Kamakura official and as an emergent force within
the context of greatly altered conditions in fourteenth-century
Japan.

Both Minamoto Yoritomo and Ashikaga Takauji attempted to
impose their rule west of the Kantō by utilizing the mature
structure of estate holdings characteristic of that region. But by
Takauji's time the estates were not only weakening under the
onslaught of a dynamic warrior class; their holders (e.g., aristocrats
and religious institutions) were soon to lose what central support
they had received from the court. Government could no longer
rely fully upon this structure for the maintenance of order. This
is not to say that the estate system had been destroyed. The estate
was still the basic unit of economic organization in the country.
But it was no longer an autonomous political unit as well. The
inviolability of estate boundaries was gone, and control on a wider
geographic scale had become mandatory. Whereas the individual
steward of Kamakura had been concerned only with the affairs of
his particular estate, the Muromachi constable had to deal directly
with the entire estate structure of his province.

Development of the Muromachi constable, then, may be ex-
amined from two standpoints: his economic relationship to the
estate system, and his position as military leader of the province.

(*kokushi-ka*) and of the estate holder (*honjo-ka*). In modern texts the term most
commonly used is *shugo ryōkoku-ka* (transition to the constable domain).

Like his predecessor in early Kamakura, the Muromachi constable was an outsider whose powers at first were little advanced beyond those formulated in the Jōei Code of 1232.[2] At the same time his personal holdings and interests were scattered and irregular. The constable was not a conqueror who had carved out a unified domain, but the recipient of a complex of rewards from the Bakufu, which consisted in large part of miscellaneous rights to estates in his and other provinces. An extreme example of scattered constable holdings was that of the Kō, who had estate lands and offices in twenty-five different locations spread over twelve provinces. A more typical case, perhaps, was the Ogasawara of Shinano with nineteen holdings in six provinces. In any event the constable was forced to deal with a variety of local conditions, mainly through the structure of the estate system.

According to the Kemmu Code, which was issued shortly after Takauji's assumption of power in 1336: "Assignment as constable will be made on the basis of faithful service in battle. With grants of award in the estates, the constable will be an official as of old."[3] One scholar has drawn attention to use of the word "official" (*rimu*) as an indication of the Bakufu's determination to keep the constable a bureaucratic officer on the Kamakura model, and to prevent his seeking to bring provincial lands under personal control (*shoryō*).[4] Within a few years, however, it became apparent that the constable had already begun to interfere in the estates. For in 1338 the Bakufu decreed:

The constables were originally appointed to govern the provinces and to comfort the people. Men of virtue were assigned to these posts, and in cases where they proved a liability to the province, they were replaced. Nevertheless various constables have been infringing upon the estates. By claiming either that they have received such and such a steward post as reward for service or that the post has been in their family for generations, they have appointed military men and have assigned vassals to

[2] See above, p. 8.
[3] "Kemmu Shikimoku," in Satō Shin'ichi and Ikeuchi Yoshisuke, *Chūsei Hōsei Shiryō-shū*, II, 5.
[4] Satō, "Muromachi Bakufu Ron," p. 16.

take charge. This is entirely improper. Henceforth we will firmly enforce the provisions of the Jōei Code. [The constable] will not interfere [in the estates] beyond his powers of *taihon sankajō*.[5]

The aim of the constable was to consolidate his position as fully
as possible. Since his holdings and interests were tied up largely
in estates, he would have to secure a stronger footing in the administrative apparatus of the estate system. At the same time he
would need more extensive civil powers in order to control warrior
incursions and to settle disputes arising over land. During the
early years of the Kamakura Bakufu such disputes and matters of
litigation were still handled through the old provincial government
(*kokuga*) structure.[6] But by the fourteenth century the offices of
the provincial government had fallen into disuse, and the Bakufu,
despite decrees like the above, was soon forced to acknowledge the
need for an increase in constable authority to deal with civil affairs
and with questions pertaining to the estates.

The Bakufu's problem now was to strike a balance between
local samurai incursions on the estate system and constable usurpa-
tions of power. Increased military activities during the war between the courts had made conditions in the central and western
provinces highly unstable. Practices such as the indiscriminate
assessment of commissariat rice and the unlawful dispersal of rewards and lands were widespread. At first there was little Bakufu
leaders could do. But when the southern war effort began to flag,
they decided to implement their decision to increase constable
powers. Actually, constables throughout the provinces were already
engaged in a variety of extralegal practices. What the Bakufu attempted to do was to limit the majority of these practices while
acknowledging the constable's right to perform certain key functions beyond the narrow limits of the *taihon sankajō*. In 1346 constable powers were officially extended to include *karita rōzeki* (the
power to deal with harvest disorders and the cutting and theft of
crops) and *shisetsu jungyō* (the power to enforce judicial decisions

[5] "Kemmu Irai Tsuika Hō," in Satō and Ikeuchi, *Chūsei Hōsei Shiryō-shū*.
pp. 11–12.

[6] The provincial administrative offices of the *ritsu-ryō* system established by the
Taika Reform of A.D. 645.

and to ensure the transfer of confiscated lands to the winning claimant, etc.).[7] These new powers helped to strengthen the constable's position considerably. Whereas the *taihon sankajō* had authorized the constable to take action in criminal and punitive cases (authority known as *kendan-ken*) only, these powers permitted him to deal with the all-important question of dispute over land and crops.

It will be remembered that about this time an ideological dispute arose in Bakufu councils over policy toward the estate system and the constable. Kō no Moronao represented the faction pressing for destruction of estate holdings and for tacit acknowledgment of warrior depredations, while Ashikaga Tadayoshi headed the group of eastern chieftains[8] calling for a policy of moderation toward the estates. When Tadayoshi was assassinated in 1352, local samurai activities once again intensified in the central provinces. And once again the Bakufu was forced to reevaluate its position in regard to the estate system. Having progressed from a policy of outright defense of all estate rights to a cautious acknowledgment of the need for increased constable powers, the Bakufu now took an epoch-making step. In 1352 it promulgated a law authorizing constable appropriation, for distribution to the warriors, of half the yearly rice income (*nengu*) from estates in the provinces of Ōmi, Mino, and Owari and, in the following month, from those in Ise, Iga, Shima, Izumi, and Kawachi, as well.[9]

Assessment of commissariat rice (*hyōrōmai*) had been a common feature of military rule from the time of Taira Kiyomori (1118–81), who instituted the practice in 1180. But such levies by the Taira and later by the Minamoto were regarded as wartime

---

[7] The Bakufu issued a list of twelve prohibitions against constable activities (*shugo-bito hihō jōjō*). According to the first prohibition: "Aside from the *taihon sankajō, karita rōzeki* and *shisetsu jungyō*, [the constable will not] interfere in administration nor disrupt the stewards and shogunal housemen." "Kemmu Irai Tsuika Hō," pp. 23–24.

[8] Tadayoshi's strength was in the council of state, which included such eastern warriors as Kira, Hosokawa, Ishibashi, and Uesugi.

[9] In the seventh month the Bakufu stated: "We have ordered the constables to assign to the military forces as supply rice this year's crop from half of [each] estate in the three provinces of Ōmi, Mino, and Owari." The other five provinces were added in the eighth month. "Kemmu Irai Tsuika Hō," p. 5.

measures only and were suspended once peace had been restored. During the early years of the war between the courts, the Muromachi Bakufu had also granted certain estate funds to warriors (*hyōrō ryōsho*) in order to ease their military expenses. Like the leaders before him, Takauji had clamped down as firmly as possible on the unwarranted seizure of income from land. The importance of this new law lay in the fact that it was to remain in effect for the specified period of one year. Thus the Bakufu legalized confiscation of 50 percent of estate income in eight provinces, not on a day-to-day emergency basis, but for a set time.

The precise intent of Bakufu leaders behind this law is open to speculation. They may have hoped to aid the estate holder by limiting warrior greed to half the annual income; or they may have wished to provide the constable with funds to recruit vassals in the provinces; or, finally, they may have aimed at bringing under their control through law a practice already rampant on an extralegal basis in many parts of the country. Whatever the intent, the principal results were an even greater increase in constable power and a devastating blow to the estate holder. For even though the Bakufu attempted to retract this law within a few years (after several extensions of the time limit), it was reinstated in 1368 on a permanent, country-wide basis.[10]

The arrangement thus established between warrior and estate holder is known as the equal-division (*hanzei*) system. According to the 1368 law, equal-division provisions were to apply to all estates except those belonging to the imperial family (*kōshitsu-ryō*), the Sekkan families (*sekkan-ke watari-ryō*), and those still completely controlled by religious institutions (*honjo ichien shoryō*). There are no complete records, but in all likelihood these exceptions did not include extensive holdings. We may therefore conclude that the equal-division system had by this time become a country-wide institution.

This division of estates by means of the equal-division law resembled in many respects a practice originating in Kamakura times, which we have already noted, called *shitaji chūbun* ("dividing the land in half"). According to this practice, an estate holder

[10] *Ibid.*, p. 43.

and a steward who had reached a point of stalemate over control of the estate went to court and received a settlement from the Bakufu calling for the division of the estate lands into two equal parts. In the early stages leading up to the equal-division system, on the other hand, the constable was empowered to assign only half the rice income to a warrior. But by the time of the establishment of the permanent equal-division law in 1368 there had occurred a subtle transition in interpretation from half the rice income to half of all income and, finally, to half the land itself. Ostensibly, then, the equal-division system and the *shitaji chūbun* were nearly identical practices. The important distinction was that the former was controlled on a province-wide basis by the constable. Needless to say the effect on constable growth was profound. Not only was the constable's influence over the estate system greatly increased; he was also given an invaluable tool (distribution of half of estate lands) for stepping up recruitment of vassals among the local warriors.

While the constable was acquiring these additional powers over both the estate system and the warriors of his province, he was engaged also in a series of personal encroachments on estate lands and income. From an early date the Muromachi constable had begun to enter estates for the purpose of levying taxes, first for the Bakufu and then for himself. The Kamakura constable, it will be remembered, was empowered to enter the estate only under special circumstances—e.g., in case of rebellion or serious crime. At the same time he was strictly prohibited by law (the Jōei Code) from forcing levies on the estate while acting in his capacity as constable. Even as Bakufu leaders admonished against this practice, however, they indirectly acknowledged that it was precisely what certain constables were engaged in. Still it was not until Muromachi that the constable really began to drain income and labor from the estates in a systematic manner. At first he entered on behalf of the Bakufu to collect tax arrears from estate holders who were tardy in their remittances. But soon the constable, under one pretext or another, was crossing estate boundaries to collect his own taxes and to recruit his own *corvée* labor (*shugo buyaku*). The Bakufu tried to check this trend. In 1346,

for example, at the same time that Bakufu leaders acknowledged
and institutionalized additional constable powers in regard to
harvest disputes, the transfer of land, and the like, they spoke out
against "grasping the people's resources under the pretext of (a
need for) military supplies and loans." [11] The constable, however,
was hardly deterred by these admonitions, and continued his taxes
and *corvée* levies to the point where they became, to all intents
and purposes, an integral part of his office.[12]

One important point about the constable's method of taxation
should be mentioned. Lacking an administrative structure of his
own, the constable was forced to rely upon the collection apparatus
of the estate system to gather in his levies. And, since he had
neither the time nor the resources to establish direct feudal relations with the farmer,[13] the constable was obliged to work through
those in a position of closer control over the basic producer. This
constituted a fundamental weakness in the constable's position.
For once the local samurai, who had inserted himself more firmly
into the estate machinery, grew to the point where he no longer
needed direction from above, he would be able with relative ease
to dispense with the constable's function as tax collector and
arbiter. In other words, while the smaller-scale local samurai was
developing a solid base in the estate through the establishment
of direct relations with the estate producer, the constable remained basically an interloper, whose usefulness would vanish
with the final collapse of the estate system itself.

[11] See p. 37, *n.* 7.

[12] Since constable taxes closely resembled those of the Bakufu, they will be
discussed in the section dealing with Bakufu finances.

[13] Some Japanese scholars are greatly concerned with the transition during this
period (the war between the courts) from what they call slave (*dorei*) labor to
landlord (*jinushi*)-peasant (*sakunin*) relations. This new arrangement, which
the scholars term *nōdosei*, was characterized by the emergence of an independent,
or self-sustaining, producer and by attempts on the part of the landlord to extract
feudal rent (*jidai*) from those producers under his control. As a result of the
disorder of the times, however, many landlords had considerable difficulty in
managing their newly emancipated charges. According to these scholars, "the incomplete nature of his feudal relations with the farmer" was one of the principal
weaknesses of the local samurai (in his role as landlord). For example, see Matsumoto Shimpachirō, "Namboku-chō Nairan no Sho-zentei," in *Chūsei Shakai no
Kenkyū*, pp. 251–97.

For the time being, however, the constable was the strong man in both the province and the estate. This can be seen clearly from his new role in disputes that arose between estate owner and local samurai. During the Kamakura era nearly all warrior inroads into the estates were made by the steward, and when the estate holder had specific grievances, he presented them directly to the Bakufu. But in the Muromachi period the holder turned instead to the constable for redress. This may have proved effective in the early years when local samurai incursions were the most serious threat to the estate. As the century progressed, however, the estate holder found himself increasingly under attack not only from the local samurai but also from the constable, who continued to impose private taxes and levies without Bakufu approval. Helpless in the face of mounting losses, the estate holder was forced sooner or later to make a final concession to military superiority and to place responsibility for the collection of estate income in the hands of the constable. This practice was known as constable receipt (*shugo-uke*) and was based on a similar arrangement that developed between estate holder and steward during the Kamakura period (*jitō-uke*). In theory the constable was to gather the annual income, deduct a charge for his services, and remit the rest to the estate holder. By agreeing to this the holder hoped to eliminate the exactions of local samurai and, at the same time, to keep the constable's deduction down to a set figure. In practice the holder had placed himself at the mercy of the constable and was only one step away from the loss of his entire income. For the temptation to withhold increasingly larger amounts as part of his handling fee was more than the constable could resist.

So excellent a means for infringing upon the estates did the practice of constable receipt become that the constable in many cases could ill conceal his desire to offer this service to the estate holder. In 1402, for example, the constable of Bingo Province, Yamana Tokihiro (d. 1435), forced constable receipt on the Ōta estate over the repeated protests of Kōyasan, the holder. Out of an annual rice income of 1,800 *koku,* Yamana was to retain 800 and to remit 1,000 to Kōyasan. Thirty-seven years later, however, the amount of unremitted rice (*mishin*) totaled more than 20,600 *koku.* This meant that, in addition to his own fee of 800 *koku,* Yamana had channeled an average of approximately 557 *koku* per year more into his own coffers. Kōyasan's annual income, meanwhile, had dwindled to less than 450 *koku.*[14]

A few words on the history of another Kōyasan holding, the Nambu estate in Kii Province, will help clarify further the nature of these devices by which the military cut ever more deeply into the remaining estate lands. In 1222 Kōyasan, in order to solve its never-ending round of disputes with the steward of Nambu estate, agreed to the establishment of steward receipt, by which the steward would, in effect, assume control of the estate and would forward 500 *koku* of annual income to the temple authorities. From the outset, however, the steward failed to send in the stipulated amount. Throughout the Kamakura period and even during the first half-century of Ashikaga rule, Kōyasan petitioned the Bakufu with little success for satisfaction of its claims. Finally, during the Meitoku period (1390–93), the monks turned to the constable of Kii, Ōuchi Yoshihiro (1355–99), for protection against the steward. Ōuchi accepted their charge and ordered the steward to remit full annual payment. But still the steward would not desist from his exorbitant withholding, and in 1393 Ōuchi divided the estate in half (*shitaji chūbun*), granting 250 *koku* outright to the steward and returning 250 *koku* to the full control of Kōyasan (division of the land in this manner following the failure of steward receipt was a common pattern). Within six years, however, Hatakeyama had replaced Ōuchi as constable of Kii and soon the Hatakeyama forced Kōyasan to place its remaining 250 *koku* under constable receipt. Forty-two years later (1441) Kōyasan's once sizable income from Nambu estate had dwindled to a mere 30 *koku.*[15]

Traditional historians have attempted to show a close connection between the development of constable domains and the collapse of the estate system, as though the former's growth were in direct proportion to the latter's decline. Modern scholarship has

[14] This example is taken from Yasuda Motohisa, *Nihon Shōen-shi Gaisetsu,* p. 216.
[15] *Ibid.,* pp. 215–16.

completely revised this interpretation along lines suggested in this chapter.[16] The Muromachi constable built his domain not by destroying the estate system but by using it. His high-handed activities in the later fourteenth and early fifteenth centuries did, in fact, contribute greatly to the collapse of the estates, but by then the constable's own domain (*ryōkoku*) was crumbling. Thus the two main supports of regional society—the constable domain and the estate structure—were inseparably bound, and the constable could not long retain his power once the estates had finally disappeared. What elements within both estate and constable domain were responsible for these important institutional changes? A full answer to this question would demand examination of all phases of social and economic growth in the early Muromachi period. For the purpose of our present discussion the key element was the local samurai.

We have traced the constable's policy toward the estates. Let us turn now to his relations with the local samurai and to his position as military leader of the province. In a sense this is an artificial division of topics, since constable-estate relations cannot really be separated from constable-local samurai relations. Nevertheless there are certain aspects of the constable's personal contacts with the warriors of his province that deserve special attention.

In the last chapter we noted the local samurai's emergence as a small- and medium-sized warrior class in the central and western provinces during the final decades of the Kamakura period. Among the factors that contributed to the growth of this class were: the blurring of distinctions between those warriors who were direct vassals of the shogun and those who were not (*hi-gokenin*); the weakening of blood ties with the east and the development of strong local attachments; and the establishment of economic foundations in the estates based on closer feudal relations with the peasant producer. The decline and finally the fall of the Bakufu, however, left many local samurai without leadership and in great confusion. In the absence of order, these warriors organized bands

[16] See Kurokawa Tadanori, "Shugo Ryōkoku-sei to Shōen Taisei," in *Nihon-shi Kenkyū*, No. 57 (1961), p. 1.

(*akutō*) to protect their personal holdings and to carry on the struggle with the estate holder. But such bands, although recurring phenomena, were simply temporary arrangements formed to deal with emergency conditions. Once order had been partially restored by the Ashikaga Bakufu, the local samurai turned to the new constable for direction and control.[17]

One of the first tasks of the constable upon appointment to the province, therefore, was to establish vassalage ties with the local warriors. The constable was able to recruit certain local samurai through recommendation of grants in award (*onshō*) from the Bakufu for meritorious service in war and through appointment as personal representatives; but on the whole the early Muromachi

[17] Growth of the small warrior in the central and western provinces was, of course, a far more complex process than has been stated here. Following is a brief summary in more theoretical terms of the nature of warrior activities from the end of Kamakura, as generally interpreted by Japanese scholars. The first bands (*akutō*), which formed shortly after the Mongol invasions, were composed mainly of members of the steward-shogunal houseman class. Their aims in banding together varied according to location and conditions, but in general called for opposition both to the estate holder and to the Bakufu's system of family headship control. The main desire of these warriors was to establish unqualified control over their personal holdings (*zaichi ryōshu-ka*). In the course of their struggles they managed to recruit the support of certain estate functionaries (*shōkan*), who were distinguished from the steward by the fact that they received orders from the estate holder and not from the Bakufu, and a number of farmers (*nōmin*). In many cases, however, the farmers found the exactions of the steward to be more burdensome than those of the estate holder and turned against the bands. These bands formed by the steward-shogunal houseman class ran into further resistance around the time of the war between the courts in the form of organized activity on the part of the estate functionaries. These men were also developing as a warrior class for the protection of their own interests, and before the invasions had comprised the bulk of *hi-gokenin,* or those who were not direct vassals of the shogun. Faced by this new opposition from organized functionaries, the steward-shogunal houseman class of warriors disbanded their random activities as bands and sought to establish firm feudal ties extending over estate boundaries. From this time they came to be known, not as stewards or shogunal housemen (although they probably still held steward posts in many cases), but as local samurai (*kokujin* or *ji-samurai*). And their new forms of organization came to be known as *tō* or *ikki*. Thus the Muromachi constable encountered several types of warriors in the estates—the local samurai, the estate functionaries and those stewards who technically had not yet reached local samurai status. The constable, of course, attempted to recruit vassals from all of these groups; but for the purposes of this study I refer in the text only to the local samurai, since they were by far the most important from the standpoint of Bakufu-constable-warrior relations.

constable did not have sufficient legal powers to attract or to hold the majority of these dynamic warriors. As a result the constable was obliged to base his policy of aggrandizement and intervention in the estates, not only on self-betterment, but on a realization of the need to satisfy local samurai demands as well. The equal-division system in particular provided the constable with an important tool for gaining warrior support. Ironically, although the constable forced the reluctant Bakufu to sanction greater regional powers, he soon found himself in a position of similar reluctancy toward the local samurai. For in granting rights and interests in the estates to the local samurai, the constable became keenly aware that he must prevent the latter from overextending himself at the expense of the estate holder, lest he thereby destroy the constable's own base. Thus we note that, when dispute arose between the two, the constable often sought settlement in favor of the holder.

Appointment of powerful samurai as personal representatives (*daikan*) was a key phase in the establishment of the constable domain. The two main types of appointment were those to the estates and those as deputy constables (*shugo-dai*) to the provinces. Since the number of relatives he could utilize was usually limited, the constable, in order to manage his scattered holdings and interests, had to rely also on the services of newly acquired vassals. By dispatching these local warriors to posts in the various estates, the constable was able to establish quick and fairly effective control over his economic base. At the same time the constable sought to strengthen his political position by assigning a particularly trusted man to act as deputy in the event of his absence from the province. And, if he held more than one appointment from the Bakufu, the constable also assigned deputies to manage affairs in his other provinces.[18] The case of the Hosokawa illustrates how this process of local samurai assignment was handled by a great constable-daimyo family.

The Hosokawa were originally from the province of Mikawa.

[18] Professor Miura points out that some constables assigned more than one deputy to a province. The Shiba, for example, had both Kai and Asakura in the province of Echizen. "Shugo to Daimyō," p. 1190.

They were collaterals of the Ashikaga and were among Takauji's strongest supporters in the early fighting against Go-Daigo. It was this early support, in fact, that accounted for much of their later success. Even when Takauji was temporarily forced to retreat to Kyushu after his return from the Kantō in 1335, he appointed the Hosokawa to the provinces of Awa and Sanuki in Shikoku to carry on the struggle in the central districts. Thus it was in Shikoku that the Hosokawa first attempted to establish their base as constable. Since, like the average constable, they were new-comers, the Hosokawa had to set about recruiting vassals to assist in the management of their holdings. This procedure had the advantage of rallying support among the local warriors. And later, after Takauji had returned triumphantly to the Capital and had bestowed additional rewards and appointments on the Hosokawa, their leaders had even further need to recruit personal represen-tatives from among the powerful warriors of Awa and Sanuki. Some of the more important appointments made by the Hosokawa were: the Yasutomi as representatives (*daikan*) to Niimi estate in Bitchū; the Samukawa as *kumon* to Tōji's Kami-kuze estate in Yamashiro; the Kōsai as deputy constable to Tamba; and the Nagashio as deputy constable to Settsu. The names of these local samurai vassals—Yasutomi, Samukawa, Kōsai, Nagashio—appear frequently in the pages of *The Chronicle of Ōnin,* an indication of the power they were able to acquire through the years as a re-sult of their attachment to the Hosokawa.

A few comments should be made about the deputy constables. These men became increasingly important figures in the history of the Muromachi period after the establishment of the constable-daimyo domains under Yoshimitsu. The tendency was for the constable-daimyo to center their interests more and more on affairs in the Capital. In the absence of these leaders, it was the deputy constables who dealt with administrative matters at home. And when the great constable-daimyo became locked in struggle during the Ōnin War, many of these deputies took over real control in the provinces, and thereby emerged as the principal agents in the final overthrow of the constable-daimyo domains.

One power that the Bakufu zealously guarded and constantly

prohibited the constable from exercising was the confiscation and reassignment of warrior lands.[19] Both the Kamakura and Muromachi governments considered this one of their fundamental rights. And while the constable in Muromachi may have suggested worthy recipients from among the host of warriors who clamored for each reassignment, the final decision rested with the Bakufu. The manner in which the Bakufu at length settled upon a recipient reveals a significant fact about the nature of warrior society. For there was a strong feeling in medieval Japan that confiscated holdings (*kessho*) should, if possible, remain in the same family. Thus, when Bakufu leaders seized the lands of a warrior guilty of crime or breach of loyalty, they were guided in their reassignment by two principal considerations: 1) the status of relatives of the guilty party; 2) the extent and nature of past interests in the confiscated land. Consequently the confiscation of lands often did not, as might be supposed, result in a radical change in proprietorship. When a family head committed an offense, for example, the interests of his branch relatives were usually left unmolested. And when the branch relative lost his lands they were usually turned over to the family head.

We can speculate from this that, despite the seeming chaos and instability in landholding during the early years of Muromachi, there was a surprising degree of continuity in ownership among local samurai families. Unlike the constable, who was a new appointee, the local samurai was, in many cases, the product of several generations of local growth and development. Yet the local samurai's position was by no means fully secured. As we have seen, he was engaged in struggle not only with the estate holder, but also with the restless farmers and with other local samurai striving to strengthen their positions. In this stage of his development the local samurai had to rely on the protection and support of the new constable, whose authority could overcome local differences and class conflicts.

Another reason for local samurai dependence on the constable

[19] This paragraph is based on Kasamatsu Hiroshi, "Chūsei Kessho-chi Kyūyo ni Kan Suru Ichi Kōsatsu," in Ishimoda Shō and Satō Shin'ichi, eds., *Chūsei no Hō to Kokka*, pp. 411–47.

lay in the general policy of the Bakufu. Unlike Kamakura, which had based its power on the maintenance of close ties with the local warrior, who was at the same time a shogunal houseman, the Muromachi Bakufu had from the outset tended to deal solely through the constable. Even as the constable himself attempted to acquire greater powers, the Bakufu turned increasingly to him for the collection of taxes, the transmission of decrees, and the like. In later years it became virtually impossible to make contact with government leaders except through the office of constable. Thus the local samurai had no alternative source of authority to which he could turn. He either accepted constable overlordship or suffered the consequences of independence in a predatory world.

Through all the confusion of the times, then, we can see a distinct pattern of warrior growth. While the constable was a temporary figure in the history of these years, the local samurai was an integral part of a long process of feudal growth on the local level. He joined the constable of necessity, but as we shall see, his loyalty remained only so long as the constable held a preeminent position. At the first sign of weakness, the local samurai would desert his lord for other camps. This in turn drove the constable to greater dependence on Bakufu prestige, a tendency that was particularly marked among the constable-daimyo from Yoshimitsu's time.

A contemporary comment on the constable that appears in the *Taihei-ki* will serve as a summation of the developments discussed in this chapter:

When the country was ruled by Takatoki of the former House of Hōjō, constables of the various provinces did not interfere in affairs beyond their authority to punish, as granted in the *taihon sankajō*. But in these times all matters, great and small, are decided by the constable alone. Charged with full jurisdiction over his province, the constable has gathered the steward and the shogunal houseman as vassals; and, by enforcing rice levies [*hanzei*], he has taken control of the estates. In short his power is equal to that of Rokuhara or the Kyushu deputy of former generations.[20]

[20] Gotō Tanji and Okami Masao, eds., *Taihei-ki*, III, 252.

The Bakufu–Constable Balance of Power

Ashikaga Takauji and his son Yoshiakira devoted their lives to the reestablishment of military supremacy after the destruction of the first Bakufu at Kamakura. Their task was made the more formidable not only by the continuing resistance of the southern court, but by strife within the ranks of the new Bakufu as well. It is a credit to Ashikaga generalship that this Bakufu, which they founded, was able simply to survive the convulsions of its early years. Not only did it survive, but by the time of Yoshiakira's death in 1367 the new military government in Kyoto enjoyed a greater degree of security and support than at any previous time. The offensive strength of the southern court was nearly spent, and only in Kyushu were the loyalists still able to maintain the upper hand. Moreover the disputes that had wracked the Bakufu at mid-century, while not entirely resolved ideologically, no longer presented an immediate threat to Bakufu unity.

There were many reasons for these improved conditions, but probably the most important was the growth of the constable-daimyo. The Bakufu's attitude toward the steady increase in constable powers was, as we have seen, reluctant and inconsistent. Nevertheless, during the first three decades of Ashikaga rule the constables acquired, either through legal enactment or through personal aggrandizement, substantial control over their domains. At the same time many small constables had fallen as a result of internal strife, and by 1367 the number of constable families in the central and western provinces had, as we have seen, narrowed to eleven.[1] These newly consolidated constable-daimyo domains, spanning in many cases two or more provinces, became the basis of a regional stability unknown since the breakdown of estate boundaries at the end of the Kamakura era.

The task now facing the Bakufu was twofold: the establishment of permanent offices, administrative forms, and policies to supplant the loose structure and conduct of government under Takauji and Yoshiakira; and the reaffirmation of command over the semiautonomous constable-daimyo.

Yoshiakira's successor, Yoshimitsu, was only a lad of ten at the time of his father's death. To the great fortune of the Bakufu the former shogun had selected one of the most capable men of the age, Hosokawa Yoriyuki (1329–92), to act as assistant (*shitsuji*) during his son's minority. It is said that Yoshiakira, while on his death bed, had summoned both the Hosokawa chieftain and Yoshimitsu. To the former he said, "I give you a son," and to the latter, "I give you a father."[2]

Within a few weeks of Hosokawa Yoriyuki's appointment as assistant in the eleventh month of 1367, Yoshiakira was dead at thirty-eight. On the twenty-ninth day of the following month the new Bakufu leader issued a series of stern edicts exhorting against governmental waste, extravagant clothing, and the exchange of New Year's gifts.[3] This puritanical attitude was eventually to create ill will toward Yoriyuki among the other constable-daimyo, but for the time being it served as a warning that Bakufu affairs were in firm hands.

---

[1] Hosokawa, Shiba, Hatakeyama, Isshiki, Yamana, Imagawa, Sasaki, Akamatsu, Toki, Ōuchi, and Togashi. See Chapter 11, "The Muromachi Bakufu."

[2] Quoted in Yomiuri Shimbun Sha, *Nihon no Rekishi*, V, 261.

[3] "Kemmu Irai Tsuika Hō," p. 41.

In the sixth month of 1368 Yoriyuki took his first major step
to establish a consistent Bakufu policy with issuance of the law
that placed the equal-division system on a permanent, country-
wide basis. In comparison to the hesitant tone of former decrees,
this law made clear the limits of the system. For, while attempting
to satisfy warrior demands and to bring Bakufu policy in line
with existing practices, Yoriyuki also sought to placate the class
of large estate holders by excluding lands belonging to the imperial
and Sekkan families and those fully controlled by religious institutions.

Yoriyuki also turned his attention at an early date to the question of taxation and land claims. The regular payment (*go-kōnōyaku*) due the Bakufu from the constable-daimyo had originally
been two percent of the constable's yearly income from estate
holdings. This figure was later increased to five percent and became the object of strong opposition and resentment on the part
of the constables. In order to establish a more favorable atmosphere
for Bakufu-constable relations, Yoriyuki restored the original rate
of two percent. At the same time he attacked the welter of conflicting land claims that had piled up during the confusion of the
Bakufu's first years. Yoriyuki was particularly alert to weed out
the decisions of Kō no Moronao, who, in his capacity as first
assistant to Takauji, had issued a number of arbitrary and illegal
decisions on ownership and income.[4]

Beyond these preliminary measures, Yoriyuki's real job was to
find a working solution to one of the Bakufu's most fundamental
problems: its inherently weak financial position. In marked contrast to the Kamakura Bakufu, which had a solid economic base
of domains in the east (Kantō *goryō*), Ashikaga holdings and
rights (*goryōsho*), like those of their constables, were scattered
and irregular. Unfortunately we do not know the exact amount
of income derived by the Bakufu from these landed interests,
but it is certain that it was not sufficient to meet the many needs
of government. From the beginning Bakufu leaders were forced to

[4] This reference to Yoriyuki's attempts to reverse the decisions of Kō no Moronao
appears in the *Hosokawa Yoriyuki-ki,* quoted in Ōkubo Toshinori, *et al., Shiryō ni
Yoru Nihon no Ayumi, Chūsei-hen,* pp. 299–300.

rely on hand-to-mouth financing. We have seen above how Hosokawa Yoriyuki deemed it wise to relax one impost on the constable. To compensate for that loss in revenue he was obliged to turn to other sources. At length, on the occasion of extraordinary expenses stemming from the coronation of the Emperor Go-En'yū in 1371, Yoriyuki levied an emergency tax on sake brewers and pawnbrokers in and around the Capital.[5] Although not an original idea (for the court and several of the larger temples and shrines had already begun to tap this rich source of income), Yoriyuki's new tax was to have an extremely important influence on the future course of the Bakufu. In order to understand why, we must briefly examine the development of these commercial enterprises during the Muromachi period.

The origins of the brewing and marketing of sake can be traced to the Heian period, but it was not until the war between the courts that this enterprise began to assume real commercial significance. This was a result partly of the general growth in commerce (especially the increased circulation of money) during the early years of Muromachi and partly of the developing taste for sake in the big cities. There are no exact figures on the profits realized by sake brewers (sakaya) in the Capital at this time, but we can assume from the enormous quantities of this beverage consumed at parties and other functions that such profits were sizable.[6] As a result the sake brewers prospered and came to accumulate vast sums of money. In order to utilize their excess capital, a number of brewers turned to the side business of pawnbroking (dosō).[7] So rewarding did this prove that in many cases the entrepreneur's function as pawnbroker came to occupy a more important position than his primary job as sake brewer. This is not to say that all pawnbrokers were converted sake dealers, but the two occupations (sakaya-dosō) did become closely related. To-

[5] This levy was made at the rate of 30 kan for each brokerage house and 200 mon for every bottle (tsubo) of sake. The decree is recorded in Kaei Sandai-ki, in Hanawa Hokiichi, ed., Gunsho Ruijū, XXVI, 78.

[6] Ono Akitsugu, "Muromachi Bakufu no Sakaya Tōsei," in Nihon Sangyō Hattatsu Shi no Kenkyū, p. 235.

[7] For a discussion in English on the dosō, see Delmer M. Brown, Money Economy in Medieval Japan, pp. 46–51.

gether the brewer and the broker stood at the highest level of affluence in medieval Japan.

While the Bakufu allowed trade guilds (*za*) centered in other occupations to seek the patronage of various aristocrats and religious institutions, it reserved for itself exclusive rights of contact with the brewer-brokers after Hosokawa Yoriyuki's first levy in 1371.[8] Twenty-two years later, Bakufu leaders issued a law in which they regularized the monthly assessment of these enterprises, and at the same time stated that there would be no further need for emergency levies.[9] But the Bakufu could never quite resist the temptation to dip into brewer-broker profits, and, despite repeated resolutions to the contrary, continued to make extra levies above the regular monthly assessments. This practice, along with many similar financial abuses, was particularly marked during the rule of Ashikaga Yoshimasa (1436–90) before the Ōnin War. According to *The Chronicle of Ōnin*, Yoshimasa, in preparation for the Great Thanksgiving ceremony (*daijōe*) of 1456, made seventeen assessments on the pawnbrokers during the eleventh and twelfth months of that year.[10]

The Bakufu maintained favorable monopolistic conditions for the brewer-brokers in order to protect their rich tax potential. In a sense it provided conditions that were too favorable, for while Bakufu leaders would have preferred the creation of more and more breweries and shops, which they could tax, the independent brewers and brokers imposed strict organizational restrictions. From the end of Ōei (around 1425–26) to the beginning of Ōnin (1467), for example, the number of brewers in Kyoto varied little from the 342 establishments listed in 1425.[11]

The usurious rates charged by brokerage houses caused anguish among all classes of society and, as we shall see, served to spark

[8] The makers of *miso* sauce (*misoya*) were also under Bakufu control, but in the records of Muromachi reference is usually limited to the brewers and the brokers. See *ibid.*, p. 233.

[9] "Kemmu Irai Tsuika Hō," p. 60. In regard to emergency levies the text states: "Even though emergencies may arise, extraordinary levies by the temples and shrines or by the shogun above the regular monthly assessments are to be permanently discontinued."

[10] *Ōnin-ki*, in Hanawa, *Gunsho Ruijū*, XX, 356.

[11] Ono Akitsugu, *Nihon Sangyō Hattatsu Shi no Kenkyū*, p. 234.

more than one uprising during the fifteenth century. The important point to note here is that the Muromachi Bakufu, constantly in need of funds, shifted a sizable portion of its revenue burden from the natural economy (land) and payment in kind to a commercial base and payment in cash.[12] This was a most significant development, for, despite the remarkable growth of commerce in Muromachi, the warrior society that the Bakufu headed was still overwhelmingly committed to land and its possession. Without question the weakness of the Muromachi Bakufu in land was one of the fundamental reasons why it never approached the strength of the preceding Kamakura or the succeeding Edo governments.

During the Kamakura period two additional taxes—on land (*tansen,* on each *tan* of arable land) and on households (*munebetsu-sen*)—had been created to defray extraordinary expenses, such as those arising from coronation or other state ceremonies and from the need for palace, temple, or shrine repairs. Yoriyuki levied the first Muromachi land tax in 1372 to collect funds for repair of the Hie Shrine's portable shrine.[13] From that time on both land and household taxes were imposed with such frequency that, like the levy on sake brewers and pawnbrokers, they became a regular part of the Bakufu's tax structure. The land and household taxes, however, differed basically from the brewer-broker levies. While the latter were collected in cash within the city limits of Kyoto, the land and household taxes were usually gathered in kind through the constable. As noted, this became one of the means by which the constable was able to enter the estate. And later, by imitating these Bakufu taxes for his own personal profit (*shugo tansen* and *shugo munebetsu-sen*), the constable was able to appropriate still another portion of the income from land.

Hosokawa Yoriyuki's most significant work, apart from his at-

---

[12] The Bakufu even separated the functions of collecting payments in kind (through the *kura bugyō*) and payments in cash (through the *nōsen kata*).

[13] The wording of this decree calls for the collection of registers (*ōtabumi*) and the assessment of thirty *mon* per *tan* of land held by religious institutions (*jisha honjo ryō*) and by stewards and shogunal housemen. *Kaei Sandai-ki,* p. 81.

tempts to place the Bakufu on a firmer tax basis, lay in restructuring the administrative organs of government. It will be recalled that Takauji had in general adopted the institutions of the Kamakura Bakufu with the important exception of the office of shogunal regent. Although his aim apparently was to imitate the early shogunal authoritarianism of Minamoto Yoritomo, Takauji also retained, in name at least, the forms of assembly government evolved by the Hōjō, such as the council of state and the board of coadjutors. The result was that government under Takauji and Yoshiakira, while functional, was not clearly defined and certainly had not been adapted to meet the changing conditions of early Muromachi.

The overriding fact confronting Yoriyuki and other Bakufu leaders was that shogunal authoritarianism, at least as conceived in the early years of Kamakura, was no longer a political possibility. The Muromachi Bakufu's economic and military bases were too weak, while the constable had seized power sufficient to render unworkable any arrangement that did not provide him with a major voice in governmental affairs. Certain constables were, of course, already in the Bakufu. Yoriyuki himself was a great constable-daimyo and, like Shiba Yoshimasa (1350–1410) before him, held the position of assistant. But this position, despite the influence enjoyed by Yoriyuki during the Shogun Yoshimitsu's minority, was not an institutionally powerful office. Rather, the assistant was a private official in the service of the head of the Ashikaga family. Although the latter might concurrently hold the office of shogun, the authority of his assistant did not, theoretically, extend beyond family councils. It was not until the assistant, with the new title of shogunal deputy (*kanrei*) came to occupy a position directly below the shogun (in his capacity as leader of the Bakufu) that this office became an integral part of Muromachi government.

The shogunal deputy of Muromachi might be likened to the shogunal regent of Kamakura times, but, whereas the regent had held real power under a figurehead shogun, the deputy was fully subordinate, in the early years at least, to an active Ashikaga shogun. From the time of Yoshimitsu the shogunal deputy formed a liaison between the shogun and the main branches of the Bakufu. And since the shogunal deputy was always selected from among the three most powerful constable families collateral to the Ashikaga—the Shiba, Hosokawa, and Hatakeyama—this office was not a Hōjō-type monopoly, but an expression at the highest level of the need for solid constable support within the Bakufu.

During the Muromachi period there were five branches of the central government below the shogun and the deputy: the administrative board, the board of inquiry, and the board of retainers from Yoritomo's time; and the council of state and board of coadjutors from Hōjō rule. The council of state had been the main deliberative assembly of the Hōjō regents, and the board of coadjutors had functioned as an adjunct to the council for the processing of legal actions related to land. As an indication of the close relationship between the occupants of these two bodies, members of the board of coadjutors generally held positions also on the council of state. But while their day-to-day operations remained approximately the same as during the Kamakura era, both bodies were now more concerned with the enforcement of decisions than with actual policy-making, since most administrative action during the Muromachi era emanated from shogunal order.[14] Finally, both the council of state and the board of coadjutors were directly under the control of the shogunal deputy.

The board of inquiry had been the main judicial arm of the Kamakura Bakufu in its early years. But after the establishment in 1249 of the board of coadjutors, which was assigned responsibility for claims involving land, officials of the board of inquiry were left to deal primarily with disputes arising over cash loans and movable property. During the Muromachi period the functions of the board of inquiry were even further reduced, so that this once powerful body had little authority beyond the gathering of records and documents. At the same time, the administrative board, which had been the principal executive organ of the Kamakura Bakufu

[14] Shogunal orders during the Muromachi period were generally formed on the basis of opinions received from the various administrators (*bugyō-nin*). Nakada Kaoru, "Kamakura-Muromachi Bakufu no Kansei ni Tsuite," in *Hōsei-shi Ronshū*, III, 650.

(in imitation of the house governments of the great Heian families), was limited during Muromachi to the management of financial affairs. This, of course, was still an important function, and Bakufu leaders at first retained as hereditary chiefs (*shitsuji*) of the administrative board members of the Nikaidō family from Kamakura days. In 1379 they switched to an Ashikaga retainer, Ise Sadatsugu (1309–91). Thenceforth, until the Ōnin War, the Ise family, by utilizing their newly acquired influence in financial affairs plus their special position as guardians to the heirs of the shogunate, became a potent force in Bakufu politics.[15]

Of all the governmental branches under the Muromachi deputy the most important was the board of retainers. The head of this body (*shoshi*), who occupied, concurrently, the post of constable of Yamashiro Province,[16] was responsible for the protection of both the Bakufu and the city of Kyoto. This meant that the chieftain presiding over the board of retainers was in a uniquely strategic position in relation to the Bakufu as well as to his fellow warriors. It is therefore not surprising that the office was available only to very powerful constable-daimyo. Originally many redoubtable families, including the Imagawa, Hosokawa, Hatakeyama, Shiba, and Toki, had supplied leaders to the board of retainers, but by the turn of the century the headship had become the special domain of four—the Yamana, Akamatsu, Kyōgoku, and Isshiki. Together with the three shogunal deputy families of Shiba, Hosokawa, and Hatakeyama, they formed the great body of constable-daimyo participants in the Muromachi Bakufu.[17]

It would be incorrect to give full credit to Hosokawa Yoriyuki for the restructuring of the Muromachi Bakufu in the second half of the fourteenth century, since this was an evolutionary

[15] This function of guardian, which was performed by the Ise family, will be discussed in a later section dealing with the relationship between Ashikaga Yoshimasa and Ise Sadachika.

[16] Only between the years 1394 and 1418 were these two offices not held by the same person. Sugiyama Hiroshi, "Muromachi Bakufu," in Tōkyō Daigaku Shuppan Kai, *Nihon Rekishi Kōza*, p. 55.

[17] These participants were known as the *sankan-shishiki* after the three shogunal deputies and the four families who occupied the headship of the board of retainers on an alternating basis.

process that spanned years both before and after Yoriyuki's rise to prominence. Nevertheless certain developments, such as the emergence of the constable-daimyo and elimination of the southern court's offensive potential, made the time following Yoshiakira's death especially opportune for the systematization of special governmental forms outside the mold of Kamakura and uniquely suited to the conditions of Muromachi. Yoriyuki did not introduce revolutionary policies; rather, he began the codification and regularization of offices and practices incipient before his appointment to high position. Still, we must acknowledge that the Hosokawa leader was particularly well equipped for this task of governmental adjustment, and did much to place the Muromachi Bakufu on its firmest political and economic basis.

The principal beneficiary of these achievements was the adult Yoshimitsu, who assumed power in his own right upon the forced resignation of Yoriyuki in 1379. There were two basic reasons for Yoriyuki's downfall: first, he had developed personal antagonisms against certain other constable-daimyo that finally flared into open opposition; and, second, he became the victim of his own creation. Yoriyuki had been one of the chief architects of a *balance* of power between the Bakufu and the constable-daimyo. Yet he himself had already occupied the post of shogunal deputy for twelve years. Further monopolization of this office by the Hosokawa would have seriously threatened the very balance that Yoriyuki had striven to bring about.

What, then, was the over-all character of this restructured Bakufu, now headed by the third Ashikaga shogun, Yoshimitsu, in terms of the economic and political developments discussed separately above? I have, for convenience, used the phrase Bakufu-constable balance of power, even though this does not precisely explain the nature of the relationship between the Bakufu and the constable-daimyo from Yoshimitsu's time until the Ōnin War. The main divergence among Japanese scholars on this point lies in their conflicting assessments of the extent of Bakufu power. Most scholars agree on the fundamental weakness of the shogun's position and on the fact that the Bakufu was able to continue only with the support of the constable-daimyo. But, while one of the two principal schools of interpretation holds that the extent of Bakufu power was defined entirely by the league of constable-daimyo supporting it, the other maintains that the power structure from Yoshimitsu on is best described as a combination of Bakufu *plus* constable-daimyo league. In other words, whereas the first school discounts the private power of the Bakufu and speaks only of the league of constable-daimyo, the second stresses the separate strengths of both the Bakufu and the constable-daimyo.[18]

Research on this question of Bakufu power has not been developed sufficiently to warrant unqualified acceptance of either of the above interpretations. The general impression of the student of this period is that the Bakufu (as an entity apart from its relationship with the constable-daimyo) gradually declined from a high point under Yoshimitsu to virtual impotence, at least militarily, during the rule of Yoshimitsu's grandson, Yoshimasa.

Whatever strength the Bakufu did have at the end of the fourteenth century can be related in large part to its geographical position in the central province of Yamashiro. In order to meet the demands of wartime necessity, Bakufu leaders had from an early date made special efforts to enlist the direct support of warriors of both the local samurai and estate functionary classes in regions around the Capital.[19] One of their principal means for gaining this support was to assign management of Bakufu holdings in Yamashiro to the various enlistees. These warriors were then to form a reservoir of fighting strength readily available to the Bakufu in time of emergency without the need to deal through the constable, as was required when making troop levies in other parts of the country. It is not clear at the present stage of research just how successful the Bakufu was in marshaling the military resources of Yamashiro. We have seen that the head of the board of retainers was given concurrent appointment as Yamashiro constable and was assigned responsibility for the defense of both

[18] Nagahara Keiji is the best-known representative of the first school, while Satō Shin'ichi is the foremost figure of the second. See Satō, "Muromachi Bakufu Ron," p. 4, for discussion of this interpretational dispute.

[19] Takauji was forced to recruit nonhousemen as well as housemen, thus jeopardizing to a certain extent the exclusive relations between shogun and direct vassals. *Ibid.*, p. 13.

Kyoto and the Bakufu. Still, the extent of this chieftain's powers
would seem to have been limited by the degree of direct Bakufu
control over local warriors. We may presume, therefore, that the
headship of the board of retainers grew in importance as the military strength of the Bakufu declined, even in the province of
Yámashiro, during the fifteenth century. Although this position
could never rank in authority with that of shogunal deputy, it is
interesting to note that the board of retainers family of Yamana was
the one that finally challenged the supremacy of the shogunal
deputy house of Hosokawa in the years leading to the Ōnin War.

The home provinces were by far the most advanced areas in the
country agriculturally and commercially. This fact presented the
Bakufu with both special advantages and special problems. Income
from the highly prosperous sake brewers and pawnbrokers of
Kyoto was a great boon to Bakufu finances. Moreover Bakufu
leaders were able to levy their land tax and their household tax
most successfully in the provinces near the Capital, not only because of the proximity of these areas, but also because of the intense
development of land and the large number of semi-independent
farmers producing there. But in order to protect the brewers and
brokers, the Bakufu had to grant them certain monopoly rights.
Equipped with such rights, these aggressive merchants were able
to indulge freely in usury and other abuses to the despair of the
small peasants, who were forced to negotiate loans on their land
in times of difficulty. Before long many holdings in Yamashiro
and nearby provinces had fallen into the hands of the money-
lenders.

Burdened with excessive taxation and harassed by the uncom-
promising rules of the usurer, the peasants of the home provinces
at first sought redress of their grievances in petitions (gōso). Later,
in the fifteenth century, they turned to armed revolt (doikki) and
to demands for cancellation of their debts (tokusei).[20] These

[20] Absconding (chōsan) was also a common practice, along with the use of
petitions, during the early years of peasant grievances in the Muromachi period.
But these practices were strictly defensive in nature. The peasants did not mount
the offensive until the revolts of the fifteenth century, at which time their three
main targets were the sanmi ittai (the estate holder, the Bakufu, and the usurer).
Yūzankaku, Shinsetsu Nihon Rekishi, VI, 37.

questions will be taken up in more detail later. The important point to note here is the extent to which the Muromachi Bakufu was limited, both materially and geographically, even on the eve of its most vigorous period under Yoshimitsu. This is not to suggest that the Bakufu wielded no influence in other parts of the country. In fact the balance of power with the constable-daimyo was based in large part on the constables' need for Bakufu prestige. But the Bakufu's practical power, even for those who would compare it favorably with the constable-daimyo league, was concentrated militarily and economically in an exceedingly small area. And because of this concentration in highly developed Yamashiro and its neighboring provinces, a series of uprisings and violence on the Bakufu's own doorstep was to shake and further weaken government during the years following Yoshimitsu.

The adult Yoshimitsu dominated Bakufu politics for nearly thirty years, from 1379 until his death in 1408. This was a truly remarkable period in the history of the Muromachi Bakufu, for at the height of his career Yoshimitsu was to exercise greater power over a wider area than any leader during the next two hundred years of Ashikaga rule. Yoshimitsu's shogunacy, therefore, marks a peak from which to examine the subsequent decline of the Muromachi Bakufu. Actually, the Bakufu's decline did not follow immediately upon Yoshimitsu's death. Central control remained significant during the rule of his sons, Yoshimochi and Yoshinori, and it was not until the assassination of the latter in 1441 that government began to deteriorate at a rapid rate. Hence the year 1441 will be our point of departure for a more detailed study in the next chapter of the events leading to the Ōnin War. What remains here is to examine the manner in which Ashikaga Yoshimitsu brought to fruition his brand of power politics through the stabilization of relations between the Muromachi Bakufu and its league of semi-autonomous constable-daimyo.

Apart from his opening of trade with Ming China, there were three main phases of Yoshimitsu's rule: his policy toward the constable-daimyo; his successful efforts to bring about unification of the northern and southern courts; and his relations with the imperial court in Kyoto after unification. All three of these phases were interrelated and were purely political in nature. Yoshimitsu's overriding aim was to strengthen central government. And in this regard there is perhaps a tendency to overrate the accomplishments of Yoshimitsu, since his shogunacy was one of the few bright periods of "strong" rule during the troubled centuries of Muromachi. Yoshimitsu's successes as a statesman and as a military leader were indeed notable, but continued research into this period will undoubtedly confirm the view that Yoshimitsu was more the master of compromise and concession than the iron-fisted dictator. He was able to control with considerable skill the various factions that tended separately to bring disunity to the land. But for all his victories, Yoshimitsu was not able to strengthen to any great extent the economic and military bases of the Muromachi Bakufu.[21]

During the six-year period from 1385 until 1390 Yoshimitsu traveled extensively throughout the central and western provinces. His expressed purpose on most of these excursions was a desire to visit various shrines and temples, but the size and quality of his retinues, which usually included several daimyo, suggests that Yoshimitsu's real aim was to observe regional power conditions.[22] In fact Yoshimitsu was concerned with three main power groups: the great religious institutions (to which he contributed liberally); supporters of the southern court; and the constable-daimyo.

The question of unification was uppermost in the minds of many Bakufu leaders. Although the southern court no longer posed a serious threat to Bakufu supremacy, it remained a potential rallying point for discontented elements and an impediment to Ashikaga aspirations in regard to both the constable-daimyo and the imperial house. Hosokawa Yoriyuki had attempted to arrange a truce with the Yoshino government through the offices of Kusunoki Masanori (d. 1390). But the southern court itself was divided over the question of unification[23] and Yoriyuki's efforts

[21] Yoshimitsu also sought to bolster his finances through trade with the rulers of Ming China. This is an interesting aspect of the Yoshimitsu period, but is beyond the scope of this study.

[22] Hattori Kentarō, "Ashikaga Yoshimitsu," in Kawade Shobō, *Nihon Rekishi Kōza*, III, 231.

[23] The antiunification faction was centered around the Emperor Chōkei (r. 1368–82), while the prounification group was led by Chōkei's younger brother,

were not successful. It remained for Yoshimitsu to bring about the final reconciliation in 1392 with a promise of return to the pre-Kemmu system of alternate succession between the junior and senior lines.[24] Prior to this achievement, Yoshimitsu had asserted his preeminence in Bakufu-constable affairs through the chastisement of two powerful families, the Toki and the Yamana. Whatever faint hopes of ultimate victory southern supporters might still have harbored were thereby dashed, and the prounification faction headed by Emperor Go-Kameyama accepted Kyoto's peace proposals.

Yoshimitsu's over-all policy was based on strict maintenance of the balance of power between the constable-daimyo and the Bakufu. When a constable family grew in size to the point where it might upset this balance or threaten the security of the Bakufu, it had to be reduced at all costs. This was a fundamental axiom of the times, held not only by Yoshimitsu, but by the constables themselves. The restructured Bakufu was based on the concept that the great provincial families would share certain powers. Any attempt by one constable to overextend his personal authority through the abuse of these powers was immediately viewed with alarm by the others. We have seen how even the distinguished Hosokawa Yoriyuki was forced to relinquish his post as shogunal deputy, which he had held for twelve years, when faced with the strong opposition of hostile chieftains suspicious of a possible monopolization of power by the Hosokawa. And a similar fate befell Imagawa Sadayo (Ryōshun), the pacifier of Kyushu, who was relieved of his position as Kyushu deputy (*tandai*) in 1395 as a result of the slanderous remarks of another constable-daimyo.[25]

Yoshimitsu was not necessarily in personal agreement with these dismissals. He seems, for example, to have retained a lifelong respect for Hosokawa Yoriyuki and to have agreed to the latter's

---

Go-Kameyama (r. 1383 until unification in 1392). Kusunoki Masanori, who favored agreement between the courts, went over to the northern side during Chōkei's reign (1369) and returned when Go-Kameyama ascended the throne. Yomiuri Shimbun Sha, *Nihon no Rekishi*, pp. 266–69.

[24] Although alternate succession was promised, it was never put into effect. The succession went exclusively to the northern line.

[25] Ōuchi Yoshihiro.

removal from power only with the greatest reluctance. It is not fully clear, in fact, exactly what pressures Yoshimitsu was under from other constables on the occasions in which he took the lead in reducing certain overly ambitious families, such as the Toki (constables of Mino, Owari, and Ise) in 1388 and the Yamana, holders of eleven provinces, in 1391. One thing seems certain: the decisions to act against these families were not made by the shogun alone, but emerged from the whole context of Bakufu-constable relations.

In the cases of both the Toki and the Yamana, Yoshimitsu took advantage of family quarrels to reduce their constable holdings. By backing one faction or another, the shogun encouraged the various relatives to fight themselves into exhaustion, at which point he was able to dictate the peace settlement.

Yoshimitsu's last great campaign was in 1399 against Ōuchi Yoshihiro, the powerful western constable whose growth threatened the Bakufu-constable balance. After victory over Yoshihiro and his supporters at the city of Sakai, Yoshimitsu returned to Kyoto to enjoy his years of greatest prestige until his death in 1408.

There is one final phase of Yoshimitsu's rule that is important to our study: his relations with the imperial court in Kyoto. So forward and even audacious did Yoshimitsu become in his attitude toward the emperor that he gave every appearance of coveting the throne for himself. Whether or not this was truly his personal ambition is open to question, but Yoshimitsu certainly did try to make use of imperial prestige to strengthen the Bakufu. This was a most important development in the history of the Bakufu before the Ōnin War, but its importance was not revealed so much during Yoshimitsu's time as it was during the rule of Yoshimasa, who became, as it were, a product of his grandfather's relations with the throne.

V

The Decline of the Muromachi Bakufu

THE ASSASSINATION OF YOSHINORI

The assassination of Yoshinori in 1441 marked a turning point in the fortunes of the Muromachi Bakufu. Although the origins of the Ōnin War and the failure of central government must, in the broader sense, be traced to conflicts within the system of constable-daimyo that were nurtured from the beginning by the nature of Ashikaga rule, Yoshinori's death was clearly the beginning of the Bakufu's downward slide. Under Yoshimitsu, Yoshimochi (1385–1428), and Yoshinori, the Ashikaga had enjoyed their period of greatest prestige. Yet the pattern for this prestige was marked throughout more by skillful politics than by overwhelming military superiority. It was Yoshimitsu who had perfected the techniques of personal surveillance and "isolate and conquer" that had made possible Ashikaga dominance of the great constable-daimyo. Backed by strong lieutenants, Yoshimochi and Yoshinori had continued their father's forceful policies. But at best the Ashikaga shoguns of this period could only hope to maintain a loose hegemony over a group of provincial chieftains whose growth was, by nature, based on decentralization. Yoshinori, in particular, seemed to keep the constables in check mainly through the force of his own personality.

The result of Yoshinori's assassination and the sequence of events surrounding it was threefold: first, a failure of shogunal leadership (accompanied, coincidentally, by a marked decline in the caliber of leadership at the shogunal deputy level as well); second, a significant shift in the balance of constable power in the central provinces; and, third, the beginning of enmity between the houses of Akamatsu and Yamana that was to contribute both to the outbreak of the Ōnin War and to its prolongation. Because of these points it is important to trace in some detail the circumstances under which Akamatsu Mitsusuke (1381–1441) assassinated the Shogun Yoshinori.

The status of the Akamatsu family under the Muromachi Bakufu was unique. A great family (gōzoku) from the province of Harima, they had thrown in their lot with the Emperor Go-Daigo at an early date and, during the fighting against the Hōjō, had played an important role in bringing about the destruction of Roku-hara.[1] Their reward for this invaluable service was only a single manor in Harima. Moreover, Norimura (1277–1350), the Aka-matsu leader, lost his post as constable of that province. Embittered, he turned to Ashikaga Takauji and became one of the strongest supporters of the northern court. As a result of the efforts of Norimura and his sons, the Akamatsu emerged as the only great family in the central provinces, apart from the Sasaki, successfully to make the transition to constable-daimyo status during the early years of the Muromachi Bakufu. The family eventually came to control the three provinces of Harima, Bizen, and Mima-saka[2] and to occupy a position among the Houses qualified to hold headship of the board of retainers.

[1] During the Kamakura period the Bakufu stationed two officers (*tandai*) in this ward southeast of Kyoto to conduct affairs in the Capital. The destruction of Rokuhara by Akamatsu and other loyalist generals in 1333 marked the end of Bakufu administration in the central provinces.

[2] The Akamatsu received Mimasaka after the defeat of the Yamana in 1391.

Akamatsu Mitsusuke succeeded to the family headship in 1427. His position was immediately threatened when the Shogun Yoshimochi attempted to "nationalize" the province of Harima in order to bestow it on his favorite, Akamatsu Mochisada.[3] Mitsusuke promptly left the Capital for Harima and entrenched himself in the family stronghold at Shirahata. Although Yoshimochi began preparations for an attack on Mitsusuke's position, he was dissuaded from launching it by a group of senior constables. Instead, he was forced to pardon Mitsusuke and, much to his chagrin, witness the suicide of Mochisada, who assumed responsibility for the crisis.[4]

Under Yoshimochi's successor, a nearly identical situation arose to threaten again the position of Mitsusuke when Mochisada's son, Sadamura, became a favorite of Yoshinori. The *Kakitsu-ki*, which is a record of the events surrounding Yoshinori's assassination during the Kakitsu (1441–43) period, suggests that the relationship between Yoshinori and Sadamura, like that between Yoshimochi and Mochisada, was homosexual in nature.[5] In any event rumors reached the ear of Mitsusuke in 1441 that Yoshinori had issued a secret directive ordering the transfer of Harima, Bizen, and Mimasaka to Sadamura. To forestall this measure, Mitsusuke plotted the assassination of the shogun. In the sixth month he issued an invitation to Yoshinori to visit his Kyoto estate under the pretext of celebrating victory in a recent battle with the Yūki.[6] Yoshinori

---

At one point they held the office of constable in as many as five provinces; but by the time of Kakitsu (1441–43) their power was concentrated in these three.

[3] Mitsusuke and Mochisada were, of course, from the same Akamatsu clan, but they were rivals for the family holdings.

[4] When Yoshimochi sought to organize his generals for an expedition to Harima, they refused to comply on the grounds that Mochisada's arrogance and vanity had been the sole cause of trouble in the Akamatsu family. Nevertheless Mitsusuke's action had been abrupt, and in order not to push the shogun too far he took the tonsure and remained in semiretirement until Yoshimochi's death the following year.

[5] *Kakitsu-ki,* in Hanawa, *Gunsho Ruijū,* p. 318.

[6] After the suicide of the Kantō *kubō* (literally, "Shogun of the East"), Mochiuji (1398–1439), in 1439, his two sons Haruō and Yasuō fled to Hitachi and sought refuge with Yūki Ujitomo (1398–1441). In the early months of 1441

accepted the invitation with no apparent suspicion of what was afoot, for his entourage upon arrival on the twenty-fourth was far smaller than usual. The feasting proceeded smoothly. The shogun indulged freely and was enjoying a program of *sarugaku* when a group of horses suddenly broke into the garden enclosure where the guests were gathered. By prearrangement three hundred men appeared to seal off the garden, ostensibly to prevent the horses' escape. In fact, they had trapped the shogun and with little ado they rushed forward to cut him down. Utterly forgetful of duty to their lord, the other guests milled about in panic and struggled to scale the walls to safety.

Such are the details of this barbaric affair according to the *Kakitsu-ki*. A number of other reasons have been advanced to explain Mitsusuke's personal decision to destroy the shogun. In 1440 Yoshinori had confiscated part of the holdings of Mitsusuke's younger brother and had bestowed it upon his favorite, Akamatsu Sadamura. Moreover, Yoshinori, who apparently found Mitsusuke physically distasteful owing to his dwarfish figure, had, on more than one occasion, insulted the Akamatsu chieftain by releasing monkeys in his presence. Finally, Yoshinori had accepted Mitsusuke's sister as a concubine and later, in a fit of anger, had ordered her execution.[7]

Despite the reasons given above, it seems unlikely that an event of such consequence as the assassination of the shogun could have resulted solely from the personal animosities of two men. It is more probable that Yoshinori's policy encompassed a far wider political design. In 1430 he had sought to gain control of the province of Chikuzen by driving out the Ōtomo. His aim at that time was to strengthen the Bakufu's base in Kyushu through an increase in directly held territory. It is very likely that his interest in Harima stemmed from the same motive—the addition of a strategic province to Bakufu holdings. Mitsusuke's record of conflict with both

the Bakufu defeated Yūki and shortly thereafter executed Mochiuji's sons in Mino.

[7] Arai Hakuseki (1657–1725) identifies the girl in question as Mitsusuke's daughter. (*Dokushi Yoron,* in *Jinnō Shōtōki,* etc., in *Nihon Bungaku Sōsho,* X, 338.)

Yoshimochi and himself provided Yoshinori with an excellent excuse for encroaching on Akamatsu lands. The desperate nature of Mitsusuke's action and the events that followed the assassination also tend to confirm the. feeling that Mitsusuke recognized a greater threat in the shogun than simply personal attack. Mitsusuke had watched with growing alarm the chastisement of other families (the Isshiki and the Toki) in recent years and probably surmised that he was next in line.

The shogun dead, Akamatsu and his men delayed a number of hours before setting out for their stronghold at Shirahata, which they reached without incident. Thus the head of the House of Ashikaga was struck down "like a dog" in the very heart of the Capital and his assassins were allowed to escape unchallenged from under the noses of the Bakufu. These astonishing developments strongly suggest that Akamatsu was not alone in his scheming. According to the queries of Go-Sukōin (1372-1456) on the twenty-fifth, there may have been important men in league with him: "There were none to disembowel themselves before the shogun and none to set out in pursuit. Could there have been a conspiracy with others?" [8] It was not until the twenty-seventh that the Bakufu finally decided upon a punitive expedition, and this did not set out until the following month.

The Bakufu army was headed by Hosokawa Shigeyuki with Akamatsu Sadamura and Takeda Nobushige (d. 1450) next in command. In reserve was a force under Yamana Sōzen (1404–73). According to the *Kakitsu-ki*, when the force reached the border of Harima, Hosokawa refused to allow his troops to invade the province.[9] Takeda and Akamatsu Sadamura pleaded for permission to continue on their own, but Hosokawa remained adamant. Thus, while the advance force hesitated, Yamana, leading troops from Inaba and Hōki, rushed into the province and stormed the Akamatsu stronghold. On the tenth day of the ninth month the posi-

---

[8] *Kammon Gyoki*, 1441:6:25, in Ōta Tōshirō, *Kammon Gyoki.*

[9] The *Kakitsu-ki* suggests a strong sympathy between Hosokawa Shigeyuki and the Akamatsu. Later events tend to confirm this. On the other hand, *The Chronicle of Ōnin* states that Hosokawa clashed with Akamatsu troops at Kanigasaka and was unable to proceed farther. No mention of this engagement is made in the *Kakitsu-ki.*

tion fell and Mitsusuke and many of his followers committed suicide.[10] The Yamana returned to the Capital in triumph where they were rewarded with the three Akamatsu provinces of Harima, Bizen, and Mimasaka.

The first result of the Kakitsu Incident (Yoshinori's assassination), as mentioned, was a failure in shogunal leadership. Yoshinori, although a man of brutal nature who offended many people, had been a strong and decisive leader. He was followed by his son, Yoshikatsu (1433–43), who became shogun at the age of eight and died a brief two years later. Yoshikatsu, in turn, was succeeded by his younger brother, Yoshimasa, also eight at the time of his appointment as shogun. Yoshimasa remained in office for more than thirty years, during which time the effective power of the shogunacy vanished. Yoshimasa himself displayed little inclination to restore the authority of the office to its former heights. Whether owing to his own nature or to the desperate times in which he found himself, Yoshimasa appeared content to enjoy a life of extravagance and luxury while the system of central government in which he occupied the highest office collapsed. Such is the outward image. It is doubtful whether a complete assessment of Yoshimasa's character can ever be made. Throughout his life Yoshimasa appears to have been influenced or dominated by a succession of people more strong-willed than he—his wife, court favorites, concubines, advisers, military leaders. It is mainly through a study of these people that I shall attempt to analyze the rule of Yoshimasa and to evaluate the role of the shogun in the Ōnin War.

It should be pointed out again that, accompanying the failure of shogunal leadership after the Kakitsu Incident, there was also a decline in the caliber of leadership at the second level of Bakufu administration—the office of shogunal deputy. No Hosokawa Yoriyuki appeared this time to take charge of the government during the shogun's minority. As we shall see, this was partly due to the limited sources from which deputy leadership could be selected and partly due to altered conditions, under which even the

---

[10] Mitsusuke's son and coconspirator, Akamatsu Norisuke, fled to Ise and requested asylum from the Kitabatake. They refused and Norisuke subsequently committed suicide.

most spirited administrator would have found it difficult to operate.

The second result of the Kakitsu Incident was a significant shift in the balance of constable power in the central provinces. It will be recalled that after the early years of the Muromachi Bakufu many of the smaller constables in the provinces west of the Kantō had disappeared. By the time of Yoshimitsu there were only ten or eleven families who had consolidated their holdings and who were developing into constable-daimyo. These were: Hosokawa, Shiba, Hatakeyama, Isshiki, Yamana, and Imagawa from among the Ashikaga collaterals; and the outside families of Sasaki, Akamatsu, Toki, Ōuchi, and Togashi. This relatively small number of great provincial constables had enabled Hosokawa Yoriyuki to develop the system of shogunal deputies, whereby the leaders of the three most powerful constable families —Hosokawa, Shiba, Hatakeyama—served, in turn, as personal assistant to the shogun. According to the policy adopted by Yoriyuki and Yoshimitsu, when a constable expanded his control to the point where he might threaten the Bakufu itself, his strength was to be reduced under whatever pretext necessary. The experience of the Yamana in 1391 and of the Ōuchi in 1399 clearly demonstrated the enforcement of this basic policy.

With the passing of time there occurred certain fundamental changes among and within the constable families that were to disrupt and finally destroy this balance of power. Not only did alignment among the various constables change, the distribution of control within the individual constable families also underwent great alteration. These two processes were closely related. Change within the constable family most often appeared in the form of succession disputes, a subject that will be discussed in detail later. Once plunged into dispute over succession, the family soon declined. As one family moved down, another moved up. In addition, there was the ever-present danger that a really major change could affect the Bakufu-constable balance. This danger became reality when the relative powers of the shogunal deputy families began to slip. The Shiba were the first to suffer and, by the time of the Kakitsu Incident, the office of deputy belonged, for all practical purposes, to the Hatakeyama and the Hosokawa. But the Hatakeyama too were on the verge of a great succession dispute that was to split the family within a few years. This would leave the Hosokawa as undisputed leaders in Bakufu circles.

The Hosokawa had always occupied a particularly strong position under the Muromachi Bakufu owing to their early start and to the central location of the provinces they controlled—for instance, Tamba and Settsu. A triangular block of provinces to the west—Harima, Mimasaka, Bizen—belonged to the Akamatsu. Since the Akamatsu were no match for the Hosokawa, this block provided an excellent buffer against any power that might arise in the west. When, as a result of the Kakitsu Incident, these provinces fell into the hands of the Yamana, this buffer zone was destroyed, and the Yamana stood in a position to challenge directly Hosokawa supremacy in the central provinces.

The Yamana had arisen as a constable power in the west during the fourteenth century. By the time of Yoshimitsu, they controlled eleven provinces, or roughly one sixth of Japan. In those days, however, great size meant danger, for it violated the shogun's fundamental policy on constable growth. Yoshimitsu's political instincts told him that the Yamana had gone too far and, in 1391, he took advantage of a family quarrel to interfere in Yamana affairs and to bring about a considerable reduction in their territory. Thereafter the power of the family was limited mainly to the provinces of the San'indō.[11] But the Yamana had by no means been crushed. Their relatively poor showing against Bakufu armies was due in large part to their lack of maturity. The Yamana had not yet fulfilled the constable's first, and most important, task— recruitment of local samurai as vassals. A passage from the *Meitoku-ki*[12] shows us that the local samurai, far from rallying to the Yamana cause, turned eagerly to the Bakufu in order to oust their former overlords:

[11] The San'indō comprises the southwestern littoral of Honshu, including the provinces of Tamba, Tajima, Inaba, Hōki, Izumo, Iwami, and Oki (an island off the coast of Hōki).

[12] Yoshimitsu's campaign against the Yamana is known as the Meitoku Incident after the year period (Meitoku, 1390–93) during which it occurred. The *Meitoku-ki* is a war tale based on this incident.

Yamana Mitsuyuki rode over to Tango and established himself at Hosokage estate in Kitsu where he decided to await the punitive force from the Capital. But not a single samurai of the locality came forth to aid him. On the contrary, they had changed allegiance and were preparing to attack him.

Thus the Yamana lost lands that were not fully theirs. Their prospects in the western provinces remained high, and during the early years of the fifteenth century they worked to consolidate a base of power in the region of Tajima, Inaba, and Hōki. Moreover, in 1435 they came under the leadership of Yamana Sōzen, a vigorous and forceful warrior bent upon restoring the family fortunes. Opportunity arose for the Yamana during the Kakitsu Incident and, as we have seen, Sōzen exploited this opportunity to the fullest. With the acquisition of the three strategic provinces of the Akamatsu, the Yamana stood once again among the ranks of the foremost constable-daimyo. Furthermore, in both size and location they had become a distinct threat to the supremacy of the Hosokawa.

In conjunction with this discussion of the reemergence of the Yamana as a power in the west, a few words should also be said about the Ōuchi of Suō and Nagato. Occupants of a strategic position on the Straits of Shimonoseki, the Ōuchi, like the Yamana, had become great constables by the late fourteenth century. Yoshihiro, the Ōuchi general under Ashikaga Yoshimitsu, added the provinces of Buzen, Izumi, and Kii to his inherited domains in Suō, Nagato, and Iwami. He served the Bakufu well both in Kyushu and during Yoshimitsu's campaigns against the Yamana. But again like the Yamana, whom he helped to defeat, Yoshihiro had grown too powerful, and in 1399 he too was destroyed.[13]

To continue the parallel, the Ōuchi, although reduced to the western end of Honshu, still retained good prospects. In their case location on the Straits of Shimonoseki, through which passed

[13] Yoshihiro had ignored a shogunal order to appear in the Capital. Instead he gathered his forces and entered the city of Sakai. Thereupon the shogun dispatched a huge Bakufu army that disposed of Ōuchi and his vassals after a brief struggle.

much of the traffic with Ming China, was particularly important. Bolstered by profits from this trade, the Ōuchi began to recover their strength, so that by the time of Yoshimasa they too appeared as a reemergent force in the west. Furthermore, it was the alliance of Ōuchi Masahiro (d. 1495) and Yamana Sōzen that was to form the foundation of the western army during the Ōnin War. The balance of constable power had indeed changed.

The third result of the Kakitsu Incident was the beginning of bitter enmity between the Houses of Akamatsu and Yamana. Mitsusuke's rebellion had been disastrous to the Akamatsu and they were naturally anxious to regain their lands and their former power. In 1444 and again in 1454 remnants of the Akamatsu family rose against the Yamana. In the second case Hosokawa Shigeyuki, working through his kinsman, Katsumoto (1430–73), managed to gain the shogun's favor on behalf of the Akamatsu. When the Akamatsu took up arms in Harima, a full-scale rebellion appeared in the offing and Yamana Sōzen was obliged to hurry down to restore order in the province.[14]

Hosokawa's repeated espousal of the Akamatsu cause was one of the major reasons for the final deterioration in relations between Sōzen and Hosokawa Katsumoto. But the matter went even further. Akamatsu Masanori (1455–96) became one of the leading generals on the Hosokawa side during the Ōnin War and, as we shall see, posed a constant obstacle to peace talks that might have ended the conflict far sooner.

It may be interesting before we leave this subject to recount the rather bizarre manner in which the Akamatsu managed to reinstate their family standing. During the years of confusion following the assassination of Yoshinori and, not long after, the death of Yoshikatsu, remnant supporters of the southern court scattered throughout Yamato, Kii, and Kawachi renewed their activities and even went so far as to brew a plot against the Kyoto government. They first secured the aid of an official who had been shabbily treated by Yoshinori. Then, on an evening in the ninth month of 1443, they broke into the palace grounds, set fire to the Seiryō-

---

[14] Both of these events will be discussed in greater detail in regard to the rivalry between Hosokawa and Yamana.

den[15] and caused a commotion that extended to the emperor's quarters. According to an account of the times, his majesty "discarded his mantle and, assuming the disguise of a lady in waiting, made good his escape." [16] As the attackers departed, they carried with them part of the regalia—the sword and the jewels. The sword was later recovered in the vicinity of Kiyomizudera, but the jewels became the property of the southern pretender.[17]

Fifteen years later, in 1458, a group of Akamatsu retainers requested service at the pretender's court. Since their former master (Mitsusuke) had been branded an enemy of Kyoto, it seemed plausible that these men had indeed defected from the north. Accordingly, their request was granted. In the course of duty they managed to gain access to the quarters of the pretender and, on a snowy night in the twelfth month, rose up, slew him, and fled with the jewels. During a series of harrowing escapades, which are recorded in both the *Kakitsu-ki* and *The Chronicle of Ōnin*, they lost the jewels again and had to call on local warriors of Yamato for help before finally returning the sacred treasure to its proper place.

As a result of this singular service to the throne, the Akamatsu were pardoned. In addition, the young Akamatsu lord, Masanori, received lands in the provinces of Kaga, Bizen, Izumi, and Ise.[18]

[15] A building in the palace compound used for ceremonial functions.

[16] *Kammon Gyoki,* 1443:9:24.

[17] At the time of unification of the courts in 1392 Go-Kameyama surrendered his claim to the throne with the understanding that the two lines would again alternate as they had before Go-Daigo's ascendancy earlier in the century. But in 1412 the northern emperor, Go-Komatsu (1377–1433), abdicated in favor of his son Shōkō (1401–28), and when the latter died in 1428 the succession went to another northern sovereign, Go-Hanazono (1419–70). Go-Kameyama's son, Ogura-no-Miya, claimed his right to the throne, but was ignored by the Bakufu, which clearly had no intention of honoring the treaty of 1392 in regard to alternation. Ogura-no-Miya thereupon founded a line of southern pretenders, who were to maintain a nomadic existence in various parts of the central provinces and even farther afield for many years thereafter.

[18] *Kakitsu-ki,* p. 325.

EARLY SUCCESSION DISPUTES

One of the most significant developments following the Kakitsu Incident was the outbreak of succession disputes among the great families. Beginning with the Ogasawara of Shinano in 1442 and the Togashi of Kaga in 1443, the problem of internal discord and rivalry eventually came to plague even the shogunal deputy Houses of Shiba and Hatakeyama, and finally the Ashikaga family itself. These disputes were by no means isolated or unrelated occurrences. Rather, they were symptomatic of profound changes taking place, not only among the families, but within the whole structure of Bakufu-constable relations. In a sense these disputes over family succession were both a cause and a result of the decline of the Ashikaga Bakufu. Bakufu and constable-diamyo were so closely dependent upon each other that a failure of one inevitably brought the downfall of the other. The quarter century from the Kakitsu Incident in 1441 to the Ōnin War (1467–77) witnessed the collapse of both the central government and the provincial lord. From the standpoint of the constable-daimyo this fact was particularly ironic. Growth of the Muromachi constable had definitely been decentralist: enfeoffment of local vassals, broadening of judicial powers, assessment of private taxes—in short, a constant effort to establish regional autonomy. Yet the constable-daimyo survived by only a few years the failure of the Bakufu after Yoshinori's death. For two decades several of the leading chieftains were able to prop up the Bakufu and to carry on the affairs of central government; but they were unable to stem the tide. Instead, they used their authority more to interfere in the disputes of other families for their own political advantage than to stabilize the Bakufu.

Underlying the succession disputes was a basic change in the custom of inheritance among the military families. During the Kamakura period, family property was commonly distributed to all offspring, regardless of sex. The result of this varied according to family size. In the case of larger families the division of estates meant the establishment of branch families. Although the family head retained certain residual powers over the various branches, distance and time proved corrosive factors. The tendency was for the branch family eventually to make complete its break from the main house.

In the case of smaller military families, multidistribution of property was apt to have a more immediate effect on family fortunes, for the recipients of these fragmented rights and holdings were often hard-pressed to make ends meet. Faced with financial distress, many were forced to sell or otherwise dispose of their interests. This process was particularly conspicuous among the steward families and was one of the fundamental reasons for the decline of the Kamakura Bakufu.[19]

In order to check the debilitating effects of this custom of divided estates, the military houses turned to single inheritance. The years of incessant warfare following the dynastic split had forced all families to close ranks in defense against the incursions of outsiders. A warrior's first responsibility was to concentrate as much military power as possible in his own hands. No longer could he afford the luxury of doling out his estate piecemeal to several offspring even before his death. A successor had to be selected to carry on the leadership of the family. Thus the practice came to be transmission of all property to one male descendant (not necessarily the eldest son). In this way the warrior sought to perpetuate the strength of his house through the vicissitudes of the times.

This practice, born of necessity, undoubtedly helped to maintain the smaller warrior family. But in the case of the constable house it created certain unavoidable dangers inherent in the size of the prize involved. It must be remembered that the interests of the greater constable daimyo extended to two or more provinces. If a mature and forceful heir was ready to take over upon the death of the family head, a smooth transition of power could be expected.

---

[19] This does not mean that all local warriors of steward size were disappearing at the end of the Kamakura period. As the stewards went down, others came up; but the newcomers were not direct vassals of the shogun and therefore had no vested interest in the Kamakura Bakufu. This new group of roughly steward-size warriors became, as we have seen, the nucleus of the local samurai class.

But in the event that the order of succession had not been made clear or that the heir was young or indecisive, dispute was sure to arise. The stakes were high and it was not simply a matter of claimants within the constable family fighting it out among themselves. Local warriors who had become vassals of the constable were likely to have just as vital an interest in the outcome of a succession dispute. Once having backed this contender or that in the hope of advancing their own fortunes, these warriors were quite prepared to go to whatever lengths necessary to secure the succession for their man. We see here again a reflection of the constable-daimyo's most fundamental weakness: he was forever a newcomer who had entered the province and had imposed his rule from above. The local warriors would back him only so long as it was to their advantage. Once the constable began to slip, he could expect no lingering regrets on the part of his newly acquired vassals.

Thus there arose, upon the death of a constable, a potentially explosive situation. The great arbiter was the Bakufu; for, despite separatist tendencies, the constable remained an officer of the central government and shogunal confirmation (*ando*) was necessary for his appointment. Under a strong shogun immediate confirmation of a successor was usually enough to check disputes before they had a chance to mature. But when the authority of the shogun declined with dramatic suddenness upon the death of Yoshinori, the effectiveness of shogunal confirmation was seriously weakened.

The strongest figure in the Bakufu after Yoshinori was the shogunal deputy, Hosokawa Mochiyuki (1400–42), who took control with a firm hand after the assassination. The office of shogun was smoothly transferred to the youthful Yoshikatsu and troops were dispatched, albeit somewhat belatedly, to chastise the Akamatsu. Unfortunately for the future of the Bakufu, Mochiyuki survived his lord by only one year. Upon his death in 1442 the appointment of shogunal deputy went to Hatakeyama Mochikuni (1397–1455).

If one wished to interpret the origins of the Ōnin War in terms of personalities rather than institutions, the character of Mochikuni would be worthy of careful study. One cannot help recalling the skill and determination with which Hosokawa Yoriyuki had directed the course of the Bakufu during Yoshimitsu's minority nearly seventy-five years earlier. Although he never forgot the private interests of the Hosokawa family, Yoriyuki was also largely responsible for stabilizing the balance of Bakufu-constable power. To him must go much of the credit for Yoshimitsu's later success.

Hatakeyama Mochikuni, on the other hand, made no attempt to revitalize the Bakufu nor to guide the young shogun (first Yoshikatsu, then Yoshimasa) toward his future responsibilities. Instead, he used his high office to interfere arbitrarily in the affairs of other families and to wage a private struggle with the Hosokawa for supremacy in Bakufu circles. At the time of his appointment to the office of shogunal deputy, Mochikuni's leadership in the Bakufu was undisputed. The shogun was a young boy of eight and Hosokawa Katsumoto, Mochiyuki's successor, only ten. As we shall see, Mochikuni not only failed to provide the direction so desperately needed by the Bakufu; within a decade he was unable to keep his own house in order. Dispute over succession to the Hatakeyama found Mochikuni, despite his prestige and years of experience, powerless to control the forces that arose to threaten the future of his family.

It is clear that the quality of Bakufu leadership, apart from the shortcomings of any particular individual, had declined drastically after Yoshinori. This condition can be traced to two basic weaknesses in the structure of the Muromachi Bakufu: the concentration of power in the hands of a few and the limited sources from which these few could be selected. In theory, the shogun had absolute power over the Bakufu; in practice, he often delegated that power to his deputy, but not beyond.[20] Generally speaking then, the most powerful official in the Bakufu at any time was either the shogun or the shogunal deputy. Of course, nonofficials could and did come to exercise considerable power as personal advisers to the

---

[20] Although Ashikaga Takauji retained most of the administrative organs of the Kamakura Bakufu, he changed considerably their various functions. Even beyond that, the tendency for the early Muromachi shogun to exercise absolute power himself, or in conjunction with his deputy, caused most of these governmental branches, such as the board of retainers, the board of inquiry, and the council of state, to dwindle markedly in importance.

shogun. One of the most noteworthy was Manzai (1378–1435), a priest of the Daigo-ji, who was an intimate confidant of both Yoshimitsu and Yoshimochi. But his was a noninstitutionalized and irregular route to power; formal authority continued to reside in the hands of the shogun and his assistant. Moreover, since the shogun was selected from the Ashikaga main line and since the choice of a deputy was limited to the heads of three houses, there was only a handful of men, perhaps as few as four, upon whom the highest authority of the Bakufu could devolve at any given time. In view of this it is surprising that the Muromachi Bakufu was able to produce as many capable administrators as it did in the early years. The limitations of this system of restricted selection were graphically demonstrated in 1445 when Hosokawa Katsumoto replaced Hatakeyama Mochikuni as shogunal deputy. At that time the highest offices in the Bakufu were occupied by a ten-year-old (Yoshimasa) and a sixteen-year-old (Katsumoto).

Shortly after the Kakitsu Incident, succession disputes erupted within the constable families of Ogasawara[21] in Shinano and Togashi in Kaga. In the case of the Ogasawara, conflict arose upon the death of the family head in 1442. A son took over with the support of powerful Ogasawara vassals; but a nephew, who claimed that his father's line was senior, petitioned the Bakufu to confirm him as successor in place of the son. The Bakufu held that the provisions of the deceased's will had been met, and denied the petition. The matter might have ended there; but the nephew had another avenue of approach. His mother was at that time a favored concubine of the shogunal deputy, Hatakeyama Mochikuni. Relying upon this intimate relationship, he appealed directly to Mochikuni, who attempted to reverse the Bakufu's previous decision and to obtain confirmation of the nephew as family head. At that point the Ogasawara family split, relatives and retainers lining up behind the two contenders, and a protracted struggle ensued which was to

[21] The Ogasawara were Seiwa Genji. Nagakiyo, the first to take the Ogasawara name, had been a supporter of Yoritomo. During the fourteenth century Ogasawara Sadamune joined Nitta Yoshisada in overthrowing Hōjō rule at Kamakura and later became a general under Takauji. From that time the Ogasawara became the most influential family in Shinano.

weaken and finally to eliminate Ogasawara influence in Shinano.[22]

Discord in the Togashi[23] family had its origins during the time of Yoshinori. The family head, who held the post of constable in Kaga, had incurred the displeasure of the shogun and, fearful of Yoshinori's vengeance, had fled the province. Thereupon the Bakufu placed his younger brother at the head of the family. After Yoshinori's assassination the former constable returned to the province and attempted to regain control. His support came from none other than Hatakeyama Mochikuni. When word reached the Capital that Mochikuni was behind the former constable, a great furor arose. The deputy constable, who was one of the younger brother's strongest supporters, committed suicide with his father and several retainers in protest.[24] Rumors circulated everywhere. Some feared a plot by the southern court, which, as noted, had become active in the home provinces after Yoshinori's assassination. Armed men raced up to the Bakufu, while nobles flocked to the palace. By the next day the uproar had subsided, although rumors persisted about the possibility of a coup by adherents of the southern court and about persons in the palace suspected of being in secret contact with them.[25]

With the two contenders in open defiance of each other, the lines were drawn for a prolonged dispute over succession to the Togashi. More significant than alignment of the Togashi and their vassals, however, was the confrontation of Hatakeyama Mochikuni and Hosokawa Katsumoto; for, as Mochikuni backed one contender (the former constable), so Katsumoto gave aid to the other (the younger brother). A quarrel for leadership of the constable family of one province had become a test of strength between the two great deputy families of Hatakeyama and Hosokawa. Under

[22] The two lines of the Ogasawara were known after the places in Shinano where they based their operations, Matsuo and Fukashi. In later years the Matsuo line gave rise to the Echizen Ogasawara, while the Fukashi line established the Ogasawara of Buzen.

[23] The roots of the Togashi family in Kaga extended back to their Fujiwara ancestors of the tenth century.

[24] Go-Sukōin notes in his diary the emotional response of people toward the deputy constable's selfless loyalty and sacrifice. *Kammon Gyoki*, 1443:2:28.

[25] *Ibid.*

such circumstances, there could be no immediate solution, and within a few years the province of Kaga was divided, the Bakufu assigning half to one side in the dispute and half to the other.[26]

I have described the Ogasawara and Togashi disputes, first, because they were early examples of the type of internal upheaval that was to plague the great constable-daimyo families of Hatakeyama and Shiba on the eve of the Ōnin War, and second, because they became areas for political competition within the ranks of the Bakufu itself. Needless to say, the disputes in Shinano and Kaga were not the only armed conflicts that occurred during these years. Fighting and bloodshed were almost daily occurrences in one part of the country or the other as lawlessness mounted with the Bakufu's decline. On every level of society, from the lowest peasant struggling against an oppressive landlord to the greatest warrior chieftain contending for power in the Bakufu, conditions of chaos and near anarchy were at hand.

The Ashikaga Bakufu, never a very powerful institution, was entering the final stages of its effectiveness as a central government. By the time of Yoshimasa, large areas of the country, including Kyushu and the Kantō, were almost entirely beyond Bakufu control. It was only in the central districts and in Shikoku and those provinces extending to the western end of Honshu that the Bakufu still functioned as the central ruling power. A glance at the chronological listings of events in primary source compilations such as *Dai Nihon Shiryō* or *Shiryō Sōran* will reveal that the Bakufu was engaged in a continuous series of military operations. Many of these operations were skirmishes of a very minor nature, but their frequent occurrence was a clear indication of the Bakufu's own inability to control the country.

Recent scholarship in Japan suggests that the Ashikaga Bakufu, in its early years at least, had far more military strength than had previously been thought to be the case.[27] The great expeditions under Yoshimitsu, for example, were not composed simply of constable divisions centered around the shogun and a small body of

---

[26] The Bakufu ordered the division of Kaga in the fifth month of 1447, thus creating two constables in the province.

[27] See Satō, "Muromachi Bakufu Ron," pp. 5–25.

his "elite" troops.[28] Rather, Yoshimitsu commanded a sizable personal force recruited from direct Ashikaga vassals below the status of constable. The quality of the Bakufu's military prepared-ness had, however, changed greatly by the mid-fourteenth century. Unlike his predecessors, Yoshimasa had not the slightest interest in fighting. He trained no troops and led no expeditions. Further-more, it is not even clear whether the Bakufu had an army of its own. The records of the times, including *The Chronicle of Ōnin*, occasionally refer to the dispatch of a Bakufu army, but details are few. In general it appears that the Bakufu assigned its fighting to commanders from the military families, who marshaled and led their own provincial troops. They were Bakufu armies only in the sense that they received their initial order to mobilize from the Bakufu. Once in the field they were likely to be concerned as much with their own interests as they were in carrying out the policies of the government.

How, then, did the Bakufu continue to exist during these years of constant warfare? Part of the answer has already been given. The Bakufu continued to exist because the great constable-daimyo still found it to their advantage not to destroy it. With the shogun no longer a forceful personality, families like the Hosokawa and the Hatakeyama were able to exercise greater power than ever be-fore. But Hosokawa and Hatakeyama represented the old Bakufu-constable balance of power. New forces were reemerging in the west—the Yamana and the Ōuchi—who did not have nearly so great a vested interest in the Bakufu and were ready to challenge its authority.

Another reason for the Bakufu's continued existence was the intangible prestige it enjoyed as the recognized center of military authority. This is a very difficult factor to evaluate. The shogun

---

[28] At the time of the Ōei disturbance in 1399 when the Ōuchi were besieged at Sakai, Yoshimitsu reportedly had at his command thirty thousand troops. Yet, as one source points out, the shogun's personal corps numbered only two or three thousand men—about half the number Ōuchi had with him in the city. The remainder of Yoshimitsu's enormous host was recruited from friendly con-stables through the chain of command: shogunal deputy—constable—deputy constable—local warrior (Yomiuri Shimbun Sha, *Nihon no Rekishi*, VI, 27). These traditional figures may be revised through future study to show that the shogun in fact had a much greater number in his personal corps.

appeared weak and powerless, yet his word could still carry the weight of law. What was the decision-making process behind the shogun? Did the shogun act independently or was he closely controlled by others? There is much evidence to indicate that the shogun was advised by a long succession of people, many of whom had no military strength to back their advice. At the same time there are frequent references in *The Chronicle of Ōnin* and other records to orders issued by Yoshimasa that appear to have been based entirely on his own decisions. In the case of a romanticized work like *The Chronicle of Ōnin,* it may have been part of the author's stylization to credit the shogun with decisions that were formulated in quite different quarters.

The purpose of this digression from our examination of pre-Ōnin succession disputes has been to make clear the state of Bakufu-constable relations just before the great Hatakeyama and Shiba quarrels. The Kakitsu Incident had marked a sharp turning point in Bakufu fortunes. Leadership, which had always been tapped from limited sources, fell into mediocre or incompetent hands. Moreover, any personal power that the Ashikaga shoguns may have commanded in the early years of the Bakufu had disappeared by Yoshimasa's time. All military matters were entrusted to the constables and other generals from their families. These men fought in the name of the Bakufu, but also for their own interests. Despite disruption in the traditional Bakufu-constable balance of power, the Hosokawa and Hatakeyama attempted to maintain the old order. Their supremacy was soon to be challenged, however, by new powers in the west. The Yamana, in particular, were bent upon extending their influence at the expense of the central families.

We have seen that, after the death of Yoshinori, Hatakeyama Mochikuni became the most powerful figure in the Bakufu. His leading rival, Hosokawa Katsumoto, was still a young boy. As the years passed, however, and Katsumoto reached his majority, he began to assert himself ever more strongly in Bakufu councils. By the time of the Togashi dispute a clear-cut contest for supremacy commenced between these two men. Together, they shared the office of shogunal deputy for more than twenty years—Mochikuni during the periods 1442–44 and 1449–51, and Katsumoto, 1445–48, and 1452–63.[29] Of the two, Katsumoto was the more skillful politician. He established a marked advantage over Mochikuni by taking for his wife a daughter of the powerful Yamana Sōzen. Faced by a coalition of Hosokawa and Yamana, Hatakeyama Mochikuni found his power shrinking rapidly. Even more damaging was the great dispute over succession brewing in the Hatakeyama family. Mochikuni himself died in 1455; but for several years prior to his death a fierce quarrel had raged over the choice of his successor. Powerful vassals—Jimbo, Yusa, Suya—had become restless and were choosing sides. Mochikuni was helpless in the face of such opposition from below. He died a broken and disappointed man.

The partnership of Yamana Sōzen and Hosokawa Katsumoto, based purely on strategical considerations, was not intended to be a permanent one. Once Hatakeyama Mochikuni had been removed from the scene, a clash between these two great constable-daimyo became inevitable. The main source of contention continued to be the status of the Akamatsu family, for the Hosokawa were anxious to reinstate the Akamatsu and check the eastward expansion of Yamana. As a result, Sōzen had to be constantly on the alert for uprisings in the territories he and his family had received as booty for chastising Yoshinori's assassins. The main trouble spot was the province of Harima, birthplace of the Akamatsu family and a hotbed of pro-Akamatsu sympathizers.

In 1444 a group of Harima adventurers (*rōnin*) urged an Akamatsu clansman into revolt. His uprising was short-lived, for Yamana Sōzen hastened down to the province and soon forced the clansman to commit suicide.[30] Twelve years later Yamana was faced with a far more serious threat. During this interim, according to the *Kakitsu-ki*, Sōzen had made himself quite unpopular in Bakufu circles with his arrogant ways. In 1454 the ever-watchful Akamatsu approached Hosokawa Shigeyuki for assistance in an

---

[29] Long after Mochikuni's death, Katsumoto assumed the office of shogunal deputy for a third time, from 1468 until his own death in 1473.

[30] *Kakitsu-ki*, p. 321. The place of his suicide is given as Arima in the province of Settsu.

attack on Yamana. Shigeyuki seems to have been the great champion of the Akamatsu. It will be recalled that it was Shigeyuki who had held his lieutenants in check during the expedition against Akamatsu Mitsusuke in 1441, thereby inadvertently providing Yamana Sōzen with the opportunity to rush in for the kill. Through his kinsman Hosokawa Katsumoto, Shigeyuki now obtained the shogun's support for a plan to assault Sōzen in his mansion on a night early in the eleventh month. The plotters were to assemble at the shogunal palace and to set forth at the signal of a bell from the Shōkoku-ji. At the last moment Katsumoto had a change of heart and slipped out of the city. Without the Hosokawa chieftain's support, the plot had to be abandoned. Shortly thereafter the two Akamatsu ringleaders went down to Harima and raised the banner of revolt against the Yamana. Sōzen returned to Tamba to gather a force and the following year marched into Harima, where he defeated the insurgents in a two-pronged attack.

Katsumoto's role in this bizarre affair is somewhat perplexing. He seems to have provided Shigeyuki with entree to the shogun and even to have supported the plot at first. But apparently he was not prepared to make the final break with his father-in-law Sōzen. The incident did cause further disruption in relations between the two Houses, however; for, although Katsumoto had foiled an attempt on his life, Yamana Sōzen harbored great resentment against the Hosokawa, particularly for the part played by Shigeyuki in backing the Akamatsu.

The Hatakeyama Succession Dispute

Although originally of Taira stock from the province of Musashi, the Hatakeyama were among the early supporters of Minamoto Yoritomo. Hatakeyama Shigetada (1164–1205) served high in Bakufu councils under both Yoritomo and his successor, Yoriie (1182–1204). In 1205, however, Shigetada was falsely accused of treason by Hōjō Tokimasa (1138–1215) and subsequently per-

ished with many members of his family in a clash that virtually
eliminated Hatakeyama influence in the Kantō.[31]

The branch of the Hatakeyama that gained prominence under
the the Muromachi Bakufu was actually a revival of the family
line as a collateral of the Ashikaga.[32] Hatakeyama Kunikiyo (d.
1364) marched westward with Ashikaga Takauji in 1333 and was
later rewarded with an appointment as constable to the provinces
of Kii and Izu. Lack of complete records makes it difficult to follow with full accuracy the subsequent development of the Hatakeyama as a constable-daimyo family. During the early years of
Ashikaga rule they served for a while in the northern provinces of
Mutsu and Dewa and under the Kantō deputy, Motouji, in Kamakura.[33] But the real centers of Hatakeyama power came to be
the regions of Kawachi-Kii and Noto-Etchū. Here the Hatakeyama
established themselves as a leading constable-daimyo family and,
along with the Hosokawa and Shiba, as one of the three great
cadet houses of the Ashikaga Bakufu. In theory the Hatakeyama
were to share, in succession, the duties of shogunal deputy with
the Hosokawa and the Shiba. In fact the office became the object
of a great rivalry between Shiba Yoshimasa and Hosokawa Yoriyuki, with no member of the Hatakeyama occupying it until Hatakeyama Motokuni (1352–1406) became deputy in 1398. From
the time of Motokuni the influence of the Hatakeyama rose in the
Bakufu while that of the Shiba declined.[34]

[31] Hatakeyama Shigetada fell a victim of the rift that developed in the Hōjō
family as they sought to gain control of the Bakufu after Yoritomo's death.
Hōjō Tokimasa claimed that Shigetada was planning rebellion and directed his
son, Hōjō Yoshitoki, to attack and destroy him. Yoshitoki was highly critical of
the flimsy charges brought against Hatakeyama Shigetada, but carried out the
attack nevertheless. This incident created great ill will between Yoshitoki and
his father and eventually led to the latter's downfall. Yasuda, *Nihon Zenshi*, pp.
122–23.

[32] In 1205 Minamoto (Ashikaga) Yoshizumi received the Hatakeyama name
and the forfeit domains of Shigetada. The Hatakeyama from this time, then,
were Seiwa Genji and branch relatives of the Ashikaga.

[33] Hatakeyama Takakuni served as deputy to the northern provinces under
Ashikaga Takauji, while Kunikiyo became assistant for Ashikaga Motouji in
Kamakura. Kunikiyo was later expelled and the Hatakeyama were replaced by
the Uesugi as the leading power behind the Kantō government.

[34] As I shall demonstrate below, Shiba power declined at an early date owing
to their unusually strong and unruly vassals.

In establishing their constable domains in Kawachi-Kii and Noto-Etchū,[35] Motokuni and his successors were faced with the usual problems of the Muromachi constable, the most important of which was the recruitment of local chieftains as vassals. Among the powerful warrior families who submitted to the Hatakeyama were the Yusa of Kawachi and the Jimbo, Suya, and Chō of Etchū-Noto. These names appear frequently in the pages of the *Chōroku-Kanshō-ki,* which is primarily a record of the Hatakeyama family in the years before the Ōnin War, and in *The Chronicle of Ōnin.* When dispute arose in the constable house, it was the failure of the Hatakeyama to control these rising warriors that made settlement of the succession problem impossible. As we shall see, alignment of the vassal families was not a simple matter. Members of the Yusa, for example, appear on several occasions in the ranks of both armies after the outbreak of hostility between the two Hatakeyama claimants. The animosities among and within these families stemmed from a long-standing struggle for land. In that sense, the quarrel over succession to the main line of the Hatakeyama became simply an excuse for the individual vassal to seek an increase in his personal holdings through the use of arms.

The outward cause of the Hatakeyama succession dispute originated with Hatekeyama Mochikuni's failure to produce a male heir to the House. Concerned over the question of family continuity and anxious to groom a successor, Mochikuni adopted his nephew, Masanaga (d. 1493),[36] and placed him in line for the Hatakeyama headship. The exact date of Masanaga's appointment is not known, but shortly thereafter one of Mochikuni's concubines gave birth to a boy. Scarcity of facts again makes it difficult to trace the course of events, to analyze the early relations between Masanaga, his young cousin and brother-through-adoption Yoshinari (d. 1490), and their father.[37] Traditional accounts tell us that Mochikuni

[35] Hatakeyama Mitsuyoshi began the Noto branch of the Hatakeyama family. He was the younger brother of Mitsuie (1372–1433), who held the post of shogunal deputy from 1410 to 1411 and from 1421 to 1429.

[36] Masanaga was the son of Mochikuni's brother, Hatakeyama Mochitomi.

[37] According to one version, Yoshinari was born *before* Masanaga's appointment as heir. Yoshinari was placed in holy orders at an early age and it was only after the adoption of Masanaga that Mochikuni capriciously decided to return his

developed an inordinate fondness for the new child[38] and would not rest content until he had installed Yoshinari as his rightful heir. In 1450 the old Hatakeyama warrior retired and sought to relinquish his holdings and posts to Yoshinari[39] in flagrant disavowal of his previous commitment to Masanaga. But the matter could not be so easily settled, for Masanaga had influential backers, including Hosokawa Katsumoto and Yamana Sōzen. Mochikuni, his power waning, found himself the victim of Bakufu intervention in family succession, a practice which he had so openly encouraged during the throes of the Ogasawara and Togashi disputes.

The *Chōroku-Kanshō-ki* speaks warmly of Masanaga's filial behavior toward his foster father despite the latter's repeated efforts to disinherit him.[40] This model conduct earned Masanaga little reward, for in the fourth month of 1454 Mochikuni finally secured a directive from the shogun confirming Yoshinari's appointment to the family headship. Powerful Hatakeyama vassals, including members of the Jimbo and Yusa, rallied to Masanaga. They put forth a rumor that Yoshinari was not, in fact, Mochikuni's real son and petitioned the shogun to reverse his decision.[41] Mochikuni retaliated by dispatching another warrior from the Yusa family to attack Jimbo. When the latter perished in defense of his mansion, his allies fled to Yamana Sōzen and Masanaga took refuge with Hosokawa Katsumoto.

At this early date we see both Yamana and Hosokawa backing the candidacy of Hatakeyama Masanaga. In view of such support, it is surprising that Mochikuni was able to induce the shogun to sanction the transfer to Yoshinari. The latter's ascendency, however, was short-lived. In addition to strong pressure from Hosokawa Katsumoto for a return to the original order of succession, Yo-

---

real son to secular life and to relinquish the family headship to him. See Watanabe Yosuke, *Muromachi Jidai Shi*, p. 291.

   [38] *Chōroku-Kanshō-ki*, in Hanawa, *Gunsho Ruijū*, p. 329.
   [39] *Daijō-in Jisha Zōjiki*, 1450:6:26, in Tsuji Zennosuke *et al.*, *Daijō-in Jisha Zōjiki*.
   [40] *Chōroku-Kanshō-ki*, p. 329.
   [41] Watanabe, *Muromachi Jidai Shi*, p. 291.

shimasa himself seems to have developed a dislike for the young Hatakeyama leader during his first few months as family head. In *The Chronicle of Ōnin* we find the shogun commenting on Yoshinari's "haughty manner" in the shogunal palace and on his personal desire to be rid of the youth.[42] The Yusa and Jimbo were not long in taking advantage of these sentiments, and when they again petitioned the shogun to censure Hatakeyama Yoshinari, Yoshimasa agreed. Upon news of the shogun's decision, fighting broke out in the Capital between the forces of Yoshinari and Masanaga. Mochikuni, bitterly disappointed by the censure of his son, set fire to his mansion and went into seclusion at the Kennin-ji, while Yoshinari, finding it impossible to continue in the Capital, went down to the province of Kawachi.[43]

Masanaga, who seems to have had a sincere desire to settle the family dispute peaceably, sent an envoy to his foster father.[44] But Mochikuni was intractable. Even before the arrival of Masanaga's envoy, the old Hatakeyama warrior left his temple asylum and slipped quietly out of the Capital. The official reason given for his departure was illness, and this may have been partly true, for he died not long thereafter.[45]

The events of the following year are not entirely clear. At some point Yoshimasa recalled Yoshinari and once again placed him at the head of the Hatakeyama. Dismissed for the second time, Masanaga fled to Kawachi and later fought a series of engagements with a force brought in pursuit by Yoshinari.[46] The fighting was inconclusive and before long the shogun called upon both Masa-

[42] *The Chronicle of Ōnin*, p. 364.

[43] *The Chronicle of Ōnin* gives Iga as Yoshinari's destination. Arai Hakuseki, although he does not give his source, corrects this account and states that Yoshinari went to Kawachi. Since the Hatakeyama had no base in Iga, whereas Kawachi was one of their home provinces, I have accepted Hakuseki's statement. See *Dokushi Yoron*, p. 343.

[44] Masanaga dispatched as envoy his relative, Hatakeyama the Lord of Awa.

[45] Hatakeyama Mochikuni died in the third month of 1455.

[46] Accompanied by Hatakeyama Yoshimune of the Noto Hatakeyama, Yoshinari set out for Kawachi in the sixth month of 1455. The fighting is fairly well documented in a dispatch which Yoshinari sent to the shogun the following month. *Chōroku-Kanshō-ki*, pp. 327–28.

naga and Yoshinari to open peace talks. For the next few years their representatives met occasionally in the Capital, but made little progress toward a reconciliation.

While Masanaga languished in the provinces, Hosokawa Katsumoto and a group of constable supporters continued to work on his behalf in the Capital. Yielding at last to pressure from these quarters, the shogun granted permission for Masanaga to return to Kyoto in the seventh month of 1459.[47] This decision served only to intensify the conflict between the two Hatakeyama claimants, for the sporadic fighting they had waged for the past four or five years in the relatively remote mountains of Kawachi and Yamato was now transferred to the close confines of the Capital. Tension in both camps continued to mount with the passing months until the shogun at length moved against Yoshinari. In the ninth month of 1460 he canceled the Hatakeyama leader's right of attendance and ordered him to vacate the family mansion in Kyoto. According to a traditional account, Yoshimasa was angered by what he regarded as an insult from Yoshinari. The shogun often sent requests to his warrior chieftains for unusual rocks, trees, and the like to supply the many building and landscaping projects in which he was constantly involved. It is reported that on this occasion Yoshinari had had the effrontery to donate several trees that were already badly withered upon arrival.[48] Outraged, the shogun ordered Yoshinari's censure and immediate dismissal from Bakufu councils. This anecdote gives an interesting glimpse into the character of Yoshimasa, but it is more likely that Yoshinari's sudden ouster was due to further pressures exerted by Hosokawa Katsumoto.

On the nineteenth day of the ninth month Yoshinari departed the Capital in the company of Honda, Suya, Kainoshō, and other vassals. He went directly to Kawachi where he was joined by one of his most powerful supporters, Yusa Kunisuke (d. 1460). At

---

[47] "The shogunal deputy and other daimyo speak out for the pardon of Hatakeyama Masanaga. It is granted and the deputy secretly sends word to (Masanaga ·in) Yamato." *Daijō-in Jisha Zōjiki*, 1459:7:23.

[48] *Ōnin Ryakki*, in Hanawa, *Gunsho Ruijū*, p. 431.

Kunisuke's suggestion Yoshinari established his headquarters in Wakae Castle, long the symbol of Yusa authority in the province. In the Capital, meanwhile, Masanaga hastily made preparations to set out in pursuit. Upon receiving a commission from the shogun to chastise Yoshinari, he marched over to Tatsuta in the province of Yamato. During the ensuing engagements Masanaga, in general, was supported by soldiers from Yamato, while Yoshinari drew his strength mainly from Kawachi.[49] Two of the Kawachi warriors who accompanied Yoshinari on his flight from the Capital, Suya and Kainoshō, were related to the Kusunoki, the loyalist family that had served the southern court so faithfully from the days of Go-Daigo's first call to arms.

Masanaga's departure had been overly hasty. He had left the Capital with little more than a nominal force, hoping to pick up adherents along the way. By the time he reached Tatsuta, however, his strength was still seriously inadequate. Reinforcements from various Yamato families were expected momentarily and the Bakufu had promised an additional contingent, but for the moment Masanaga was in a vulnerable position.

On an evening early in the tenth month a warrior from Kawachi arrived at Masanaga's camp to report rumors of an attack planned for that night by a raiding party from Wakae. Masanaga and his generals discounted the report on the grounds that the enemy could not possibly cover the distance between Wakae in Kawachi and Tatsuta in Yamato on such short notice. In this they were mistaken, for at dawn a force under Yusa Kunisuke fell upon Masanaga's startled troops. During the fighting that followed Yusa made a valiant effort, but the exhausting march and unfamiliar terrain placed him and his troops at a distinct disadvantage. In the dim morning light Yusa's force was put to rout. One by one the attacking captains fell—the Okabe brothers, the Honda—and finally Yusa himself. When news of the disaster reached Wakae, Yoshinari was thunderstruck. Only the impassioned plea of a re-

---

[49] Two Yamato stalwarts who provided invaluable service to Masanaga were Tsutsui Jun'ei and Jōshin'in Mitsunobu. They do not appear to have been Hatakeyama vassals.

tainer prevented him from turning back to aid his scattered troops.[50] With barely three hundred men Yoshinari abandoned Wakae Castle and fled to Mount Take, where he threw up defense works and prepared to guard his position.[51]

Masanaga's victorious troops swept into Kawachi. After occupying Wakae Castle and pausing for reinforcements, they camped at Hirokawa for the assault on Mount Take. Yoshinari's position, however, was unusually strong, and soon Masanaga was obliged to settle down to a prolonged siege. Throughout the winter and spring of 1460–61 the two forces sat facing each other. Early in the sixth month Yoshinari, pressed by a shortage of provisions and harried by his impatient commanders, dispatched a night attack party of two hundred men. Once again Masanaga's camp was taken by surprise. The attackers lost their advantage, however, when part of the group was delayed on mountain trails and failed to join the assault on time. In the first encounter Yoshinari's men overran an enemy outpost, killing Jimbo and several other leading generals. But when they pushed on to the encampment at Hirokawa they ran into the main concentration of Masanaga's forces. Their efforts were ill-coordinated and, lacking a smoke screen that had failed to spread down to Hirokawa, the attackers were soon forced to retreat in disorder back up the mountain. Yoshinari's losses were heavy, among them several leaders of the Suya clan.

The siege dragged on through the fall and a second winter, with the defenders possessing little strength for further forays down the mountain. Masanaga, meanwhile, received powerful reinforcements from the Bakufu. In the fourth month of 1462 the

[50] Just as Yoshinari was about to set out for the scene of battle, a monk named Jisō, who had been with Yusa's contingent, rode up. He reported that all was lost and implored Yoshinari not to become involved in a hopeless cause. *Chōroku-Kanshō-ki*, p. 333.

[51] The *Chōroku-Kanshō-ki* is highly critical of Yoshinari's strategy or lack of strategy in this engagement: "Yoshinari was a brave leader . . . but his planning was hot-blooded and reckless, and thus he was defeated." The author maintains that Yoshinari should have reenforced his Wakae position for a defensive stand there. As it turned out, this is precisely what he was obliged to do later at Mount Take in less friendly territory and with a greatly reduced force. *Chōroku-Kanshō-ki*, pp. 333–34.

shogun dispatched forces from twenty-eight provinces, including contingents of the Hosokawa, Yamana, Takeda, Kobayakawa, and Sasaki. On the fifteenth day Masanaga began a series of assaults on the mountain from three directions (while Yoshinari's supporter Ochi kept the southern route to Kii open).[52] But the position remained impregnable. It is reported that one of Masanaga's allies personally led seven attacks in a single day and seven times was repulsed. On the seventh assault the defenders were so weakened and exhausted that Yoshinari himself snatched up a sword and joined his men in turning back the storming troops.[53]

The key to Yoshinari's defense of Mount Take was the southern route to Kii. So long as this remained open he could count on receiving enough provisions to enable his embattled warriors to hang on despite a serious shortage of hands. But after still another year of stalemate, Masanaga, on the advice of Jōshin'in from Nara, succeeded in establishing an outpost on a nearby peak and was able to block the Kii Road. From that time on Yoshinari's supplies began to shrink rapidly, and in the third month of 1463, after nearly two and a half years on the mountain, he quietly led the remnants of his force out of the battered fortress and down the slope to the forests below.

For the next few years Yoshinari wandered through the provinces of Kii and Yamato. At one point he spent several months with the monks on Kōyasan until harassment and threat from Masanaga finally drove him to the hills of Yoshino, a natural sanctuary for fugitives from the Capital. Supported by only a small band of loyal vassals, Yoshinari was no match for Masanaga, who had received further reinforcements from Hosokawa Katsumoto and was now in full control of Kawachi. Only Yoshinari's elusiveness prevented Masanaga from tracking down and destroying him.

When news of the evacuation of Mount Take reached Kyoto

[52] Ochi supported Hatakeyama Yoshinari. Like Tsutsui and Jōshin'in on Masanaga's side, he does not appear to have been a vassal of the Hatakeyama. The names of these three warriors—Ochi, Tsutsui, Jōshin'in—appear frequently in the chronicles. They seem to have been constantly involved in the intermittent strife and warfare that plagued Yamato and its neighboring provinces throughout these years.

[53] *The Chronicle of Ōnin*, p. 365.

there was great rejoicing.[54] Lords gathered at the shogunal palace and at the mansions of Hosokawa Katsumoto and Ise Sadachika (1417–73) to celebrate the long-awaited victory. In the twelfth month of that year (1463) the shogun ordered Masanaga to return to the Capital. After posting a garrison at Wakae Castle, Masanaga departed the provinces and arrived triumphantly in Kyoto during the first month of 1464.

Masanaga had been recalled to succeed his patron, Hosokawa Katsumoto, in the post of shogunal deputy. The transfer of office did not actually take place until the eleventh month, since Katsumoto still had unfinished business and was obliged to devote most of the year to it. The events of those days—Masanaga's return, his participation in great affairs of state and, finally, his appointment as shogunal deputy—represented not the final victory for Masanaga, but the fruition of Katsumoto's carefully laid plans. Masanaga had indeed won an important battle. His star, for the moment, was on the rise while Yoshinari's seemed to have sunk permanently beyond the horizon. In fact, the goal for which both Hatakeyama contenders were fighting so desperately had become, in terms of real power, meaningless; for the Hatakeyama were no longer masters of their own fate. Forces beyond their control had entered the family dispute both from above and from below and had rendered permanent solution to the succession problem virtually impossible. The Hatakeyama were never again to enjoy jurisdiction over the extensive lands they once had governed. Their great vassals, who were struggling so bitterly on behalf of both Hatakeyama leaders, would never allow a settlement until their own desire for land had been fulfilled. And fulfillment of this desire could be realized only at the expense of the Hatakeyama themselves.

At the same time that the Hatakeyama were experiencing this great social upheaval in which "those below" overthrew "those above" (*gekokujō*), they were about to become pawns in the

---

[54] Ise Sadachika, for example, was feasting at the mansion of Akamatsu Masanori when couriers arrived with news of Yoshinari's withdrawal. He went immediately to the shogunal palace to relay the good tidings to Yoshimasa. *Inryōken Nichiroku*, 1463:4:16, in Bussho Kankōkai, *Nihon Bukkyō Zensho*.

struggle for power forming between Hosokawa and Yamana. We have seen how the former Hatakeyama leader Mochikuni had set the pattern for interference in constable succession disputes during the crises in the Ogasawara and Togashi families. Now the Hatakeyama themselves were about to become victims of the same game. At first both Hosokawa Katsumoto and Yamana Sōzen had supported Hatakeyama Masanaga. The benefits of this joint support, however, were reaped entirely by Katsumoto. In his position as shogunal deputy, Katsumoto had a major voice in Bakufu decisions. Thus he was able to don the mantle of official patron of Masanaga. Masanaga's return and installation as deputy in 1464 was, for Katsumoto, a personal triumph.

With Katsumoto doing so well in support of Masanaga, it was just a matter of time until Sōzen, for tactical considerations if for no other reason, would be forced into support of Yoshinari. This part of the story, however, belongs to the opening phases of the Ōnin War. Let us turn now to events taking place during these years in the House of Shiba.

THE SHIBA SUCCESSION DISPUTE

The Shiba succession dispute is not nearly so well documented as that of the Hatakayama. The *Bunshō-ki,* which deals with the Shiba quarrel, is an exceedingly short work and is so stylistically remote from the other war tales that it scarcely seems to deserve inclusion in this category. Much of the *Bunshō-ki* is devoted to Buddhist and Confucian moralizing, with the result that little space remains for historical information. Hence we must turn to other sources to piece together the events surrounding the Shiba dispute. Both *The Chronicle of Ōnin* and the *Ōnin Ryakki* are useful for the periods of Bunshō (1466) and Ōnin (1467–68), while entries in journals such as the *Hekizan Nichiroku* and the *Daijō-in Jisha Zōjiki* help to fill in facts about the earlier years.

Descendants of Seiwa Genji[55] from the province of Mutsu, the

[55] Ieuji, the son of Minamoto Yasuuji, adopted the name Shiba at the end of the thirteenth century and became the first of this family line.

Decline of the Muromachi Bakufu   97

Shiba joined their kinsman, Ashikaga Takauji, in his struggle against loyalist forces during the dynastic split of the fourteenth century. Shiba Takatsune (1299–1366) contributed particularly valuable service to the Ashikaga cause in the north, where he defeated Nitta Yoshisada in Echizen in the summer of 1338. As constable of Echizen and Wakasa, Takatsune ranked among Takauji's leading generals. But he later became involved in the internecine disputes that wracked the Ashikaga family at mid-century and soon found himself in opposition to the shogun.[56] After Takauji's death Takatsune was able to reinstate himself in the good graces of Takauji's son and successor, Yoshiakira, and lived to see his own son, Yoshimasa (not to be confused with Ashikaga Yoshimasa), become first minister of the new shogun in 1362.

Yoshimasa represented the high point of Shiba power during the Muromachi period. A leading figure in the Bakufu under both Yoshiakira and Yoshimitsu, Shiba Yoshimasa added the provinces of Etchū, Noto, Tōtōmi, and Shinano[57] to his inherited constable holdings of Echizen and Wakasa. In many respects the history of the Bakufu during the remaining years of the fourteenth century (until Yoshimitsu reached his majority) can be reduced to a record of the careers of Shiba Yoshimasa and Hosokawa Yoriyuki. As we have seen, the third shogunal deputy family, the Hatake-yama, had little voice in public affairs during this period. Rivalry between Yoshimasa and Yoriyuki was the dominant factor in Bakufu affairs. After Yoshimasa's death in 1410, however, Shiba strength began to ebb. The family produced one more shogunal deputy in Yoshiatsu (1396–1433), who held the post from 1429

[56] When Ashikaga Takauji and his brother Tadayoshi quarreled in the 1350s, Shiba Takatsune sided with Tadayoshi.

[57] Three of these provinces did not remain under Shiba jurisdiction. As we have seen, Etchū-Noto became one of the centers of Hatakeyama power, while the Ogasawara emerged predominant in Shinano. It is very difficult to trace the shifts in constable domains during the early years of the Muromachi period. At present this can be done only by piecing together references from scattered sources. Professor Satō Shin'ichi of Tokyo University is now collecting material on this subject to supplement his excellent study of the Kamakura constable in *Kamakura Bakufu Shugo Seido no Kenkyū*.

to 1431, but were unable to approach again the power they had enjoyed under Yoshimasa.

The fundamental problem facing the Shiba was how to control their unruly vassals. Of all the great constable-daimyo families, they held fealty over the most formidable array of vassal chieftains. In the three provinces of Echizen, Owari, and Tōtōmi, which became the permanent areas of Shiba authority, the family was obliged to contend with the burgeoning power of Kai, Asakura, and Oda, all of whom would provide excellent case studies in the growth of the daimyo during the period of war in the provinces (*sengoku,* from the end of the Ōnin War until reunification at the end of the sixteenth century).[58] Even at the time of our story these vassal warriors had achieved a large degree of autonomy; and when the Shiba head died in 1452 without a male heir, their imposing presence as clan elders made the reestablishment of central control in the Shiba family a remote goal.

The succession went to Yoshitoshi, the son of a branch relative, who was known from that time as Shiba Yoshitoshi (1430–90). The new family head seems to have aimed from the outset for a revival of Shiba power. In so doing he encountered the formidable opposition of Kai Tsuneharu (d. 1459), a ranking Shiba vassal. Records are few, but Kai appears to have been a strong-willed person, as set upon maintaining the autonomy of the vassal families as Yoshitoshi was upon drawing them safely back to the central House. What is more, Kai had personal influence in the Bakufu, as he was later to demonstrate in a clash with Yoshitoshi.

The first few years following Yoshitoshi's succession passed quietly enough, but around 1458 the new Shiba chief ran into serious difficulty with Kai and the other vassal heads. To stem their opposition to his leadership, Yoshitoshi turned for assistance to the Bakufu. He secured the support of three officials, Kira, Ishibashi, and Arakawa,[59] and for a while appeared to have gained the upper hand. But Kai's younger sister was a concubine of Ise Sadachika, and Kai now went with Oda and Asakura to persuade

[58] The differences between the pre-Ōnin and the post-Ōnin daimyo will be discussed in a later section.

[59] Watanabe, *Muromachi Jidai Shi,* p. 290.

Sadachika to back them against Yoshitoshi. In Sadachika the Shiba vassals gained a powerful ally, and before long shogunal censure was imposed upon Yoshitoshi. Discouraged over this new turn of events, Yoshitoshi retired to the Higashiyama section northeast of the Capital and secluded himself in the Tōkō-ji, where he remained for more than a year (from the twelfth month of 1456 to the second month of 1458).[60] During Yoshitoshi's self-imposed retirement others spoke out in Bakufu councils for a more realistic settlement of the Shiba affair.

Hosokawa Katsumoto argued that the Shiba quarrel was causing unfavorable repercussions throughout the country and urged that Kai be brought into line behind his lord.[61] On Katsumoto's advice the shogun persuaded Yoshitoshi to return to his mansion. This was hardly a final solution to the problem, however, simply a temporary arrangement to preserve the peace. In 1459 the shogun saw an opportunity to engage Yoshitoshi's services and, at the same time, to divert his attention from Kai. A few years earlier Yoshimasa had dispatched his younger brother, Ashikaga Masatomo (1436–91), to the Kantō in an attempt to bring order to that troubled land. But Masatomo had made little headway against his chief rival, the so-called Koga *kubō*.[62] Yoshimasa now decided to send an expeditionary force under Shiba Yoshitoshi to provide aid for the beleaguered Masatomo. Yoshitoshi set out on the Tōkai Road and went to Ōmi; but there, instead of continuing eastward, he veered north and crossed the Echizen border to launch a full-scale assault on Kai Tsuneharu. The *Hekizan Nichiroku*, which contains a fairly detailed account of this action, claims that Yo-

---

[60] *Ōnin Ryakki*, p. 428.

[61] *Hekizan Nichiroku*, 1459:5:26, in Kondō Keizō, *Kaitei Shiseki Shūran*. I have used the information contained in the entry for this date to reconstruct the following account of Yoshitoshi's campaign in Echizen.

[62] After the defeat in 1439 of the Kantō *kubō*, Ashikaga Mochiuji (1398–1439), the eastern provinces lapsed into a long period of unrest and anarchy. Mochiuji's son, Shigeuji (1434–97), attempted to restore order in Kamakura. He was expelled, however, by the powerful Uesugi family and fled to Koga in Shimōsa, where he became known as the Koga *kubō*. In 1457 the shogun sent his brother Masatomo to assume leadership at Kamakura. But owing to the turmoil in the east Masatomo was not able to get beyond Horikoshi in Izu. Here he settled and was known from that time as the Horikoshi *kubō*.

shitoshi had under his command 10,000 troops and 50 war vessels for operations by land and by sea. Kai, with only a token force of 200, seemed doomed; but in the midst of the fighting a great wind arose that destroyed much of Yoshitoshi's fleet and threw his troops into wild confusion. The defenders saw their opportunity and burst forth to rout Yoshitoshi's disorganized host. According to the *Hekizan Nichiroku*, Kai's 200 inflicted 800 casualties on Yoshitoshi's 10,000.

Yoshitoshi's advantage was gone. He still held Kai in a desperate position despite the failure of his surprise offensive, but his flagrant disobedience of Bakufu orders had brought down the wrath of the shogun, who promptly sent off a punitive force from Ōmi[63] to bring Yoshitoshi to task. In the meantime, Kai died in Echizen. His death is briefly noted in the chronicles.[64] No reason is given, though the wording indicates that Kai died from natural causes and not on the field of battle.

Although Yoshitoshi's principal adversary was gone, his own position had become untenable. As the Bakufu's Ōmi force closed in, Yoshitoshi hastily withdrew from Echizen and fled to the western provinces. There he sought and received asylum from Ōuchi Masahiro in Suō.[65] The relationship between Ōuchi and the Shiba, primarily an eastern power, is not clear. Perhaps it stemmed from the previous century when Shiba generals had marched westward to fight Loyalist armies in Kyushu. The records say only that Yoshitoshi "sojourned in the west for five or six years." [66]

With Shiba Yoshitoshi in disgrace, the Bakufu temporarily installed his son as family head. Two years later, in 1461, the son was in turn replaced by another Shiba collateral, Shibukawa Yoshikado (henceforth, Shiba Yoshikado). The great vassals fell in line behind Yoshikado, and the Shiba succession dispute, on the surface at least, appeared settled. In fact, the settlement was at best a temporary alignment. The big three vassals—Kai, Asakura, Oda—backed Yoshikado only as an alternative to Yoshitoshi, who had

[63] *Daijō-in Jisha Zōjiki*, 1459:5:14. This force was followed by troops from Etchū and Noto a week later. *Ibid.*, 1459:5:21.

[64] For example, *Hekizan Nichiroku*, 1459:8:13.

[65] *Ōnin Ryakki*, p. 428.

[66] *The Chronicle of Ōnin*, p. 359.

sought to reduce their autonomy. Yoshikado was little more than the nominal head of a house divided, while the concept of a united Shiba had long since become a fiction. Rent from within by forces it could no longer control and prey to the disorder of the times, the once proud Shiba of Yoshimasa had fallen on evil days. And within a few years the family was to become even more deeply divided as the opposing factions came under the control of Yamana and Hosokawa in a test of strength preliminary to the Ōnin War. I shall return to the Shiba, therefore, at the time of Yoshitoshi's dramatic return from the west in the winter of 1465.

FAVORITISM, EXTRAVAGANCE, AND FAMINE UNDER YOSHIMASA

In the years of turmoil and conflict that surround the Ōnin War Ashikaga Yoshimasa emerges an enigmatic and intriguing figure. Traditional historians have assailed him as the villain whose misrule, extravagance, and caprice plunged the country into a period of endemic civil war. More recently, Japanese scholars engrossed in the momentous social and economic changes of the Muromachi era have almost entirely discounted Yoshimasa's role as a prime instigator of the Ōnin War. While not condoning his prodigal ways, they see little connection between the shrunken world of his authority and the fundamental historical processes at work throughout the country at each level of society. To them Yoshimasa is best regarded as a product of his times, who fulfilled a role inevitably his by birth during a period of "dynastic decline." According to their view, the petty intrigues, reversals, and recurrent crises of the shogunal court that spice *The Chronicle of Ōnin* and other records are a commentary on the fallen state of the Bakufu, but hardly the determining events of the age.

As a result of the work of these postwar scholars in the still pioneer field of Muromachi studies, few can deny the essential validity of their reevaluation of Yoshimasa's historical role. In the present examination of the origins of the Ōnin War I have stressed the failure of Bakufu leadership after the death of Yoshinori, not as a result of the personal shortcomings of any individual, but as due to the Bakufu's limited system of leadership selection. I have also noted that even a strong leader would have faced nearly insurmountable obstacles in attempting to revitalize the Bakufu. In this sense Yoshimasa was a product of his times.

But can we dismiss him with such clichés? Can we fully understand the times of which he was a product if we ignore the activities of the shogun and his clique of personal advisers? To do so, I believe, would be to misinterpret seriously the true nature of the Ōnin War. For while we may seek to explain the convulsions of this age from the more fundamental historical processes at work, the great war as it was finally fought was in many ways incongruous. It was not a war of revolution except in the incidental sense that rising vassals were prepared to annex the lands of their faltering constable lords. Nor was it a war aimed at the overthrow of the government. The Bakufu itself, for all practical purposes, had no military strength, yet neither of the major belligerents at any time sought to displace it. Finally, the arena of battle for much of the war was confined almost entirely to Kyoto and to those areas selected for their strategic bearing on the fighting in the Capital,[67] even though the powerful decentralist trend of the times had rendered the city a mere symbol of its former authority.

In the last statement we have, I believe, a key to the nature of this seemingly senseless struggle. So great was the idea of a central military government (Bakufu), which derived its authority from a symbolic imperial line, that men were impelled to fight for goals that were no longer attainable. From the establishment of the Kamakura Bakufu in the late twelfth century, Japanese society had been dominated by the military caste. Go-Daigo's return to the imperial ideal in the fourteenth century was nothing more than

---

[67] Fighting did break out in other parts of the country; and, as I shall point out, it was the spread of unrest and conflict to the provinces that contributed to the termination of the Ōnin War. But much of this provincial fighting resulted from the opportunism of underlings. The fact remains that the principals concentrated their strategy almost exclusively on the Capital.

a brief, anachronistic pause in the more significant pursuit of the new military ideal.[68]

Ashikaga Takauji seized power through the reinstitution of a Bakufu conceptually (although not structurally) identical with that of Yoritomo. The conditions that Takauji faced, however, were far different from those of the earlier period, and, as we have seen, he chose to establish his Bakufu on the basis of a federation of provincial barons (constables) and central government. In attempting to strengthen his constables, Takauji weakened immeasurably the power of the Bakufu itself through the dispersal of authority and holdings. And thus he laid the foundation for growth of the constable-daimyo, that transitional and paradoxical figure devoted to the development of regional autonomy, yet in the end unable to survive without the support of the Bakufu.

In other words the Bakufu before the Ōnin War remained a vital force *regardless* of the extent to which its military strength had dwindled. No matter how flagrantly a great baron like Yamana Sōzen might flout the orders of the shogun and pursue his own course of territorial aggrandizement, he was still willing to commit his entire force to a protracted struggle over a few acres of land in Kyoto.

Where, then, did the real strength of the Bakufu lie? Through the darkest and most discordant years of the medieval period it persisted as the dominant ideal in the minds of men and, aside from a few brief lapses, it persisted in name as well. As scholars of comparative history have pointed out, this is not a unique phenomenon during times of feudal development.[69] After the fall of the Roman Empire the imperial ideal was maintained for centuries under Byzantium in the East, and was the ideological stimulus for at least one great restorative attempt by Charlemagne in the West. There are, however, several aspects of this ideal of central government during protracted chaos and anarchy that are

---

[68] By imperial ideal I refer to direct rule by the emperor, which may never have actually been realized in Japan, but was still an ideal. Military ideal means military rule of the country through the authority of the emperor.

[69] See Rushton Coulborn, ed., *Feudalism in History*, pp. 20–23.

peculiar to the history of medieval Japan and that may partially explain the nature of the Bakufu at the time of the Ōnin War.

I have suggested the incongruous character of the war, of the fact that no one at any time attempted to displace either the shogun or the Bakufu, despite the weakness and incompetence of both. This poses an intriguing question: granted that the concept of a central military government held sway throughout the medieval period, how can we explain why men were ready and willing to destroy the Kamakura Bakufu when it became unworthy, yet did not even challenge the central existence of the Ashikaga Bakufu once it had reached a similar state?

An obvious answer lies in the relative strength and structure of the two governments. The Kamakura Bakufu of the early fourteenth century, while corrupt and decadent, was still a functioning organization. The Hōjō family itself occupied nearly half (thirty) of the constable appointments and owned vast paying estates throughout the land, while the Bakufu still governed the two most important administrative centers—Kamakura and Kyoto —and had a formidable regional organization as well. The tyranny of Hōjō rule could be removed only by revolutionary means. Someone had to give the Kamakura Bakufu a push before it would fall.

This was not the case with the Ashikaga Bakufu under Yoshimasa. The personal holdings and income of the Ashikaga family had dwindled to such an extent that the shogun was forced to devise whatever makeshift means he could to stimulate the inflow of revenue. And while the Ashikaga, through their collaterals (for example, the Hosokawa, Hatakeyama, and Shiba), held many constable appointments, there was a vast difference between the fully bureaucratic constable of Kamakura times and the nearly autonomous constable-daimyo of the Muromachi period. Finally, the administrative organization of the Ashikaga Bakufu had shrunk to the point where it is questionable whether it really controlled even its own seat in Kyoto.

Therefore one may argue that there was no need to "push" or destroy the Ashikaga Bakufu since, despite the extravagance and arbitrary behavior of Yoshimasa, there was no tyranny or, for that matter, no effective government, to destroy. The continued existence of the Bakufu interfered little with the warlike activities of the great chieftains.

There is no question of the logicality of the origins of the Ōnin War, nor of the fact that it began as a clash of arms between the two most powerful constable-daimyo and their supporters, with the Capital city as their battleground. But why did the two armies choose to struggle so long in Kyoto without attempting either to mount full-scale offensives in the provinces or to brush aside the shogun and to establish a provisional Bakufu of their own? When finally, in the later stages of the war, fighting did spread on a large scale to outlying areas, it was not so much fighting over the so-called central issue of victory or defeat as it was the uprising of individual vassals against their absentee masters who continued to dispute this issue in the Capital. In fact, one of the main reasons for the termination of the war after eleven years was the steady departure of troops for the provinces, not to open new fronts, but to deal with these uprisings in their own domains. We may presume that many warriors would have been willing to prolong the stalemate in Kyoto even longer had they not been forced, for personal reasons, to return home.

Why did these men continue to fight after so many years of frustration on both sides? They fought partly because they were constable-daimyo and could not dissociate themselves from Bakufu affairs despite the extent of their own autonomy and the corresponding weakness of the Bakufu; and partly, I believe, because of the special ideal of central government of the Muromachi period based on the unique relationship of the Ashikaga Bakufu to the imperial court.

Minamoto Yoritomo was the first to formulate the military ideal. While openly arrogating many of the powers formerly enjoyed by the court, he was scrupulously careful to exercise these powers in the name of the emperor. Yoritomo took great pains to dispel the impression that he had usurped imperial authority; rather, he sought to show that at all times he was acting as an agent and as a loyal subject of the emperor. The relationship of military ruler to sovereign established by Yoritomo became a fundamental political rule for all Japanese governments during succeeding centuries.[70]

Another important aspect of Yoritomo's military ideal was his determination that the military government, while deriving its authority from the emperor, be kept physically and spiritually separate from the court at Kyoto. He founded his Bakufu at Kamakura and made every effort to inculcate military values among his followers in order to avoid the debilitating influence of the court. After power had been seized by the Hōjō regents, members of the Fujiwara family and then princes of the blood were brought from Kyoto to serve in the empty capacity of shogun. Through these nobles, court values did eventually infiltrate and weaken Kamakura society. But this influence was indirect; throughout the Kamakura period the real rulers of the Bakufu remained distinctly separate from the emperor and his Kyoto court.

Like Yoritomo, Ashikaga Takauji wished to establish his Bakufu in the east. Owing to the circumstances of the war of succession, however, he was obliged to set up administration in Kyoto in close physical proximity to the court. Even so, Takauji did attempt to draw a clear line between courtier and warrior by reaffirming the military virtues. Under Takauji and his son, Yoshiakira, there was little fear that the shogun and his entourage would succumb to the softness of court life. Both Ashikaga leaders were eastern warriors who devoted most of their energies to fighting. They were soldiers on the move, not diplomats or statesmen with time for the subtler pursuits of the Capital.

At the death of Yoshiakira care of the Bakufu during Yoshimitsu's youth was, as we have seen, entrusted to the eminent minister Hosokawa Yoriyuki, a puritan who inveighed against luxury and extravagance. Yoriyuki's young charge was a person of quite, different tastes. Unlike his forebears, Yoshimitsu grew up entirely within the environs of the Capital. He received high court rank at an early age[71] and thereafter never ceased his quest for greater honors and more imposing titles.

[70] On the subject of Yoritomo, see Minoru Shinoda, *The Founding of the Kamakura Shogunate, 1180–1185.*

[71] In 1375, at the age of eighteen, Yoshimitsu was appointed to Junior Third Rank.

Yoshimitsu had a flair for the expensive and the ostentatious. At the age of twenty-one he began work on his Muromachi palace, the Hana-no-Gosho, a lavish structure of courtly scale that earned its name from the profusion of flowers and unusual blooms that are said to have filled its gardens at all seasons. Upon its completion in 1381 the Emperor Go-En'yū proceeded in full attendance to the Hana-no-Gosho for the ceremonies of exorcism and dedication. After His Majesty had bestowed a wine cup on Yoshimitsu, he and his guests launched into a round of entertainment that continued for five days and included dancing, court football, boating, and poetry. As a climax to this grand affair, the emperor made a special grant of title to many of Yoshimitsu's favorites and close court admirers.[72] It was, in all, a time of singular triumph for the young shogun.

As Yoshimitsu subdued and dominated his unruly barons during the final years of the fourteenth century, he came to dominate the imperial court as well. Those nobles who did not openly assist him were afraid to speak out against his pretentious ways, lest they should lose their estates and even their lives. Go-En'yū deeply resented the servile attitude his courtiers were forced to adopt and was himself frequently involved in discord with the shogun.[73]

Yoshimitsu's pretensions were enormous. In every way he sought to fashion himself in the mold of nobility. He not only acquired the niceties of court etiquette and accomplishments, he dressed and lived in the manner of the noble, and even changed his official seal from the military to the aristocratic style and adopted the Sinified title, *kubō*.[74] In 1394 he became chancellor (*dajō daijin*), thus assuming a rank held only once before by a military man (Taira Kiyomori). It seemed indeed that he would settle for nothing less than the throne. In 1408 Yoshimitsu invited the emperor and all the great dignitaries to his monastic retreat at Kita-

[72] Usui Nobuyoshi, *Ashikaga Yoshimitsu*, pp. 39–40.

[73] *Ibid.*, pp. 50–53.

[74] *Kubō* is used in the records from this time interchangeably with "shogun." It is also associated with the Bakufu's deputy in Kamakura, the so-called Kantō *kubō*. Yoshimitsu was infatuated with all things Chinese, and at one point even accepted the subordinate title "King of Japan" in his correspondence with the emperor of China.

yama. During the feasting he rested on a mat aligned with His Majesty's, while his favorite son, Yoshitsugu, occupied the position of an imperial prince on a level above the courtiers, including the imperial regent (*kampaku*).[75] Only fate prevented Yoshimitsu from pursuing further his apparent goal of installing Yoshitsugu as emperor, for in the fifth month of that year the master of Japan was stricken with illness and died.

It is doubtful whether Yoshimitsu's sole purpose in usurping the prestige of the throne was his own overweening pride, for he was a shrewd and pragmatic man. Despite personal success in dealing with the great families, Yoshimitsu saw clearly the inherent weakness of the Bakufu. The Ashikaga could not hope to hold the barons in check indefinitely by political stratagem alone. He, and surely his successors, would need more to rely upon than simply a delicate balance of power between constable and Bakufu. Thus he sought to bolster the Bakufu by establishing as completely as possible its identification with the imperial House. In his view the "marriage" of shogun and emperor would render his own authority unassailable.

At the same time Yoshimitsu encouraged his barons to partake of the pleasures and rewards of metropolitan life. The longer they remained in the Capital, the more easily their activities could be observed. Thus lured by a heady social atmosphere where chieftain could mingle with noble, the constable set up full-time residence in Kyoto, leaving his deputy in charge of affairs at home. Since those who remained in the provinces would have little chance to obtain special favor or assignment, few could afford not to move. In this manner the Capital became studded with the mansions of the constables, who saw greater gain in attendance at court than in attention to provincial administration.

While these developments may have eminently suited the policy of Yoshimitsu, they were to have unforeseen and, in the long run, ill effects on the future of the Ashikaga. For Yoshimitsu

[75] Yoshimitsu favored his second son, Yoshitsugu, far above his heir and successor, Yoshimochi. On this occasion Yoshimochi was assigned a distant seat while Yoshimitsu and Yoshitsugu occupied their exalted positions attired as though they were emperor and crown prince. See Yomiuri Shimbun Sha, *Nihon no Rekishi*, VI, 17–18.

had created an atmosphere of exaggerated and distorted political importance in Kyoto, analogous in many ways to the state of affairs in the Fujiwara-dominated Capital during the final years of Heian. Long after real power had passed to the provincial warrior, the Fujiwara continued to concentrate on political intrigue at court, as though they could thereby regain the authority that once had been theirs. At that time the weight of tradition surrounding the imperial House had sustained the deception of Kyoto's importance in the minds of the Taira as well as the Fujiwara until it was finally shattered by Minamoto Yoritomo.

From the time of Yoshimitsu the great leaders once again looked inward toward the Capital while momentous changes were taking place in the provinces. Although aware of the importance of establishing ever more firmly their provincial bases, the constable-daimyo became addicted to metropolitan life and came, paradoxically, to center their quest for regional autonomy on the increasingly ineffective conduct of affairs in Kyoto.

Yoshimasa was truly a product of his grandfather's attempts to merge the shogunal and imperial Houses and to create an inbred climate of political centralization for the constable-daimyo in Kyoto. Yoshimochi, though not a forceful personality, had maintained Bakufu hegemony with the aid of first-rate lieutenants, and Yoshinori had prevented the break-up of that hegemony through vigorous policy. But Yoshimasa fell heir to the mounting ills and, conversely, the deceptive strength of Yoshimitsu's designs. The shogunate to which Yoshimasa succeeded was in a state of rapid decline, and he displayed little concern for its military revitalization. Yet by breeding and temperament Yoshimasa filled the role of the Kyoto shogun. He had aristocratic tastes and a flair for kingly extravagance. He was at once the perfect tool for scheming daimyo and fawning favorite, and the means for blending the Ashikaga with the imperial family.

The world of Yoshimasa, then, was the world of the Capital. For the leaders of the age all plans and ambitions were centered in Kyoto. If there were issues to be settled, they would be settled here. If a Yamana and a Hosokawa were to clash, they would clash here. They would not seek to overthrow the shogun any more than they would seek to overthrow the emperor, for both stood symbolically for a' unique merger of imperial and military ideals at the head of this vital city that had to be controlled at all costs.

The fundamental dependency of constable-daimyo on Bakufu, the merging of shogun with imperial House, the concentration of leading warriors in Kyoto society—these facts go far in explaining the nature of the Ōnin War and why it was fought for so many years in such limited space.

Let us turn now to a closer examination of Ashikaga Yoshimasa and his favorites. Born in 1436, Yoshimasa was the second son of the Shogun Yoshinori and his consort, Hino Shigeko (1410–63). In accordance with the custom of the times, younger sons of the shogun were generally placed in holy orders at an early age and were relegated to a life of monastic retirement. The Ashikaga regarded this as sound policy, from an economic as well as a political standpoint. For one thing, it was expensive to maintain additional offspring on a level befitting their relationship to the shogun. Moreover, a discontented second or third son could become a focal point of trouble if allowed to roam the corridors of the Bakufu unattended.

In Yoshimasa's case, however, fate played a hand. As we have seen, his older brother, Yoshikatsu, survived their father by only a few months and Yoshimasa himself succeeded to the shogunacy in 1443 at the age of eight. Needless to say, a child of this age could hardly have assumed control of the Bakufu. Administrative affairs were left largely in the hands of the shogunal deputy, while the young shogun remained under the care of his guardians. From birth Yoshimasa had known little more than the company of women and court attendants. One of the most important influences during the child's youth was undoubtedly his mother, Lady Shigeko. She appears to have been a sensible woman, although, as we shall see, she was not reluctant to partake of her son's lavish generosity in later years.

Lady Shigeko's family, the Hino, occupied a special position under the Ashikaga Bakufu. A branch of the Fujiwara, the aristo-

cratic Hino had remained with the northern court at the time
of Go-Daigo's flight to Yoshino. Their great rise to prominence
began during Yoshimitsu's rule when the family managed to in-
stall one of their daughters as wife of the shogun.[76] From that
time it became customary to select Hino women for shogunal
consorts, much as it had been the custom to use Fujiwara women
during the Heian period, and Saionji women during the Kamakura period, as wives for the imperial family. History abounds
with the disastrous consequences of interference by maternal
families, and in the case of the Hino these consequences were
to be forcefully revealed with the advent of Yoshimasa's consort,
the notorious Lady Tomiko (1440–96).

Aside from the Hino, the most influential family in private
circles of the Bakufu was the Ise clan. In the late fourteenth century the Ise, vassals of the Ashikaga, had replaced the Nikaidō as
hereditary chiefs of the administrative board. Successive Ise leaders
were able to enhance further their status and authority by assuming the unique role of shogunal guardian. Yoshimitsu was the
first to be placed in the care of the Ise during his formative years,
and thereafter it became traditional to assign the shogun's young
sons to upbringing in an Ise household. Shortly after his birth,
Yoshimasa became the charge of Ise Sadachika (1399–1473).
Actually, Sadachika's official career did not commence until his
appointment as chief of the administrative board in 1460; but it
is appropriate at this point to say a few words about this colorful
figure who was to have such a strong, although baneful, influence
over the young shogun.

If we are to believe *The Chronicle of Ōnin*, Ise Sadachika was
at the very core of the corruption and excess that marked the
years before the Ōnin War. Lecherous, greedy, immoral, he was
ever available for bribery or graft and was prepared to interfere in
the greatest state affair on behalf of a crony or upon receipt of
cash payment. Moreover he enjoyed a most intimate relationship with the shogun. It is said that Yoshimasa looked upon the
Lord of Ise as his second father, from which we can gather that

[76] Yoshimitsu took as his wife Hino Nariko and, after her death, Hino Yasuko.
See Miura Hiroyuki, "Hino Tomiko," in *Rekishi to Jinbutsu.*

the latter had a ready ear for even his most preposterous schemes. Through the chronicles we see this devious man hovering at the side of the shogun, whether during the revelry of a drinking bout or in the privacy of Yoshimasa's own chambers, prepared to offer the most capricious advice on any matter that had captured his fancy. Sadachika's most flagrant abuse of authority was displayed during the Shiba succession dispute, when, through the urgings of his wife and, later, of his mistress, he secured the shogun's benediction first for Shiba Yoshikado and, within a few years, for Shiba Yoshitoshi, whom he had previously caused to be banished. This abrupt reversal of favor brought down the wrath of both Yamana and Hosokawa and sent Sadachika scurrying from the Capital in 1466. But before long he was back among the shogun's circle of favorites.[77] By that time the Capital was at war and there was little opportunity for a return to earlier intrigues.

Mention should be made of a curious trio of favorites whose names are unimportant but whose activities typified the early years of favoritism in the shogun's court. The trio consisted of Imamairi-no-Tsubone, a concubine who became Yoshimasa's first great passion; Karasumaru Suketō, related to the shogun by marriage; and Arima Mochiie, a sycophant who had ingratiated himself at court. A contemporary punster, playing on the syllable "ma" that was common to the names of all three, dubbed them the "Three Ma" or the "Three Devils." They were universally despised, so blatant was their abuse of privilege and their craving for wealth. One journal records that posters displaying their likenesses were tacked to trees about the Capital and served as targets for the people's loathing.[78]

At first O-Ima, as she was called, held complete sway over the affections of the young shogun. Neither the admonitions of his mother nor the threats of his generals could deter Yoshimasa from humoring her every whim. No one in the shogunal entourage dared incur her displeasure and for a while it seemed as though the authority of the Bakufu lay solely with her. But O-Ima's posi-

[77] Sadachika returned to the Capital in 1467 at Yoshimasa's request, but retired four years later.

[78] *Gaun Nikken Roku*, 1455:1:6, in Kondō Keizō, *Kaitei Shiseki Shūran*, III.

tion was seriously threatened by Yoshimasa's marriage to Hino Tomiko in 1455. And when, four years later, Lady Tomiko produced a son who died shortly after birth, it was rumored that O-Ima had cast an evil spell over the child:

The shogun's favored mistress has thwarted the consort and now her power is like a bright flame that none can approach. This woman conducts herself as though she were a great minister, and there is no end to the suffering she has caused people. What is more, in her jealousy she has cast secret spells that have brought disaster to the consort.[79]

Even Yoshimasa could not ignore these charges and presently he banished O-Ima to a small island on Lake Biwa, where she was later killed by Tomiko's men.

Lady Tomiko was one of the more strong-willed women in Japanese history. Unfortunately, aside from the incident recounted above, there is little information about her early years as shogunal consort. It is certain that she was able to capture a goodly share of her husband's affections, for they were soon to become nearly constant companions on the round of ceremonial and social events launched by the shogun several years before the war. Her greatest disappointment at the time was her failure to produce an heir to the shogunacy. I must reserve until the next section the story of how Lady Tomiko finally did give birth to a son and thereby helped to precipitate the Ōnin War. We can gain an even better idea of this lady's character through her activities during and after the war.

Utilizing what remained of the Bakufu's authority after the commencement of war, Tomiko entered the moneylending business on a grand scale. She accepted bribes from all—daimyo, noble, merchant—and handled her money so shrewdly that a common saying of the day credited her with having accumulated the "wealth of the realm." [80] On one occasion she made an enormous profit by establishing barriers at entrances to the city for the alleged purpose of raising funds for repair of the palace. And as an illustration of her affluence and, at the same time, as a commen-

[79] *Hekizan Nichiroku,* 1459:1:18.
[80] Yūzankaku, *Shinsetsu Nihon Rekishi,* VI, 64.

tary on the fallen state of the imperial family, it is reported that Tomiko personally defrayed most of the expenses of the coming-of-age ceremony and celebration for the eldest son of Go-Tsuchimikado (1442–1500), the future Go-Kashiwabara (1464–1526), in 1480.

One final figure who should be mentioned among Yoshimasa's coterie of favorites is Kikei Shinzui, the Zen priest of the Shōkoku-ji. Among the temples of the land, the Shōkoku-ji occupied a place of particular importance for the Ashikaga shoguns. It was built in 1383 by Ashikaga Yoshimitsu, who planned it as his own special Zen center and who even managed to secure ranking for the new structure as one of the *Gosan,* or Five (Famous Zen) Temples, of Kyoto.[81] The Shōkoku-ji was located adjacent to the shogun's Muromachi quarters and from Yoshimitsu's time was used by the Ashikaga leaders for a variety of functions and purposes. During the early months of the Ōnin War the Shōkoku-ji was the center of much activity on the part of both armies. But before the year (1467) was out, it was destroyed by fire and was not rebuilt until the time of Hideyoshi.

In the years before the war, Shinzui occupied the office of Inryōken (a form of secretary) at the Rokuon-in of the Shōkoku-ji. We do not know a great deal about Shinzui, although he was very close to Yoshimasa and met him often. Shinzui, like Ise Sadachika, was therefore in a position to have an important influence on Shogunal decisions. And in fact he became involved in the same affair concerning the Shiba succession dispute that sent Sadachika fleeing from the city in 1466. At that time Yamana Sōzen was particularly anxious to punish Shinzui, probably, as *The Chronicle of Ōnin* points out, because the priest was a kinsman of the Akamatsu.[82] In any event, Shinzui's most important role in history was as compiler of the pre-Ōnin portions of the *Inryōken Nichiroku,* one of the principal source journals of this period.

[81] The *Gosan* originally consisted of the Nanzen-ji, Tenryū-ji, Kennin-ji, Tōfuku-ji, and Manju-ji. Yoshimitsu placed the Nanzen-ji in a special position above the others and inserted the Shōkoku-ji in second place among this group of noted Zen temples.

[82] *The Chronicle of Ōnin,* p. 363.

The opening pages of *The Chronicle of Ōnin* give, in hyperbolic terms, perhaps the most vivid picture of the extravagance and corruption of Yoshimasa's Bakufu in the years before the war. Although Yoshimasa may not have been the greatest profligate in Japanese history, there is something especially theatrical about the way in which he was able to maintain life on a grand scale within the narrow confines of his metropolitan world as discipline and order collapsed around him. We see the shogun surrounded by his favorites, immersed in luxury-loving pursuits and forced to resort to the most abusive forms of tax-draining and fiscal contrivance in order to cover costs. Much in the behavior of Yoshimasa and his cronies is reminiscent of the periods of dynastic decline in early Chinese history, and the parallel with omens that portended the fall of the House of Chou is duly recorded in *The Chronicle of Ōnin*.[83]

From the standpoint of historical analysis there is probably little to be gained by delving too minutely into the extravaganzas and lavish displays of Yoshimasa; for it is not the details of the extravaganzas, but the fact that there were extravaganzas and that somehow the Bakufu was able to finance them that is significant for an understanding of the times. We read in *The Chronicle of Ōnin,* for example, of the extraordinary number of emergency levies made during these years, of the hardships they caused, and of Yoshimasa's frequent use of the debt-cancellation, or act of grace (*tokusei*) decree. This type of decree, which was intimately related to the whole problem of tax exploitation and chaotic monetary conditions, has become, along with the peasant uprising (*doikki*), the object of intensive research on the social and economic changes occurring during the later fifteenth century. But these studies are focused more sharply on the years after the Ōnin War than on this pre-Ōnin period; hence discussion will be reserved until later.

The aim here is to examine briefly some of the more celebrated examples of Yoshimasa's extravagance during these years of foreboding and natural disaster, not for the purpose of suggesting a

[83] *Ibid.*, p. 357.

new interpretation but to convey through the chronicles something of the mood prevailing on the eve of the great war.

Lavish building projects seemed to appeal particularly to the leaders of Muromachi Japan. Even to those not especially known for their prodigal ways, the lure of a new palace or a fine mansion often proved irresistible, despite the drain on government finances. Emperor Go-Daigo, for example, had no sooner returned to the Capital after the defeat of the Hōjō, than he launched an expensive program of palace construction. There was a real need for new imperial quarters after the devastation of civil war, but when it came to the most crucial issue of the day, the settlement of warrior claims, Go-Daigo acted with far less vigor.

Part of the answer to this recurrent building urge on the part of Muromachi leaders lay in the essential fragility of Japanese wooden constructions, which were extremely vulnerable to fire or rapid decay, especially in these disordered years. Given the constant need for new buildings, some of the greater spendthrifts, such as Yoshimitsu and Yoshimasa, devoted much of their time and resources to the creation of ever more elaborate structures suited to their own tastes and pretentions. Yoshimasa, following his grandfather's lead, made frequent calls upon his chieftains to contribute unusual materials gathered from the provinces to aid in this project or that, and employed a variety of devices to accumulate the necessary funds. His greatest undertakings before the Ōnin War were the refurbishing of the shogunal palace (Hana-no-Gosho), which had originally been built by Yoshimitsu, and the erection of a new mansion at Takakura for his mother, Hino Shigeko.

During his early years as shogun, Yoshimasa had lived in a variety of places, including Karasumaru Suketō's mansion and a new residence of his own at Madenokōji that had consumed considerable time and money in the building. Yet in the spring of 1458 he began extensive repairs on Yoshimitsu's long-neglected shogunal palace with the aim of moving his headquarters there. To meet expenses, he resorted to a new series of levies on the various daimyo and religious institutions. He could not have selected a worse time for the commencement of this costly project nor for the building of his mother's mansion at Takakura, which he started shortly thereafter. The years of Chōroku, from 1457 until 1460, witnessed a succession of natural calamities, including flood, pestilence, and famine, that left much of the countryside barren and in great distress. A contemporary account from the *Hekizan Nichiroku*, dated the sixteenth day of the third month of 1460, vividly recounts the suffering of country-folk during these years, and follows with an incident of striking contrast involving the frivolity of members of a more privileged class:

When the sun went down I set out for home, and as I passed through Rokujō I saw an old woman cradling a child in her arms. After calling the child's name over and over, she finally ceased and began to wail. I looked closely and saw that the child was already dead. The woman fell over onto the ground in lamentation and people passing by inquired of her origins.

"I am a homeless wanderer from Kawachi," she replied. "The drought there has lasted for three years and the young rice plants no longer sprout. Officials perpetrate excesses and taxes are collected, but not a penny is lent out. If I had not left I would have met my death. Therefore I had no choice but to go to another province to seek food from others and to beg. As it is I have not been able to provide for this child and now it has come to this."

She began to wail again with great sobs. I took out the spare alms money I had and gave it to her, saying, "Take this money and hire someone to bury the child. I will return now and conduct a service to provide him with a Buddhist name and to pray for his salvation in the next world." The mother was very pleased with my words.

While still in a mood of sorrow over this experience, I came across a group of lords out viewing flowers. They numbered more than a thousand on horse and a myriad others in carriages. One could not cope with a force of that size. They looked down haughtily on pedestrians and railed at the soldiers in front of their horses. They were in a frolicsome mood, stealing flowers, and some had drawn their swords and were singing drinking songs. Others, who had vomited and were unable to walk further, were lying on the road. There were many such incidents occurring. Those who were witness to these happenings shuddered, while others coming upon the scene withdrew in surprise. They feared the powerful.[84]

[84] *Hekizan Nichiroku*, 1460:3:16.

So great was the suffering in those days and so wasteful and unnecessary the building programs of Yoshimasa, that the Emperor Go-Hanazono (1419–70) himself felt obliged to express his deep concern. In poetic phrases he addressed his errant shogun:

> The suffering people struggle for ferns on Mount Shouyang
> While everywhere their ovens are banked, and their bamboo
>   doors shut.
> It is spring and the second month; yet there is no joy
>   in verse.
> For whom are the colors of the land bursting forth?[85]

Yoshimasa was genuinely ashamed at these words and for a while suspended his building projects. But soon he was at it again. He spent huge sums on his mother's mansion, and installed in its rooms, according to *The Chronicle of Ōnin*, sliding panels valued at twenty thousand *kan* each.[86] He also engaged the exclusive services of Oguri Sōtan to paint murals of the eight views of the Hsiao and the Hsiang.

Yoshimasa's taste for the flamboyant was shared by his wife Tomiko, and around 1464 they launched a great round of processions and extravaganzas. During her early years as shogunal consort, Tomiko had been completely overshadowed by the favorite mistress, Imamairi-no-Tsubone. Now, her power secure, Tomiko was seen often at Yoshimasa's side, as they moved from one massive entertainment to another. In the spring of 1464 the shogun staged a grand, three-day performance of *Nō* at Tadasugawara, featuring the Kanze school of performers headed by On'ami (d. 1467), the nephew of Zeami (1363–1443). The distinguished On'ami had participated in a similar program arranged in 1433 by Yoshimasa's father, the Shogun Yoshinori, and he now emerged from retirement at the age of sixty-seven to perform before a dazzling array of notables from both the aristocratic and the military worlds.

In the third month of the following year Yoshimasa and Tomi-

---

[85] *Chōroku Kanshō-ki*, p. 237. The word *ferns* in the first line implies that the lack of food has driven the people to seek such things as bark and roots for sustenance.

[86] *The Chronicle of Ōnin*, p. 409.

ko led the lords and generals on a flower-viewing excursion outside the city to Kachō-zan in what was undoubtedly the most magnificent procession of the age. A contemporary diarist, Shinzui of the Shōkoku-ji, has recorded the brilliance of their entourage:

At the sound of four drums [on the fourth day] the flower-viewing procession set out in a splendor that was breathtaking to behold. The world itself seemed to be transformed and all present agreed that it was a rare sight indeed, a sight such as one might hope to see once in a lifetime. The processioners passed eastward from the Hōkaimon at Muromachi-Kitakōji . . . to Kachōzan, where they engaged in a linked-verse contest. Afterwards they moved on to Nyakuōji. Lord Hatakeyama [Masanaga] was in command at Kachōzan. . . . It looked very much as though there would be rain, but, to the surprise of everyone, none fell. The flowers of the land all burst forth in profusion.[87]

They returned from Nyakuōji on the night of the fifth and the following day continued their flower-viewing in a procession to Ōharano. But this time it did rain, and the enthusiasm of many participants was considerably dampened, as they were forced to trudge home in the mud.

The Chronicle of Ōnin tells us of the sumptuous feast, consisting of a myriad delicacies to be consumed with eating sticks formed from gold and rare woods, that accompanied the flower-viewing procession. In fact this affair marked the very summit of Yoshimasa's early brilliance, which he himself aptly captured in his contribution to the linked-verse session at Kachōzan:

> The world in bloom
> And naught else but the flower's hue.

[87] *Inryōken Nichiroku*, 1465:3:4.

PART TWO

The Ōnin War

The dates usually given for the Ōnin War are 1467–1477, or from the outbreak of hostilities in the Capital until the withdrawal of the last western armies from its charred ruins eleven years later. But 1477 is not universally accepted as the terminal date of the Ōnin War, since much of the fighting spread immediately to the provinces and continued there under the direction of many of the same protagonists for several decades.[1] This was particularly true in the case of southern Yamashiro, where the two Hatakeyama, Masanaga and Yoshinari, resumed their interminable struggle and even helped foment the great peasant uprising of 1485. According to those who would extend the duration of war until some time later in the century, it is meaningless to study only the years of fighting in the Capital, since one battle is

[1] Professor Suzuki Ryōichi, for example, places the end of the Ōnin War at 1493. This is the year in which the shogunal deputy, Hosokawa Masamoto (1466–1507), deposed the Shogun Yoshitane (1465–1522) and installed the figurehead Yoshizumi (1478–1511). According to Suzuki, the Shoguns Yoshihisa and Yoshitane had carried on campaigns related to the Ōnin War. See "Sengoku no Sōran," in Iwanami Shoten, *Iwanami Kōza Nihon Rekishi*, VIII, 4–5.

often indistinguishable from another. The more important phase of the war was that which succeeded the withdrawal of the western forces from Kyoto and which brought into play the complexities of military activity as a form of catalyst within the whole structure of changing social and economic conditions in the provinces.

This is obviously an important interpretation. Beyond the initial disposition of troops and the question of broad shifts in strategy, the day to day fighting in Kyoto from 1467 until 1477 can be of little interest to anyone other than the military historian. On the other hand, if the Ōnin War is thought of as a continuing process that extended into areas such as southern Yamashiro in the 1480s and became part of the profound changes taking place among the various social classes of that region, its historical significance is immediately enhanced. The war is then seen not simply as a holocaust that laid waste the Capital and brought to an end effective central government, but also as part of the next stage of feudal development in Muromachi Japan. I shall examine the first phase of the Ōnin War—its outbreak and progress in the Capital—in this chapter and reserve until later a discussion of those developments that followed the transfer of warfare to the provinces after 1477.[2]

The proximate political events leading to the Ōnin War are enormously complex. We have already seen the beginnings of conflict and struggle among the great constable-daimyo families of Hatakeyama, Shiba, Hosokawa, and Yamana. These families were to become even further embroiled with the commencement of dispute over succession to the shogunal house itself. It is necessary here to trace as coherently as possible the interplay of ambitions and animosities that finally brought war and carried it to its conclusion, in the Capital at least.

During the years of Kanshō, from 1460 until 1465, the powers of the land began to gather into two great camps behind the

---

[2] There was some fighting in the provinces from the outset of hostilities. The distinction being made here is that after 1477 a number of leading constable-daimyo, such as the two Hatakeyama, transferred their center of military operations to the provinces.

Hosokawa and the Yamana. Hosokawa Katsumoto, it will be recalled, had become the dominant figure among the leaders of the shogunal deputy families, whereas Yamana Sōzen headed the resurgent forces of the western provinces, whose potential had been recognized and temporarily destroyed by Yoshimitsu and Hosokawa Yoriyuki as early as the fourteenth century.

In one sense the confrontation of Hosokawa and Yamana may be regarded as a struggle between the party out of power and the party in, since Yamana Sōzen undoubtedly envied the preeminent position of Katsumoto in Bakufu councils. It would be a mistake, however, to picture Sōzen in the role of the revolutionary advocate of *gekokujō* ("those below overthrow those above"), as is often done on the basis of a passage from the *Chirizuka Monogatari* in which he is shown warning an old campaigner to forget about past deeds and to concentrate solely on existing power relations.[3] Apart from romanticized anecdotes such as this, there is very little to suggest that either Hosokawa or Yamana was anything but a warring chieftain out for military victory and greater political advantage.[4]

At first Yamana and Hosokawa had been closely allied, and Katsumoto had even taken for his wife one of Sōzen's daughters. But with the elimination of other contenders for power in the land, notably Hatakeyama Mochikuni, these two constable-daimyo came naturally to enter into rivalry with one another. There were no ideals or ideology involved in this rivalry; both men were pragmatic and entirely opportunistic. If Katsumoto, for example, took one side of an issue, Sōzen was sure to join the other. Succession disputes presented excellent opportunities for them to back the re-

---

[3] Quoted in Yomiura Shimbun Sha, *Nihon no Rekishi*, VI, 110.

[4] This opinion is corroborated by Professor Satō. See "Shugo Ryōkoku-sei no Tenkai," pp. 122–23. Professor Suzuki in his study of the Yamashiro Uprising of 1485 suggests an interesting distinction between the "Hosokawa line" (Hatakeyama Masanaga) and the "Yamana line" (Hatakeyama Yoshinari) in their respective attitudes towards the estate system, which resembles the old ideological dispute between Kō no Moronao and Ashikaga Tadayoshi. But Suzuki's interpretation does not really establish a fundamental ideological difference between Hosokawa and Yamana; rather, it points to a variance in their tactical approaches to the confiscation of estate lands. This will be discussed in more detail later.

spective contenders, and in the mid-1460s they were given the chance to support different aspirants to the shogunacy itself.

Yoshimasa was then approaching the prime of life. He had not yet reached his thirtieth birthday and was in the process of enjoying, as noted in the last chapter, a spectacular round of pleasure-seeking and grand entertainment. Yet shortly thereafter he seems to have grown despondent and to have wished to rid himself of the burdens of office. We can assume that Yoshimasa despaired of ever setting to rights the troubles that beset his Bakufu. Far better to be done with all responsibility and to devote the remaining years to aesthetic pursuits. The main obstacle to fulfillment of this desire was Yoshimasa's lack of a male heir to the House, for his wife had not yet been able to provide a successor who survived infancy. Accordingly, Yoshimasa turned to his younger brother Yoshimi (1439–91), who had entered holy orders under the priestly name of Gijin, and requested that he return to lay life and assume the shogunacy.

Yoshimi was at first reluctant to accept his brother's proposal through fear that the birth of a son to the shogun at a later date might place him in an extremely awkward position. Yoshimasa, however, was determined to carry out his plan and swore to Yoshimi that, even should a son later be born, he would be placed in holy orders at the time of infancy and would in no way disturb the order of succession.[5] Impressed by his brother's pledge, Yoshimi at length agreed and in 1464 returned to the Capital to prepare for the ceremonies that would place him in line for the shogunacy. His strongest supporter at that time, and possibly the one who had persuaded him to abandon the cloth, was Hosokawa Katsumoto, whom the shogun appointed to act as official guardian or protector to the new Ashikaga heir.

Within less than a year Yoshimi's earlier fears were realized as the shogun's wife, Tomiko, gave birth to a male child, known in his adult years as Ashikaga Yoshihisa (1465–89). Despite Yoshimasa's pledge to his brother, Tomiko quite naturally wished to secure the succession for her own son. And from what we know

[5] *The Chronicle of Ōnin*, p. 358.

of Tomiko's strength of character we could hardly expect her to have hesitated for even a moment in pressing with the utmost vigor the candidacy of the infant Yoshihisa. In the words of *The Chronicle of Ōnin,* "it was this desire on the part of Lady Tomiko to place her son in line for the succession that eventually led to disturbance in the land."[6] Since Hosokawa Katsumoto was behind Yoshimi, Tomiko now approached Yamana Sōzen to champion the cause of Yoshihisa.

Thus in the year 1465 there arose a major succession dispute over the highest military office in the land. As the great chieftains took sides, others found they could no longer afford to remain neutral. Neither Yamana nor Hosokawa had formerly adopted all-out positions on the most pressing problems of the day, such as the disputes within the Houses of Shiba and Hatakeyama. In fact they had on occasion joined hands, as in their mutual support of Hatakeyama Masanaga. Now Katsumoto had become Masanaga's sole patron and Yamana was forced to assume responsibility for the other Hatakeyama contender, Yoshinari. In like manner many unrelated conflicts and intrigues came to be polarized within the great power struggle emerging between Hosokawa and Yamana.

Perhaps the most involved dispute and the one that in most ways typified the political excesses of the age was the quarrel for headship of the Shiba. We have seen how Shiba Yoshitoshi was denied his position as family head through the efforts of his great vassals, Kai, Asakura, and Oda. Thanks to Kai's personal ties with Ise Sadachika, one of the shogun's favorites, Yoshitoshi had been challenged and, after an abortive attempt to destroy Kai in Echizen, had been forced to flee to the west in 1459. The family headship thereupon went to Shiba Yoshikado. But during the years of Yoshitoshi's exile an interesting turn of events occurred. Sadachika, who had previously favored Kai's younger sister, now became enamored of another young lady who, as chance would have it, was the sister of Shiba Yoshitoshi's concubine.

Sadachika's advice in shogunal councils changed abruptly at this point from support for Yoshikado to patronage of Yoshitoshi. At length, in the twelfth month of 1465, he secured pardon for

[6] *Ibid.*

Yoshitoshi and made possible his return to the Capital after an absence of six years.

The final element of confusion in this already bewildering complex of relations emerged with Yamana Sōzen's announcement of preparations to take Shiba Yoshikado as his son-in-law. When the shogun several months later acknowledged Yoshitoshi as head of the Shiba in place of Yoshikado and sought to transfer the provinces of Echizen, Owari, and Tōtōmi to the former's jurisdiction, Yamana immediately began to muster troops to defend the dispossessed Yoshikado.

The main *provocateur*, of course, was Ise Sadachika. Having thus thrown the Shiba into turmoil, he now proceeded to cause a flare-up between the shogun and his brother.[7] Yoshimi, fearing for his life, fled the shogunal palace and took refuge in Katsumoto's mansion. This incident occurred in the ninth month of 1466. So blatant had Sadachika's interference in the affairs of state been that voices from all quarters began to clamor for his chastisement. It was rumored the following day that Yamana had dispatched a war party to attack him; but the Ise chieftain, accompanied by several of his cronies, including Shinzui of the Shōkoku-ji, had already fled the city that morning by the Ōmi Road.

With Ise and his group gone, some of the tension in the Capital receded. Yoshimi was persuaded to return to his former place, and the shogun granted reinstatement to Shiba Yoshikado. Nevertheless troops had been mustered by the various chieftains and many could not be restrained from rampaging wildly through the city streets. The men of Yamana and Asakura were particularly boisterous. In the entries of a contemporary diary recorded shortly after Sadachika's flight, the warriors of these two families are seen routing the retainers of Ise, destroying their property, attacking the pawn shops and sake dealers, and engaging in general burning and looting.[8]

Nor was there long to wait before the next major outbreak of

[7] According to *The Chronicle of Ōnin*, somebody told the shogun that Yoshimi was patronizing Shiba Yoshikado. The implication is that the rumormongers were Sadachika and his cohorts. *Ibid.*, p. 363. See also *Go-Hōkōin Masaie-ki*, 1466:9;6, in Hiraizumi Kiyoshi *et al.*, *Go-Hōkōin-ki*.

[8] *Daijō-in Jisha Zōjiki*, 1466:9:9.

The Ōnin War   129

trouble. In the final month of 1466 Hatakeyama Yoshinari, after many years of trial and struggle in the provinces, returned victorious to Kyoto. This was due partly to Yoshinari's own military prowess and partly to the personal efforts of Yamana Sōzen, who had made secret overtures to Lady Tomiko to arrange for Yoshinari's pardon.

"As lingering vestiges of the old year departed . . . the New Year (1467) arrived in the Capital. The year-name 'Bunshō' was discarded in favor of 'Ōnin'." [9] Yet there was little to bode well for the New Year. Even as preparations were made for the great feasts and festivals, armed men were on the move. The shogun, fearful of Yamana's wrath, canceled his traditional visit on the second day of the first month to the mansion of the shogunal deputy, Hatakeyama Masanaga. Shortly thereafter he also canceled Masanaga's appointment and ordered return of the family provinces to Yoshinari.

The fortunes of Yamana were on the rise. His son-in-law, Yoshikado, was once again head of the Shiba, while Hatakeyama Yoshinari, back in the Capital with the shogun's blessing, was preparing to move against the dispossessed Masanaga. Sōzen demanded that Hosokawa Katsumoto abandon his support of Masanaga; but when the shogun complied by dispatching a stern note of warning to Katsumoto, the Hosokawa chieftain promptly summoned troops to his mansion for warlike preparations.

The shogun was now thoroughly alarmed. He ordered both Yamana and Hosokawa to remain out of the Hatakeyama dispute, stipulating that the first to defy this order would be declared a rebel by imperial decree. It is interesting to note that such a statement, even from the effete Yoshimasa, could still carry weight among the warriors of this lawless age. Neither Yamana nor Hosokawa could afford to test the shogun's determination on this point. Sōzen did try to strengthen his position by arranging the transfer of Their Majesties, the emperor and his cloistered father, to the Muromachi Palace, where the Yamana influence was still in the

[9] *The Chronicle of Ōnin*, p. 367.

ascent. Even as he did so the Hatakeyama crisis reached its break-
ing point. Masanaga abandoned the family mansion, which was
tactically unsuitable, and moved his position to Goryō Shrine north
of the city. There, at dawn on the eighteenth, Yoshinari attacked
with superior numbers through the surrounding forests. Katsumoto
scrupulously obeyed the shogun's injunction, despite Masanaga's
pleas; but Sōzen was unable to restrain himself and managed
secretly to give material support to Yoshinari. The result was a
thorough rout of Masanaga's hard-pressed troops.[10]

For weeks thereafter, apart from an occasional skirmish, there
was peace in the city as Yamana's boisterous men celebrated the
victory at Goryō. In the third month, however, Katsumoto ceased
his attendance at the shogunal court, and, from increased troop
movements in the area of his quarters, it became apparent that the
Hosokawa leader was preparing for a major move. Finally, on the
twenty-sixth day of the fifth month, his soldiers attacked the mansion of one of Yamana's leading generals, Isshiki Yoshinao, and the
great war was on. In the early deployment of troops Hosokawa and
his supporters aligned themselves generally to the east of Muromachi, while the Yamana took their position to the west. Accordingly, their respective hosts were known as the "eastern" and the
"western" armies. Since Yamana was indeed a leading daimyo
from the western provinces, the use of such terminology, in his
case at least, was quite appropriate.

One of the most puzzling aspects of this first stage of warfare
was that Katsumoto, recently out of favor, somehow managed to
regain Yoshimasa's confidence. There were many within the shogun's circle strongly opposed to the Hosokawa. Yet on the first day
of the sixth month Yoshimasa commissioned his brother Yoshimi
to subdue the Yamana and, at the same time, granted Katsumoto
use of the shogunal colors. There is a vague reference to this turn
of events in one of the journals, but no concrete information on
how the Hosokawa chieftain was able to ingratiate himself.[11] As

---

[10] *The Chronicle of Ōnin* is extremely critical of Katsumoto's failing to aid a
comrade in distress. *Ibid.*, p. 373.

[11] "A curious thing has occurred recently. The shogun is sympathetic to
Hosokawa. I must investigate and record the details, but in general that is how
the rumor goes." *Go-Hōkōin Masaie-ki,* 1467:5:25.

subsequent events were to reveal, the shogun himself had no personal love for Katsumoto. Nevertheless Yamana was now the "rebel." As though to make this perfectly clear, Katsumoto shortly thereafter escorted the emperor and his father to the Muromachi Palace[12] just as Yamana had done during the Hatakeyama crisis several months earlier.

The Chronicle of Ōnin places the total number of troops mustered in the Capital at 277,500: 161,500 for the Hosokawa and 116,000 for the Yamana. Owing to a lack of corroborative records we must accept these figures, even though *The Chronicle of Ōnin* is not noted for its numerical accuracy. It would seem that the eastern army did have a decided edge in numbers. This was offset to some extent by Yamana's early tactical advantages and by the arrival in mid-summer of more than twenty thousand troops under Ōuchi Masahiro and Kōno Michiharu to supplement the ranks of the western army.

One interesting aspect of the deployment of troops was the manner in which the various families chose sides. Succession disputes naturally caused the division of a number of Houses: not only the Shiba and the Hatakeyama, but the Togashi of Kaga and the Sasaki of Ōmi as well. The Sasaki family had split years before into the Rokkaku and Kyōgoku branches. At this time the Rokkaku joined the Yamana, while the Kyōgoku fought for the Hosokawa. The Yamana received strong western support from the Ōuchi as well as the Kōno of Iyo. Still, there was no absolute geographical division of forces. The Hosokawa side, for example, had western backing through the Takeda[13] of Aki, while the Toki of Mino provided Yamana with an eastern flavor. Needless to say, the Akamatsu remained allied with the Hosokawa throughout. Akamatsu Masanori, in fact, was one of the principal commanders of the eastern forces.

At the outset of hostilities the western army held a distinct ad-

[12] This was part of a much more complicated affair in which Katsumoto attempted to purge the shogunal palace of Yamana sympathizers. See the section entitled "Imperial Procession to the Muromachi Palace" in *The Chronicle of Ōnin,* pp. 385–88.

[13] The Takeda also disputed the province of Wakasa with the Isshiki, who were stalwarts of the western army.

vantage, despite their numerical inferiority. They controlled six of
the seven approaches to the city and had the eastern army squeezed
into a cramped area in the northeast corner. Under such circumstances Hosokawa and his men had great difficulty in maintaining
their lines of supply, and were forced to take to the streets in order
to widen their scope of operations. With the passage of time, however, the eastern army came gradually to assert the upper hand.[14]
In the early part of the following year (1468) Hosokawa's con-
federates even turned the tables on the western forces by blocking
their supply lines in the Fushimi-Inari region south of the Capital.
Some months later they also took the offensive in the suburbs of
Saga and Funaoka to the northwest of Kyoto, as the fighting continued to spread beyond city limits.

The bitterest and most destructive warfare took place in the
city during these early years. Losses were enormous, since in-
cendiarism accompanied each struggle. One temple or mansion set
ablaze would gut a whole district, and before too many months had
passed the principal areas of conflict in the city had become little
more than barren fields. A further source of anxiety to citizen and
soldier alike was the activity of the *ashigaru*, mercenaries engaged
by both armies to assist in the door-to-door fighting. *The Chronicle
of Ōnin* does not say much about the *ashigaru*, but from other
sources we gather that they were responsible for an enormous
amount of looting and destruction.

Although Hosokawa emerged the stronger contender, he, like
Yamana, was never able to marshal the extra strength necessary to
win a decisive victory. Within a few years the fighting in the
Capital had settled down to an interminable round of minor skirmishes conducted from fixed fortifications, and both commanding
generals came to despair of ever finding a satisfactory solution. At
one point Hosokawa shaved his head and even sought entry into
holy orders, while Yamana attempted to slice his aged belly. It

[14] A good part of the success of the eastern army was due to the fact that
Hosokawa and his allies controlled most of the central provinces. They also
received support from various local samurai of Yamashiro who owed direct allegiance to the shogun. See Inagaki Yasuhiko, "Ōnin-Bummei no Ran," in
Iwanami Shoten, *Iwanami Kōza Nihon Rekishi*, VII, 199.

must be noted that these gestures held little real significance, for neither man suggested any sincere basis for a settlement. On the contrary their activities continued to extend ever farther from the Capital with its stalemate and frustration. Then, in 1473, both Yamana and Hosokawa died within a period of months, Sōzen at the age of seventy and Katsumoto at forty-four. They were turbulent men in a turbulent age, and the eulogistic remarks recorded on their behalf are few. *The Chronicle of Ōnin* notes simply that Yamana's time had come, while Hosokawa, owing to his hot-blooded nature, would have met death about this time one way or the other.[15]

One tragicomic aspect of the Ōnin War was the series of misadventures that befell Ashikaga Yoshimi. The succession dispute involving the shogun, his brother, and the young lad Yoshihisa had supposedly been the "principal cause" for conflict between the Yamana and the Hosokawa. Yet from the beginning it became apparent that Yoshimi, for one, was to be the merest pawn in the hands of the contending warlords. Shortly after the commencement of fighting, Katsumoto escorted him to the shogunal palace, where he remained for several months under the same roof with the shogun, his wife Tomiko, and Yoshihisa. We can only imagine the animosities generated by this close contact, especially between Yoshimi and Tomiko. The shogun had, as yet, made no open move to alter the order of succession. Nevertheless Yoshimi was most apprehensive about his brother's intentions. In the eighth month he returned to his own mansion, and shortly thereafter departed the Capital for Ise.

Yoshimi sojourned in Ise until spring of the following year, 1468, when at the urging of the shogun he finally agreed to return to the Capital. But reconciliation between the brothers was short-lived, and before the year was out Yoshimi again found himself embroiled in intrigue, this time between Yoshimasa and Hosokawa Katsumoto.[16] In the eleventh month he fled to Mount Hiei,

---

[15] *The Chronicle of Ōnin*, p. 418.

[16] Somebody told the shogun that Katsumoto planned to replace him with Yoshimi. In order to dispel this impression, Katsumoto arranged for Yoshimi's flight, which eventually led to the western camp. *Ibid.,* p. 412.

where he was greeted by supporters of the western army and commissioned as Yamana's "shogun." Before many months had passed, however, Yamana turned to a new source of legitimacy and this time embraced the cause of the southern pretender, Ogura no Miya. In 1473 Yoshimasa placed his son, Yoshihisa, in the office of shogun, and for the remainder of the war years the disfranchised Yoshimi wandered the provinces, a victim of cruel schemes and broken promises.

The attitude and behavior of the Shogun Yoshimasa during these years is virtually unfathomable. At one moment he seeks to eliminate his brother, at the next attempts to win back his friendship. He grants official sanction to Hosokawa, yet more often than not his sympathies appear to be with Yamana. And what were his reactions to the bloodshed and anguish that surrounded him? We know of the famous incident in which he refused to allow the clash of arms outside to interfere with his pleasures for the evening.[17] Still, it is obvious that in his own cynical way Yoshimasa was deeply affected by the uncontrollable sequence of events in which he was engulfed. This is perhaps most clearly revealed in the profound change in his aesthetic canons after the war. Far removed from the flamboyance of earlier days, Yashimasa now turned to the restraint and refinement that is exemplified by his retreat at Higashiyama.[18] This is the image with which we are familiar— Yoshimasa the connoisseur. But it was not the only image of this complex personality.

The most significant aspect of the war following the deaths of the two commanders in 1473 was its spread to the provinces. Some of these provincial quarrels were directly related to the over-all strategy of the armies in the Capital, while others involved the usual opportunism, such as attacks by Ōtomo and Shōni on Chikuzen Province in Kyushu during Ōuchi's absence. The most meaningful struggles (not including peasant uprisings) were those

[17] *Ibid.*, p. 392. "Smoke from the temples and houses covered the area in all directions. The shogun's wife and the other ladies and maids lost interest in what they were doing and began to clamor about going for a while to Kuruma, Kibune, and northern Tamba. But the shogun was not in the least perturbed and, in his usual high spirits, was at a drinking party."

[18] Tanaka Yoshishige, *Ashikaga Jidai Shi*, p. 210.

in which assistant or subordinate chieftains seized the holdings of their absentee masters, who were still engrossed with the fighting in the Capital. We are primarily concerned in this study with those seizures involving appropriation of constable lands by the deputy constable. Closer examination of this key result of the Ōnin War must be reserved until a later section. Here we can note the final elements in the tragedy of the constable-daimyo: failure of the Bakufu upon which he relied; and long neglect of his base provinces, especially during these years of incessant struggle in Kyoto.

As the war dragged on year after year, many weary combatants came to yearn for a return to peace. Yet each time negotiations were begun, the old unsolved problems would reemerge: neither Yamana nor Akamatsu was willing to relinquish claims to the provinces of Harima, Bizen, or Mimasaka; the two Hatakeyama were still as implacably opposed as ever; and the shogun's brother, convinced that he had been wrongfully deprived of the succession, remained an exile from the Capital.

Nevertheless the outward flow of troops from the city continued, as men returned to deal with trouble in the provinces. The last to persist was Ōuchi, who continued to demand a settlement between the shogun and Yoshimi. Finally Ōuchi too grew weary, and in the eleventh month of 1477 he fired his position and marched away with the remaining generals of the western army.

A Selective Translation of
The Chronicle of Ōnin

TRANSLATOR'S NOTE

In presenting a selective translation of *The Chronicle of Ōnin* I have been guided by three main considerations: readability, accuracy, and interest value. *The Chronicle of Ōnin* has not, to my knowledge, been made a principal object of study until now by any scholar, either in Japan or elsewhere. Hence I have not had the benefit of such lengthy annotations and glosses as are often provided for more familiar tracts in Japanese history.

But perhaps the greatest obstacles that face the prospective translator of a work such as *The Chronicle of Ōnin* are the reconstruction of lengthy battle scenes and the rendering and identification of proper names and places. In fact, many of the battle accounts that appear in the middle and later sections of the text are not only repetitive and highly stylized; they defy scholarly reconstruction, owing to an overabundance of obscure place names and personages. Since both accuracy and interest value would therefore be at a minimum in any treatment of these accounts, I have omitted them from the present translation.

Place-name identification, particularly in the capital city of Kyoto, presents special problems for any student of the Ōnin period. While omission of those sections dealing with the endless round of skirmishes and street fighting that followed the early stages of hostilities in the city removes much of the burden of tedious and often fruitless search for places, it has been necessary to identify certain key points and landmarks. For this purpose I have used a set of maps published in 1901 and constructed specially as a guide for this period in Japanese history by Imazume Sadasuke. My descriptions based on these maps must be accepted with caution, for there are no completely authoritative maps of the Ōnin capital in existence.

In order further to improve the readability of the text, I have omitted, in every instance possible, ornamental titles and appellations added to the names of the illustrious. In those cases where only surname and title appear I have retained the title to differentiate the personage from others bearing the same surname. Finally, I have attempted to eliminate most variant names, such as those borne in childhood or those adopted by Buddhist laymen.

To give the reader a sense of perspective, I have tried to describe key city locations in terms of their relation to the shogunal palace and the adjacent Shōkoku-ji enclosure, situated in the Muromachi section of northeastern Kyoto.

The Chronicle of Ōnin: *I*

EXTRAVAGANCE BEFORE THE CONFLICT

In the first year of Ōnin, 1467, the country was greatly disturbed, and for a long time thereafter the five inner provinces and the seven regions[1] were all in turmoil. The fault lay with his lordship, the Shogun Yoshimasa, who was the seventh ruler from Takauji. Instead of entrusting the affairs of the country to his worthy ministers, Yoshimasa governed solely by the wishes of inexperienced wives and nuns, such as Lady Tomiko, Lady Shigeko, and Kasuga-no-Tsubone. Yet these women did not know the difference between right and wrong and were ignorant of public affairs and the ways of government. Orders were given freely from the muddle of drinking parties and lustful pleasure-seeking. Bribery was freely dispensed: after men like Ise Sadachika or

---

[1] The five inner, or home, provinces were Yamashiro, Yamato, Kawachi, Izumi, and Settsu. The rest of Japan, in earlier times, was divided into seven circuits or ways: the Saikaidō, Nankaidō, San'yōdō, San'indō, Tōkaidō, Tōsandō, and Hokurikudō. They comprised all of what today would be considered Japan proper, except for the island of Hokkaido.

Shinzui of the Rokuon-in had been approached, a landholding which should have been granted to a hitherto favored defendant would be given, instead, to the claimant. Moreover, if the magistrate's office confirmed a holding, Lady Tomiko would reverse the decision and present the same land in reward to someone else.

As a result of this chaotic state of affairs, both branches of the Hatakeyama family [Yoshinari and Masanaga] had three times received censure and had three times been pardoned during the twenty-four years from 1444 until this year, 1467. These censures and pardons were issued without regard either to misconduct on the one hand or to loyalty on the other. According to a popular saying bantered about by the townsfolk, "Censure is imposed where there is no offense and pardon is granted where there is no loyalty." Furthermore, both lines of the Shiba family [Yoshitoshi and Yoshikado] had been censured and pardoned twice within the brief space of twenty years. Behind all this devious maneuvering was Ise Sadachika, who craved pleasures of the flesh, engaged in lustful affairs, and accepted bribery.

There were other signs that forewarned of a great conflict. Both court noble and warrior were steeped in luxury, as were people in the city and even those in distant provinces. The opulence of the great houses and the suffering of the masses were beyond description. Thus the masses were anguished and distressed, and they cried out as did the people of Hsia who resented the outrages of King Chieh:[2] "Who will perish today? Perhaps it will be you and I." If there were loyal subjects at this time, why did they not come forth with remonstrances? On the contrary, their attitude was "let the country break asunder, if it is going to break," or "let society perish, if it is going to perish." People sought only wealth and honors so they could disport themselves in a manner more brilliant than others.

While one grand ceremony every five or six years was cause for alarm among the Houses, as many as nine in a row were held at this time. First, there was the splendid *on-haiga* procession of the

---

[2] King Chieh was the last ruler of the legendary Hsia Dynasty (2205–1766 B.C. or 1994–1523 B.C.). He was overthrown by T'ang, the founder of the Shang Dynasty (1766–1122 B.C. or 1523–1027 B.C.).

generals of the shogunal family;[3] second, a performance of *saru-gaku* by Kanze at Kawara in the third month of 1464; third, the accession ceremony of Emperor Go-Tsuchimikado in the seventh month of the same year; fourth, the flower-viewing excursion to Kachōzan, Nyakuōji, and Ōharano in the third month of 1465; fifth, the ceremony at the Hachiman Shrine in the eighth month;[4] sixth, the visit to the Kasuga Shrine in the ninth month; seventh, the Great Thanksgiving festival of the twelfth month; eighth, the visit to the Ise Shrine in the third month of 1466; and ninth, the flower procession.[5]

A feast of a thousand delicacies was prepared for the flower-viewing excursion. The shogun's attendants were supplied with eating sticks of gold, while other guests received sticks carved from scented wood and inlaid with precious metals. People ran about madly preparing their costumes. So great was the expense, they were forced to put all their holdings in pawn and to sell their valuables. Taxes were levied on people in the provinces and collection of the land and household taxes was pressed. Farmer and landlord suffered dreadfully. Without the means to continue planting and harvesting, they abandoned their fields and turned to begging and lived in misery on whatever their hands and feet could bring them. Most of the hamlets and villages throughout the country reverted to uncultivated fields.

During the time of Yoshimitsu the tax on pawnbrokers was levied at each of the four seasons. Yoshinori increased the number of collections to twelve a year, while Yoshimasa, in preparation for the Great Thanksgiving festival, made nine emergency levies during the eleventh month alone and eight during the twelfth. Moreover, in an effort to cancel his debts, the shogun decreed as many as thirteen *tokusei* during this period. Such measures were unknown in former times. As a result brokers and officials lost everything.

[3] A visit by the various chieftains to the shogunal palace for the purpose of paying their respects at the New Year.

[4] This event was held annually on the fifteenth day of the eighth month.

[5] The exact time or reason for this event is not clear. Even Arai Hakuseki, who has carefully listed the other ceremonies and excursions, has nothing to add that might help explain this occasion.

Heaven had already displayed omens portending a great disturbance. At about ten in the evening on the thirteenth day of the ninth month of 1465 a brilliant object streaked across the sky from the southwest to the northeast. Heaven and earth rumbled and it seemed as though the universe would suddenly break and the world would be torn asunder. It was dreadful. In China, when the Chou Dynasty[6] was about to collapse, a comet appeared in the sky to mark a decline in the rites of the seven ancestral temples. People knew in their hearts that the House of Chou was falling, but there was no one to speak out. And in the case of our country, how strange it was that at the same hour of the same day in the following year, 1466, the object flew back to its original place. According to one story, it was a *"tengu* shooting star."[7] Someone wrote a letter and went around showing it as one purportedly dropped by the *tengu*.[8] People laughed and called it a hoax, but, strange as it may seem, the letter's forecasts on the whole came true. Among these was the prediction that Tesshoki, Sōsetsu, and On'ami[9] would soon join the *tengu*. And, sure enough, all died that year.

. . .

KUMAGAI'S MEMORIAL

There was at that time a vassal named Kumagai who lived at Shiotsu in Ōmi Province. He possessed the three virtues of wisdom, benevolence, and bravery, and was a man versed in both the art of the pen and the art of the sword. Aggrieved by the improper practices of the government of his time, Kumagai carefully drew up a list of remonstrances and presented it as a memorial to

---

[6] Chou Dynasty (1122–255 B.C.).

[7] A meteor that descends with a loud noise.

[8] *Tengu* were mythical beings with wings and exceedingly long noses.

[9] Tesshoki (1380–1458) was a noted composer of *waka* style poetry under whom Sōsetsu (d. 1455) studied. On'ami (d. 1467), as we have seen, belonged to the Kanze School of Nō performers. Although the next sentence states that all died in the same year, biographical sources indicate that this is not true. Only On'ami, in fact, died in the year 1467.

the shogun. When Yoshimasa read Kumagai's memorial, he was instantly offended by these model words and became greatly angered: "He is not mistaken in any of the charges he brings. But it is an outrage for one who is not in the government to take the law into his own hands and to present a rebuke in this manner. According to the *Shih chi*,[10] if a man occupies a post to which he has no claim, the country will be disrupted." With that he banished Kumagai Saemon and confiscated his estates. It was a shameful thing for the shogun to do.

And when Yoshimasa learned that people were discouraged by the unfair treatment dealt Kumagai and had begun to neglect their duties, he thought how difficult it was to be shogun. Although barely forty years of age, he no longer had any interest in the affairs of government, and decided to have his younger brother, the abbot of the Jōdo-ji,[11] return to secular life and succeed to the shogunacy. Then he, Yoshimasa, could retire and enjoy the pleasures of later life to his heart's content. It is said that when Confucius reached seventy he followed the bent of his heart, but did not go against the proper order of things. This was not the case with Yoshimasa. Once having decided to relinquish the shogunacy, he forthwith ordered his brother to return to the Capital. The abbot, however, replied that holy vows were not to be taken lightly and three times refused to return. Thereupon Yoshimasa sent a messenger to assure his brother that he would not be deprived of the succession even if a son should later be born into the shogunal house.[12] From the time of swaddling the child would be made a monk. To prove his sincerity, Yoshimasa swore in writing by the gods of heaven and earth, both great and small, that he would abide by these words. In view of the solemnity of this oath, the abbot saw little room for doubt. And so, discarding his holy

[10] Principal work of the early Chinese historian, Ssu-ma Ch'ien, whose dates are placed at roughly 145–90 B.C.

[11] The Jōdo-ji is located in the town of Omichi in Aki Province. It is a Shingon temple, reputedly built by Shōtoku Taishi. The brother was Yoshimi, discussed above in "The Ōnin War."

[12] Yoshimasa did not have a male child of his own at the time.

robes, he returned to secular life. After undergoing investiture, he received the name Yoshimi and moved to the home of his relative, Sanjō. From the location of this dwelling Yoshimi came to be known as "Imadegawa-dono." [13]

Both hereditary and outside lords stood watch at the mansions of Yoshimasa and Yoshimi and spent day and night, morning and evening, preparing their costumes for attendance at the installation of the new shogun.

Birth of the Young Lord

Then, unexpectedly, the shogun postponed his retirement. People rumored that this was because Lady Tomiko was with child, and before long she did give birth. It was a boy,[14] and glad tidings were sent forth to the country on shafts of *yomogi*[15] shot from mulberry bows, while priests and laity throughout the Capital joined in proclaiming: "How wonderful! A young lord of great fortune!"

Lady Tomiko, meanwhile, brooded over how she might establish her own son as the successor. She thought bitterly of Yoshimi, whom she despised, and wished for some miracle to change things. It was this desire of Lady Tomiko to place her son in line for the succession that eventually led to conflict in the land.

For daring and resourcefulness there were none among the daimyo or the lesser lords who could compare with Yamana Sōzen. Not only was he head of a powerful warrior family, he had a number of sons-in-law among the other daimyo as well. With these thoughts in mind, Lady Tomiko decided that she would secretly appeal to Yamana and would seek his aid in advancing her son's fortunes. She composed a letter in her own hand: "I entrust the affairs of the young lord to you. Please do your best to assure success for him in life. Having been blessed with this child so unexpectedly after thirty springs makes me feel as though I have

[13] This building was located on the corner of Imadegawa and Mushakōji, within a block of the shogunal palace in the northeastern part of the city.
[14] Ashikaga Yoshihisa.
[15] In English, "mugwort."

lived long enough to see the blossoming of the *udonge* flower.[16]
It is a sad thing and by no means my desire that this young prince
I have so miraculously given birth to should be made to take the
tonsure and wear robes of black. Please do not reveal this matter
to others." Closing respectfully, she dispatched the letter to Yamana.

Upon receiving it Yamana thought carefully: "Hosokawa Katsumoto, as Yoshimi's guardian, is like a father to him. Moreover,
there are none who can rival him in the councils of state. If Yoshimi should became shogun, it will not bode well for me. Katsumoto is my son-in-law, yet he supports my enemy, Akamatsu Masanori. I cannot forgive him for that. Therefore I must be prepared.
Through Lady Tomiko's order I have been entrusted with the
care of the young lord. If I back Hatakeyama Yoshinari and drive
out Masanaga, Katsumoto will surely support his ally, Masanaga.
Then both Katsumoto and Masanaga will find themselves burdened with the same guilt, and I will be able to destroy the families allied to them, from the Akamatsu down. Therefore I must
immediately assemble my forces." To Lady Tomiko he replied that
he would accept her charge.

DISORDER WITHIN THE HOUSE OF SHIBA
AND THE HATAKEYAMA AFFAIR

In the fourth month of 1466 disagreement between Yoshitoshi
and Yoshikado over succession to the House of Shiba broke into
open dispute. The seeds of this dispute were planted in the fourth
month of 1459[17] when Yoshitake, the Shiba chieftain, died unexpectedly without leaving a male heir to the House. At that time
Yoshitoshi, a son of Ono Mochitane, received the title Assistant of
the Military Guards, Right Division, and assumed headship of the

---

[16] The *udonge* is a legendary plant believed to have grown in India and
Ceylon. It was said to bloom once every three thousand years, an event that
portended the commencement of a Buddhist age or the coming of a savior.

[17] This date is most likely incorrect. Other biographical sources place Yoshitake's
death at 1452.

family. Before long, however, the family elders became dissatisfied. Kai, Asakura, and Oda, hereditary vassals of the Shiba, resented the new lord's arbitrary attitude toward them. Determined to oust Yoshitoshi and to prevent him from becoming shogunal deputy, the three petitioned Ise Sadachika. They were able to put strong pressure on Sadachika, whose concubine was Kai's younger sister, and soon obtained a shogunal directive calling for Yoshitoshi's dismissal. Shibukawa Yoshikado took Yoshitoshi's place as head of the Shiba and, with the Shiba title Chief of the Military Guards, Right Division, became eligible for the office of shogunal deputy. Meanwhile, Yoshitoshi went to the western provinces and, for a period of five or six years, remained under the patronage of Ōuchi Norihiro.

Around that time Ise Sadachika acquired a new mistress whom he adored passionately. As it happened, the girl was a sister of Yoshitoshi's concubine. Thus Yoshitoshi found himself in a position to approach Sadachika on a very intimate basis. At the same time Yoshitoshi's son, Matsuōmaru, who was a disciple of Shinzui of the Rokuon-in, called upon this priest to help his father obtain pardon.

The relationship between Ise Sadachika and the shogun was extremely close. Yoshimasa, who had received his childhood name from Ise, looked upon Sadachika and his wife as his father and mother, and listened carefully to their words. But Sadachika ignored the possible ill effects of hasty advice and, along with Shinzui, made repeated appeals for the pardon of Yoshitoshi. Alarmed, Sadachika's son, Sadamune, approached his father and said: "It is unwise to assume chief responsibility for the fortunes of Yoshitoshi. The outcome could be serious and might even lead to strife in the land." Far from heeding this grave remonstrance, Sadachika responded by disowning his son. Indeed, loyal words go against the ear and good medicine is bitter to the mouth. In just the same manner Kiyomori had rejected the advice of Shigemori[18] and had defied the imperial will to bring ruin on his House.

[18] Taira Shigemori (1138–79) was the eldest son of Kiyomori. He is generally remembered for his attempts to control his impetuous father.

People later said that Sadamune also spoke like this for the sake of his lord and his House.

They say that the plum at its season does not await the spring breeze; thus nothing can affect its bloom. And while calamity inflicted by heaven is beyond the power of man, this calamity in the House of Shiba arose from the heart.

Upon receiving pardon, Yoshitoshi departed the western provinces and arrived at the Capital during the winter of 1465. On the twenty-ninth day of the twelfth month, in the company of his father, Dōken, he called at the residences of Yoshimasa and Yoshimi where the daimyo were arranged according to the usual rules of etiquette. The attitudes of people had changed, and they now received Yoshitoshi warmly. Sadachika, meanwhile, pressed for the dismissal of Yoshikado; and finally, in the summer of the following year [1466], messengers were dispatched to inform Yoshikado, who had committed no offense whatsoever, that he need no longer attend the shogun's court and that he must turn over the Kadenokōji mansion[19] to Yoshitoshi.

Embittered to think they might lose face over this affair through no fault of their own, Kai, Asakura, and other Shiba vassals hastened to report the news of Yoshikado's censure to Yamana Sōzen and to request his aid. Sōzen, who had promised his daughter to Yoshikado and was preparing for the forthcoming marriage, listened carefully to their statement. "This is monstrous," he raged. "I don't care what the shogun has ordered. I will enter Yoshikado's mansion and will wait to do battle with the envoys!" With that, he sent off a call for troops from the provinces.

At the same time Yoshikado summoned an army under Oda Yojūrō, younger brother of the deputy constable of Owari, and requested aid from the provinces of Echizen and Tōtōmi. Although the Shiba did not have a large number of vassals in the Capital, Kai, Yuu, and Ninomiya raised watchtowers and barricades around the Kageyukōji mansion and prepared to engage the enemy. There

---

[19] The Shiba mansion was located at the intersection of Kadenokōji and Muromachi, approximately four or five blocks to the southwest of the shogunal palace.

had been no crisis of this gravity since the time of Kemmu [1334–35]. Unable to tell friend from foe, the Houses all sought protection by sending to their domains for military support.

Thirteen of Yamana Sōzen's vassals, including Kakiya and Ōtagaki, presented a joint note of admonishment to their lord: "We realize that you have every right to be angry over the Shiba affair. But your agreement with Yoshikado is strictly a private matter, while the shogun's order is based on obligation to your master. We read that both Wang Ling[20] and Fan K'uai[21] of the former Han abandoned their aged mothers in order to render loyalty to Kao-tsu. Now what are we to think of those who disobey their lord and concern themselves only with selfish interests? In the text of Shōtoku Taishi's constitution the lord is likened to heaven and the subject to earth. If 'earth' seeks to overthrow 'heaven,' it will surely spell disaster. In like manner, violation of the shogun's order will bring nothing but shame upon your House.

"To avoid embarrassment in the present situation, we suggest that the maiden who has been promised to Yoshikado be presented, instead, to the shogun. This will be perfectly plausible, since there is already the precedent of a lady from this House having entered the service of his lordship. If this petition is not accepted and warfare ensues, we will retire and enter the priesthood, and from this day forth will confine ourselves to the dwelling at Kokawa[22] on Kōyasan."

The heartfelt sincerity of this admonition was laudable. When Yamana had finished reading, he tossed the paper forward for all to see: "Such loyal words are beyond reproach. But it is not in my nature to command according to 'the way.' They say if water is muddy on top, then the current below will not be clear; and when

---

[20] Wang Ling (d. 184 B.C.) joined forces with Liu Pang, or Kao-tsu (247–195 B.C.), founder of the Han Dynasty. Noted for his filial behavior, Wang was placed in a dilemma when the enemy seized his mother. The valiant lady solved the problem by committing suicide with a sword.

[21] Fan K'uai (d. 189 B.C.) was also an early supporter of Liu Pang and later received high honors for services rendered to the new ruler of China.

[22] Kokawa is the site of a famous temple visited from early times by notables journeying through Kii Province to Kōyasan. It was destroyed by fire during the Ōnin War, but was later restored.

government is disordered, the people will find no peace. I will ride forth and vent my anger by striking down those fellows who plot against the Shiba. And even though I violate the wishes of the shogun, it should cause me little harm.

"During the Kakitsu period, Akamatsu Mitsusuke slaughtered the Shogun Yoshinori, who was still in the prime of life. Hosokawa Shigeyuki, Rokkaku, Takeda, and others rode forth in swarms to Harima, but were turned back by Akamatsu in the battle of Kanisaki. Thereupon they withdrew to Hitomaruzuka and sat facing the enemy as the days passed. In the meanwhile, I invaded from Tajima, stormed Mitsusuke's stronghold at Kinoyama,[23] and completed the mission by taking the head of the shogun's enemy. In view of that achievement, I should surely have been granted a degree of indulgence. But within six or seven years Mitsusuke's younger brother, Hikogorō, was called up and was sent into Harima. Thereupon I too entered the province at the head of a body of troops and forced Hikogorō to commit suicide. According to the *Book of Rites,* a man cannot live under the same heaven with his father's enemy. Even the most rustic fellow is sure to harbor malice against such a person. Yet the shogun appears to be unconcerned with either the foe of his late father or the wrath of his father's spirit.

"Even though I go against the shogun's wish, if each of you proceeds carefully and gains favor with those in high office, you should suffer no ill consequences. There is no need for those men to go to the dwelling at Kokawa!" Standing up, Yamana slammed shut the screen and ranted in a loud voice from within: "I am a daimyo! What should I do when there is injustice and disloyalty— go to the shogunal deputy and plead my case with the other daimyo? Should I, because of their mistakes, be deprived of my right of attendance? Or should I forgive what has happened? Never! Ise Sadachika, through his scheming, has manipulated the deputy families. After first disrupting the Hatakeyama, he has now thrown the Shiba into disorder. In view of this there can be no turning back. If today he seeks to control the fortunes of Shiba

[23] Both Kanigasaka and Hitomaruzuka are located in Akashi-gun, while Kino-yama is in neighboring Iibo-gun.

Yoshikado, tomorrow he will try the same with my descendants. Stay where you are, then. I alone will enter Yoshikado's mansion and we will slice our bellies together."

The ancient texts state that if a father ignores his child's advice, the child should change his words and obey; if a ruler rejects his subject's counsel, the subject should remain silent and obey the ruler. Thus Yamana's retainers made ready to go against the shogun's command, unable to oppose their lord's wishes. And when it was heard that the shogun had gathered troops and was about to attack the Shiba mansion, Yamana kinsmen, and the Toki, the Isshiki and the Rokkaku clamored and shouted and the country was thrown into an uncontrollable uproar. This poem was scribbled on a wall:

> Yoshitoshi is like the fisherman at Futami-no-Ura,
> He relies only upon the young maiden of Ise.
>
> Yoshitoshi had best stay in Kyushu,
> And not come forth to this empty shell of a world.
>
> Nowadays there is no one but recites the Ise Tale
> of Narihira.[24]

Within twenty or thirty days, just as Yamana had wished, Shiba Yoshikado was pardoned and his right of attendance was restored. His companions on horse at that time were Kai in the van and Asakura in the rear. There was a poem written on a wall:

> By joining with the power of another House,
> The son of Shibukawa has spread his influence abroad.[25]

Somebody told the shogun that Yoshimi's espousal of Shiba Yoshikado had been the cause of this disturbance. As Yoshimasa

[24] Like the other poems in *The Chronicle of Ōnin*, these lines contain a series of puns, usually of a caustic nature, that cannot be adequately expressed in English. In each case I have translated the surface meaning only, leaving for the notes explanation of the more significant word plays. The principal play here is on the word Ise, which is both the province where Futami-no-Ura is located and the surname of Ise Sadachika. *Wakame* means "young maiden," but also a kind of seaweed.

[25] There is a play of words on *take*, which can mean both "bamboo" and "another house." Yoshikado's father was of the Shibukawa family.

was about to sever relations with his brother, Yoshimi went secretly to the mansion of Hosokawa Katsumoto. He was accompanied by only two aides: Isshiki Noritada and Isshiki Chikamoto.

Word also spread that the shogun was about to charge Ise Sadachika and Shinzui with responsibility for bringing disorder to the realm, and that the two would surely lose face. Moreover, it was reported that Yamana had already dispatched a punitive force to attack them. So on the sixth day Shinzui, Sadachika, and the Lord of Bizen fled with their wives along the Ōmi Road. The monk Arima, allied as usual with Sadachika, followed after them, while Shiba Yoshitoshi departed on the same day for the northern provinces.

An article-by-article statement of the misconduct of Sadachika was issued on the ninth under the collective signatures of those daimyo sympathetic to Yamana. At the same time the shogun delivered an order calling for Sadachika's banishment. Yamana Sōzen was particularly insistent that Shinzui be killed. Was this determination of Yamana to seek out and destroy Shinzui related to the reinstatement of Akamatsu Masanori? [26] In any event, the shogun also sent out an order for Shinzui. But, of course, both he and Sadachika had fled beforehand. Ise Sadamune was then appointed to take the place of his father, Sadachika.

On the eleventh Yoshimasa dispatched the minister of the center, Hino Katsumitsu,[27] as an envoy to Yoshimi. In a handwritten message, which Katsumitsu delivered, the shogun proclaimed that he held no ill will whatsoever and called upon Yoshimi to return to his place. Although under the circumstances Yoshimi should have replied with equal candor, he flatly refused to return. Thereupon Isshiki Norinao came forward and spoke: "According to the records of the minister of the center's office, this is the first document in the shogun's own hand that has been transmitted since the days of Takauji. Since you have already taken delivery of this unusual paper, it would be most unseemly not to return." Accordingly, Yoshimi agreed to go back to his former place. Both Katsu-

---

[26] Shinzui was a member of the Akamatsu clan, Yamana's arch enemy.

[27] Hino Katsumitsu, Tomiko's brother, was one of the shogun's closest advisers.

mitsu and Hosokawa Katsumoto were impressed with Norinao's handling of the matter. And when it was learned that Katsumoto would accompany the shogun's brother on his return, people were greatly surprised.[28]

Peace reigned once again in the Capital; and just when it appeared that nothing further could possibly happen to disrupt the tranquillity, Hatakeyama Masanaga's cousin, Yoshinari, received a pardon and returned to the city. Yoshinari, who had long been cut off and in seclusion, was pardoned through the scheming of Yamana Sōzen. When Masanaga and Katsumoto became allies, Sōzen had supported Yoshinari with the aim of destroying Masanaga and, subsequently, Katsumoto as well. During the time of Kyōtoku (1452–54), when he was heir to Hatakeyama Mochikuni, Yoshinari's personal conduct had been reprehensible. Perhaps this was due to the work of *temma hajun*.[29] In any event, Yusa, Jimbo, and other Hatakeyama vassals turned against Yoshinari and allied themselves to Masanaga, whom they insisted be made family heir. When Yoshimasa learned of this, he thought, "I personally would like to censure Yoshinari for his haughty conduct here," and therefore readily agreed.

Yoshinari was outraged at the shogun's decision. He found it impossible under the circumstances to remain in the Capital, and, in a fit of youthful indignation, he went down to the province of Iga.[30] Meanwhile Yoshinari's father, Hatakeyama Mochikuni, who had been ill of recent years, chose that time to enter his personal sanctuary at the Sairai-in of the Kennin-ji.[31]

When Masanaga received the shogun's order appointing him to replace Yoshinari, he approached his uncle with the hope of settling the family dispute. But Mochikuni had left the Capital by the time Masanaga's envoy, Hatakeyama the Lord of Awa, arrived to confer with him. People attributed this sudden departure to ill-

---

[28] Presumably the honor of such a high-ranking guard was usually reserved for the shogun alone.

[29] In Buddhist terminology, an evil person.

[30] As stated in the text of this study, Yoshinari undoubtedly went to Kawachi and not Iga.

[31] Located in the Higashiyama section east of the Capital, the Kennin-ji was one of the principal Zen temples of this period.

ness, but one member of the Hatakeyama clan, a man named
Nishikata, was mortified over his lord's withdrawal. With their
pillows aligned, Nishikata, his son, and seven followers who had
remained behind committed suicide. To the heir, Yoshinari, they
sent a farewell poem:

> Although we leave our bodies among the mountains of the east,
> Our names will be in the west with the moon at dawn.[32]

Afterward, the shogun ordered Yoshinari and Masanaga to meet
together for peace talks. Yoshinari presently returned to the Capital, but once again went against the shogun's wishes and this time
withdrew to the province of Kawachi where he established himself
in the fortress at Wakae.[33] Masanaga, upon receiving a directive
calling for the chastisement of Yoshinari, gathered troops in the
nearby provinces and marched over to Tatsuta.[34] When Yoshinari learned that his enemy had only a small force, he arrayed a
powerful army, including Yusa Kunisuke, Honda the Lord of
Mikawa and Honda the Lord of Tōtōmi. Masanaga did indeed
have but a small force. While people wondered what would
happen, Masanaga, not in the least alarmed, prayed before the
Tatsuta Shrine.

A warrior named Baba, who had just arrived with a large force,
was appointed to lead the attack of Yusa's army. Because of Yoshinari's presence, Yusa, as deputy constable, had ordered Nakamura to remain at Wakae. In Nakamura's absence it was generally
assumed that the Okabe brothers would take over the van of the
army. But now the assignment had been given to the new arrival,
Baba. "If it were a routine matter," thought the Okabe, "we
wouldn't mind. But how regrettable it is that we should be deprived of leading the army." Thus, when Baba moved forward as
planned, then hesitated, Okabe Yaroku and Okabe Yahachi rode
in front of his position. "Leading the attack is a serious business!"
they shouted. "Watch this!" After fighting for a while in front of

[32] Nishikata means "western direction." The play, of course, is on use of the
words east and west. Their souls presumably also went west after death to Amida's
paradise.

[33] Built by the Yusa family in Naka-Kawachi-gun.

[34] In Ikoma-gun, also Kawachi Province.

a shrine, both brothers were killed. Upon seeing this, Honda the Lord of Mikawa and Honda the Lord of Tōtōmi moved over to where the brothers had fallen and soon they too went down. Finally Yusa himself turned back after hearing of the death of the two Honda and perished with the others.

In the fortress at Wakae, Yoshinari was persuaded not to follow his defeated generals in death. With barely a hundred men, he took refuge on Mount Take near the foot of Kongō Mountain and constructed outer fortifications at various places around Kontai-ji, Kankō-ji, Kanshin-ji, Kanshō-ji, and Kunimi Mountain.[35] Masanaga, his army augmented by a contingent from the shogun, pitched camp at Hirokawa.[36] With Masanaga were the commanding general and assistant shogunal deputy, Hosokawa Shigeyuki; Hosokawa Katsuhisa; Hosokawa Shigeharu; Hosokawa Katsunobu; Hosokawa Katsuyoshi; Yamana Koretoyo; Takeda Nobutaka; Nobutaka's younger brother, Kuninobu; and forces of Ukai, Mochizuki, Seki, Nagano, and the governor of Ise. Masanaga's generals strained each day to break down the enemy's defenses. At one point Yamana Koretoyo, leading a force from Bingo, attacked the position seven times and was seven times repulsed. By the final assault, those within the fortification were exhausted. Yoshinari himself snatched up a sword and cut his way forth to repel the attackers. As the sun went down, Koretoyo was forced to withdraw and return to camp.

But Yoshinari's strength was spent. Slipping away from Mount Take, he retired to the fastness of Yoshino. Some years before, the prince of Ogura[37] had also taken refuge in these mountains to avoid arrest. Although the circumstances were different in this case, Yoshinari was in flight from the shogun's displeasure, and Yoshino looked like a promising haven.

When Yamana Sōzen learned of Yoshinari's valor at the battle of Mount Take, he wept. "There is no one in the land today who can rival him in the use of arms. His defeat was most unfortunate,"

---

[35] Yoshinari held two main positions at Mount Take and Kontai-ji in Minami-Kawachi-gun, with outposts in the surrounding locations.

[36] A fortification built around Hirokawa Temple in Minami-Kawachi-gun.

[37] The southern pretender.

thought Yamana. "In the beginning I was chiefly responsible for Yoshinari's difficulties. Yet even though his House has come upon these evil days, he remains steadfast. Who can match him in military prowess? If Yoshinari and I should come to an understanding, no one in the Capital would be able to raise a hand against us." Meanwhile, Yoshinari was speculating along similar lines. Among the families aligned against him, he could find no soldier who was the peer of Yamana Sōzen. If, perchance, he and Sōzen should become allies, who then could challenge them?

As a result of this mutual regard, Yamana Sōzen and Hatakeyama Yoshinari began a private exchange of letters. Seeking to obtain permission for Yoshinari to return to the Capital, they made frequent appeals to both the minister of the center, Hino Katsumitsu, and his sister, Lady Tomiko. They even went so far as to plead their case with the courtiers. But all to no avail.

Despite these setbacks and the fact that he had disobeyed a shogunal order in connection with the Shiba affair, Yamana Sōzen was still a man of great influence. Hosokawa Katsumoto, although an enemy at the time, was nevertheless his son-in-law, while Isshiki Yoshitsura was married to his granddaughter and Toki Mochimasa was an ally. Aside from these stalwarts, there was no one who could stand in his way. "Therefore," thought Sōzen, "if I join forces with Hatakeyama Yoshinari, Masanaga will be alone and there will be peace in the land." Accordingly he instructed his elder sister, the nun Ansei-in, to go every day to Lady Tomiko and ask: "Of what disloyalty is Hatakeyama Yoshinari guilty that he has been deprived of his right of attendance? He remains secluded in the mountain forests awaiting the country's pardon. If he were granted permission to return immediately to the Capital, he would become a strong supporter of the young lord, Yoshihisa."

Yoshinari, meanwhile, took advantage of the disturbance caused by the Shiba quarrel and left Kitayama in Kumano[38] to enter Kawachi Province during the first part of the ninth month of 1465. Yusa Naganao, the deputy constable of Kawachi, set about

---

[38] Kumano comprises the southeastern portion of Kii Province.

fortifying Wakae Castle under orders from Masanaga to mount a defense against Yoshinari. He dug double and triple moats, laid in a huge stock of military provisions, and set up massive defense works. He had a force numbering four or five thousand men. Yet, without fighting a single battle, Naganao withdrew from Wakae Castle and fled to his father-in-law, the priest Tsutsui, in Nara. Thereupon Yoshinari entered Kawachi without interference. He had the son of his deceased vassal, Yusa Kunisuke, undergo the coming-of-age ceremony and designated the boy Lord of Kawachi, the title previously held by Naganao.

Just then it was announced that, as a result of Lady Tomiko's pleas on his behalf, Yoshinari had been pardoned. Yamana Sōzen greeted this news with triumph and promptly sent off word to Kumano. Thus Yoshinari, freed in a moment after many years of exile, returned to the Capital on the twenty-fifth day of the eleventh month. His gaily attired procession winding along the road consisted of more than five thousand riders, each the match of a thousand men. They pitched camp at the Jizō-in in Sembon[39] and, on the first auspicious day, Yoshinari, after calling at the Muromachi Palace, went directly to Yamana Sōzen's mansion. Bowing deeply in appreciation, Yoshinari addressed his host: "Thanks to your efforts, I have now been reinstated." Yamana offered congratulations and expressed his great satisfaction at the Hatakeyama chieftain's return. They continued their celebrations throughout the night.

That morning Yoshinari had written on the door flap of his lodging at the Jizō-in:

> Two things Yoshinari has received:
> The foot of Yamana and her ladyship's[40] *sake* cup.

As lingering vestiges of the old year departed, the New Year arrived in the Capital. The reign name "Bunshō" was discarded in favor of "Ōnin," [41] while in the palace celebrations were held

[39] Sembon, also called Suzakuōji, is the main avenue which, according to the original planning, was to divide the Capital into eastern and western sections of equal size.

[40] Tomiko.

[41] Ōnin means literally "in response to virtue or humanity."

for the festival of the New Year and the congratulatory offerings. The shogun and his followers—the three shogunal deputies, the four heads of the board of retainers, and chieftains both far and near—carefully donned their finery according to the established custom, and the deputy, Masanaga, went solemnly about his preparations for the coming fete of the shogun.[42] Arrangements had already been completed for the shogunal procession to Masanaga's mansion on the morning of the following day, the second. But, apparently as the result of a slanderous attack by Yamana, Yoshimasa decided to call off the procession. And before long he ordered cancellation of Masanaga's right of attendance.

"During the past four or five years I have participated at the forefront of eight great celebrations," said Masanaga, as he reflected upon this turn of events. "I have served with diligence and have received singular praise from the shogun. Why should I now be censured? I simply cannot understand."

THE STRUGGLE BETWEEN YOSHINARI AND MASANAGA

Upon learning of Masanaga's dismissal, Yoshinari was greatly pleased. He saw no reason why Masanaga should remain in the Capital for even half a day. "In fact," thought Yoshinari, "since the mansion he is now occupying belonged originally to me, I will move in. As one who has been censured he can hardly object, even though he may secretly have planned to remain the night."

At last the opportunity had come for Yoshinari to ride forth, oust Masanaga, and vent his pent-up resentment of many years. Yusa, Honda, Sumiya, and Kainoshō heartily agreed.

Meanwhile, Masanaga's deputy, Jimbo Naganobu, learned of Yoshinari's plan: "My lord, Masanaga, is himself about to attack Yoshinari's position. In view of this new development, I had best send a force to take charge of the mansion. Better still, I will go there myself." Thus Jimbo left his dwelling at Nijō-Kyōgoku and

---

[42] At the time of the New Year various chieftains took turns entertaining the shogun at their mansions. These affairs were known as *ōban*.

went up to the Butsuda-ji, which was situated in front of and in a position to be held together with Masanaga's mansion.[43] He carefully erected barricades and watchtowers and circled the area with inner and outer moats.

Well aware of Masanaga's fame as a commander and, even more important, of his support from Katsumoto, Yoshinari hesitated. Instead of attacking directly as planned, he spent his days in lengthy consultations. Soon it was the middle of the first month. The Yamana fete was held as usual on the fifteenth, and after the festivities allies and friendly daimyo gathered together. They went first to Yoshimi and urged him to go with them to the Muromachi Palace. Upon receiving his consent, they set forth without further preparation.

Among the Yamana supporters were Kira Yoshikatsu; Shiba Yoshikado; Hatakeyama Yoshinari; Hatakeyama Yoshimune; Hatakeyama Norikuni; Hatakeyama Masashige; Hatakeyama Masazumi, Hatakeyama Masamitsu; Hatakeyama Norimitsu; Isshiki Yoshitada; Isshiki Yoshitō; Isshiki Masauji; Isshiki Masakane; Isshiki Masahiro; Isshiki Chikanobu; Isshiki Tsuramasu; Isshiki Norinaga; Nikki Norimasa; Toki Shigeyori; Chiyo-jumaru, the son of Akamatsu the Lord of Izu; Sasaki-Rokkaku Kame-jumaru; Sasaki-Rokkaku Masatsuna; Togashi Kōchiyomaru; Togashi Ienobu; as well as Sōzen's eldest grandson, Masatoyo; Yamana Masakiyo; Yamana Noriyuki; Yamana Eichin; Yamana Toyomitsu; Miyata Norizane; Miyata Toyoyuki; and Kazusa Masayuki. The above party of thirty-odd daimyo surrounded the shogunal palace and presented their petition: "Hatakeyama Yoshinari has been pardoned and has returned to the Capital. He now wishes to move into the family mansion at Madenokōji, but is prevented from doing so by Hosokawa Katsumoto who has joined forces with Masanaga to disturb the peace. Now these two have gone against the shogun's order and have sown the seeds of treason. You should send an envoy to inquire into the facts and to advise Katsumoto

---

[43] The main Hosokawa mansion was roughly six blocks south and west of the shogunal palace, between Kasuga and Oimikado on Madenokōji. The Butsuda-ji was across Kasuga street, directly north, while Jimbo's mansion at the intersection of Nijō and Kyōgoku was the equivalent of a long block farther southwest.

that he must stop aiding Masanaga. If this is done there will be peace in the land once again."

The shogun agreed and presently dispatched an envoy to Hosokawa. Katsumoto, however, refused to acquiesce to demands that he abandon Masanaga. He sent back word that he would reserve decision until a later date.

The situation had become grave indeed. At the shogunal palace night and day watches were posted to guard against a possible raid from the Hosokawa, while on the Hosokawa side troops were stationed at various approaches to protect the family position. Among the daimyo who rallied to the Hosokawa were Kira Yoshitada; Kira Yoshitomi; Akamatsu Masanori; Akamatsu Sadasuke; Akamatsu Matsumaru; and Yamana Koretoyo, Sōzen's younger brother and the adopted son of the late Yamana master of the ministry of people's affairs, who was slaughtered by Akamatsu Mitsusuke along with the Shogun Yoshinori. At the time Koretoyo had been allowed to succeed his father, thanks to the good offices of Hosokawa Katsumoto. Aware of his indebtedness, Koretoyo abandoned his own family and rode forth to the support of the Hosokawa. Others who assembled were Sasaki-Kyōgoku Seikan; Sasaki-Kyōgoku Katsuhide; Sasaki-Kyōgoku Masanobu; Takeda Nobutaka; Takeda Kuninobu; and Togashi Tsurudomaru. Among the Hosokawa clan were Hosokawa Shigeyuki; Hosokawa Katsuhisa; Hosokawa Dōken; Hosokawa Masakuni; Hosokawa Noriharu; Hosokawa Nariharu; Hosokawa Katsunobu; Hosokawa Katsuyoshi; Nikki Narinaga; and Nikki Masanaga.

At the Hosokawa mansion[44] men removed shutters and sliding doors and erected dirt-covered walls. With Katsumoto's foster son, Rokurō, in command, the Hosokawa and their allies assembled in the garden. They clustered about tightly, five or six thousand strong, their helmet emblems aglisten, their armored sleeves clanging together. Yasutomi Mototsuna led three thousand men along the Nishiōji to hold the western fortification of the Iriedono,

[44] The Hosokawa owned a number of dwellings in the northeastern part of the city, but from later context it becomes clear that the reference here is to Katsumoto's mansion on Nishiōji, about three blocks northwest of the shogunal palace.

while another three thousand under Naitō Sadamasa deployed for action at the Anrakukō-in.[45] They fastened helmet bands and tightened girth straps as their mounts pawed the ground impatiently.

Yamana Sōzen, meanwhile, continued to guard the homes of the shogun and his brother, Yoshimi. While in the shogunal palace, Yamana repeatedly warned that there would be no peace in the country until Masanaga, Katsumoto, and their cohorts were subdued. Despite this stern warning, however, the shogun absolutely refused to proceed against the Hosokawa. There was this poem on a wall:

> When spring comes, the once-beaten Hatakeyama
> Will again sow the seeds of dissension.[46]

THE BATTLE AT GORYŌ[47]

Hatakeyama Yoshinari, meanwhile, decided to prepare for action with his own forces. He stationed more than a thousand troops of Honda, Kainoshō, and Taira under Kainoshō and Yusa at the entrance to the Iriedono facing west. Forces from the other Houses, including Kai, Asakura, Kakiya, and Ōtagaki, formed in a solid line from Ichijō-Muromachi to the Kōshōin-dono.[48]

When informed of this state of affairs, the shogun realized that there could be no peace in the country so long as the families continued to muster troops and to seek mutual alliances in this way. Thus he decreed that the Hatakeyama dispute be settled between the two contenders themselves without the interference

---

[45] The deployment suggests a north-south position from the Anrakukō-in (directly across the street from Katsumoto's mansion) to the Iriedono, three blocks south.

[46] Since *hatake* means field, the play of words is on the sowing of seeds in a field. The verb *uchikaesu* in this poem means to cultivate and also to strike back after defeat.

[47] Goryō Shrine is directly north of the Shōkoku-ji enclosure.

[48] This would place Yoshinari's forces in a three- or four-block line roughly parallel to and east of the position assumed by Hosokawa and his supporters.

of others. Yamana Sōzen protested angrily: "For four days we appealed for assistance, but to no avail. Now we are told that we must stop making trouble!" Yoshinari, on the other hand, greeted the shogun's words with equanimity: "This is just what I have wanted. It has been my desire for many years to decide the succession in combat with Masanaga alone. Tomorrow I will lead my men in an attack on his position at Kasuga-Madenokōji and settle the matter once and for all. Let all observe my mettle!"

At the same time the shogun sent Ise the Lord of Bitchū and Inō the Lord of Shimōsa with a confidential message for Katsumoto, informing him that he would be branded an enemy of the Bakufu if he persisted in aiding Masanaga. Still Katsumoto refused to comply. Thereupon the shogun's brother, Yoshimi, summoned Hosokawa Noriharu and told him repeatedly that Katsumoto must break off relations with Masanaga. Noriharu agreed to do his best. "I will make every effort to persuade Katsumoto to comply. And if unsuccessful, I will personally resign my position," he said and returned to report on his meeting with Yoshimi. Katsumoto pondered deeply over the matter, for he was not the kind of person to confuse the relationship between lord and subject. Moreover he was under great pressure both from his uncle Dōken and from Noriharu. At length he agreed to abandon his aid to Masanaga.

Upon learning of Masanaga's decision, Jimbo Naganobu approached Masanaga and said: "Through our agreement with Katsumoto we have been able to rely on his aid, until now, in the event of a conflict with Yoshinari. The Kyōgoku have also been our allies. But now Katsumoto has acceded to demands that he give us no further assistance. What is more, the enemy, along with a number of partisan supporters, is based in the Bakufu quarters. He will surely make use of secret reinforcements no matter what the shogun's order may be. Since our mansion is in a level field that does not possess strategic advantages, a battle in which we were obliged to sustain the onslaught of a powerful force could be disastrous. They say you should advance or retreat according to the situation. If we abandon this place and go up to Kami-Goryō we should be able to hold on for a while by making use of the bush for small defense works. And even if we get into difficulty, Katsumoto won't just sit there and watch us get brutally slaughtered before his own fortifications. In addition, Yasutomi Mototsuna and I have been sworn brothers from the days of our youth. How could he forsake us even if Katsumoto honors the shogun's order and continues to refuse us aid? Finally, should the situation appear untenable even after these possibilities, we could still force our way to the imperial palace. With the shogun in custody of the enemy, the palace probably won't be very well guarded and we would be able to take possession of His Majesty. Then, in the event of fighting, our allies, and later everyone else, would rally to us. These are my views. Please ask the others how they feel."

Masanaga agreed with satisfaction to Naganobu's suggestions. Setting fire to the Hatakeyama mansion, he rode forth in the company of Jimbo, Yusa, and Jōshin'in Mitsunobu of Nara. Also with Masanaga was Hamuro Noritada,[49] who, as usual, remained steadfast to the Hatakeyama leader. Noritada accompanied them on this occasion in case it should become necessary to put into effect Jimbo Naganobu's plan to take possession of the emperor.

During the night of the seventeenth of the first month they entered the forest at Goryō. Some of the supporting forces wondered what Masanaga's plan could be. If he went by way of Eastern Kawara, they believed, he would surely meet defeat. Alarmed by this prospect, they scattered and fled. As a result fewer than two thousand truly loyal warriors joined Masanaga in his encampment at Goryō.

Yamana was greatly surprised at the news of Masanaga's withdrawal to Kami-Goryō the night before. "What will happen," he thought, "if they manage to force their way into the imperial palace?" He reported his fears to the shogun, who in turn sent a messenger to suggest to Their Majesties that they transfer their residence to the Bakufu. Thus, rather abruptly, the emperor and his father set out with the regalia for the shogunal palace. The attending nobles, none wishing to fall behind, flocked to the procession, while at the shogunal palace a surging mass of splen-

[49] Hamuro, as a member of the civilian aristocracy, would be useful in dealings at the imperial palace.

didly attired retainers and armed warriors filled the garden outside the gate.

Yoshinari, sensing victory, had no other thought than to pursue his fleeing opponent. Early in the morning of the following day, the eighteenth, he marched on Goryō. Since the Goryō forest was bounded on the south by the thicket and moat of the Shōkokuji and on the west by Hosokawa's fortifications, Yoshinari attacked from north and east. Yusa the Lord of Kawachi leaped from his horse and rushed to the forefront of the attack. He was soon joined by other warriors, who abandoned their mounts and struggled to be among the first to reach the enemy. They quickly set fire to Shōmon-ji village[50] beside the *torii;* but just as they were doing so a storm blew down from Atago Mountain. Swirling snow and flames blew into the eyes and mouths of the attackers. Losing all sense of direction they milled silently about.

Seeing the predicament of Yoshinari's men, the defenders watched carefully for their chance. Then, with the peerless soldier Taketa Yoji in command, they let loose volley after volley of arrows and cut the attackers down. All of the leading troops fell, including Tsuboi of the Sakado Genji, the general who had ridden in the van of Yoshinari's force, and a native of Kawachi who claimed to be a descendant of the Emperor Montoku. Neither shield nor armor could withstand the merciless barrage of arrows poured forth from the approach to the thicket.

A pathetic thing happened during the attack. A young lad of thirteen or fourteen appeared, lightly made-up, with blackened teeth, and attired in splendid armor. Raising the side of his *hakama,* he unsheathed a short golden sword and moved to the head of the troops. "If there is anyone with a spirit of loyalty for Masanaga, let him come forward and test my arms!" he shouted and was about to set forth when an arrow from the thicket pierced his breast and down he fell. Several men, apparently the boy's comrades, placed the lifeless body on a shield and carried it back to the lines. According to the townsfolk viewing the battle from the streets, those who recovered the body were men of Kawachi— Wada, Sumiya, Kainoshō—the last of the line of Kusunoki.

[50] At the southwest corner of the Goryō Shrine.

The young warrior was a son of the intrepid Sumiya Magojirō, who had earned renown at the battle of Mount Take the year before when Yoshinari's hawk disappeared in a patch of woods. During a search it was learned that the hawk had turned up in the enemy camp. Thereupon Sumiya marched boldly over to Masanaga's position at Hirokawa, retrieved the bird, and returned it to its master.[51] People believed that the son would have followed in his father's footsteps, and as they grieved the loss of this valiant lad there was not one among the onlookers whose lips were dry.[52]

With Yoshinari's attacking force in dire straits, Asakura Takakage raised aloft his banner of the sun and moved in with fresh troops. But Masanaga's band, although small, was resolute. From early morning until dusk they repulsed each onslaught. And even though Yamana Masatoyo later came up in relief, it became clear by day's end that the attackers had failed. Realizing the futility of nighttime battle, both sides withdrew at dusk, and men and horses rested in opposing camps.

That night Jimbo Naganobu sent a messenger to Yasutomi Mototsuna: "We are exhausted from the day's battle. Yet there is little we can do, since the shogun has directed the families to suspend aid. So that is the way it must be. Would you please send me a cask of sake? I will present it to Masanaga and will attend to his final banquet. Then we will cut our bellies together. One more thing. A number of our arrow-bearers got lost at Kawara this morning and never reached camp. Could you supply us with some arms?"

When informed of Naganobu's message, Katsumoto thought carefully. He realized that his long-standing pact with Masanaga could not be taken lightly, that it would be difficult to refuse support simply on the grounds of a temporary order from the shogun. At the same time, Katsumoto, as a general of unparalleled care and

[51] There is a vivid account in the *Chōhen Ōnin-ki* of the elder Sumiya's death during the battle at Hirokawa, when Yoshinari's men stormed down from Mount Take and attempted to take Masanaga's position. Sumiya, who had killed a number of the enemy, was himself impaled by a long spear. Although dead, he remained propped in an upright position with his eyes wide open, and even after the fighting had ended no one dared go near him.

[52] Apparently their lips were wet from the tears coursing down their cheeks.

resourcefulness, knew that in this particular battle there was little hope of turning the tide in favor of Masanaga. The enemy had the shogun and his brother safely in their care and were automatically receiving the support of the families. More important, they had possession of the emperor and his cloistered father. Even if Katsumoto went personally to the aid of Masanaga, it would matter little in the end.

But what if Masanaga should first make the enemy think they had gained an advantage? Later, when their guard was down, Masanaga could strike, take the shogun, and rally his allies and sympathizers. After occupying the shogunal palace he would be able to humble his opponents one after another by declaring them enemies of the shogun. Finally, Masanaga could have the shogun issue a directive calling for the chastisement of Yamana, Yoshinari, and the others.

Katsumoto knew that Masanaga and Jimbo were the type of men who could envision such a scheme. Without composing a formal reply, he returned the messenger with a single humming arrow. Masanaga and his men understood the sign. Thereupon they gathered up the enemy bodies taken during battle, placed them in the sanctuary of the Goryō Shrine, and set fire to the structure. Then, crawling through the thicket of the Shōkoku-ji, they scattered and made good their escape.

Yoshinari's men were also exhausted and the families sent a relief of from ten to twenty thousand men. Setting ablaze a bonfire, they saw in the nighttime glow the flames from the enemy's camp. With a surge of victory they shouted: "Get them all! Don't let any get through!" But the flames were too strong and they were forced to withdraw. Later, when the fire had abated, they went to the sanctuary and found it in ruins. Was Masanaga among the mass of bodies before them? Many said they had seen the Hatakeyama leader directing operations in the sanctuary throughout the day. Until recently he had been shogunal deputy, revered by the people and highly respected for his management of many great state affairs. To meet an end such as this—the pity of it all.

What can be said of Katsumoto's cowardly behavior? The oath of the warrior demands that he be prepared to offer his life whatever the risk. Even though he may never have seen or heard of the person before, it is shocking that a warrior should so flatly refuse aid. And how much more shocking it is when there is a pledge of many years involved. To think that he could allow before his very eyes the slaughter of a man who had burned his mansion and had come for help. People concluded scornfully that this was the most dastardly behavior ever. Thus we have an example of how wrong a judgment can be when formed through ignorance of events to follow. There were these poems on a wall:

How futile of Masanaga to rely upon the Hosokawa after wearing his ancient armor as far as Goryō.

Such reliance, without the knowledge that there is no water in the Hosokawa, has caused the Hatakeyama fields to be burnt and destroyed.

To turn to another House that lacks sympathy is to bring estrangement more rapidly than a wicker scoop loses water.[53]

While people spoke in this manner with prejudiced view, those who supported Katsumoto replied: "His is truly the way of the loyal subject. It is of course regrettable that Masanaga perished due to a failure of arms, and perhaps aid should have been sent. But when Yoshimasa demanded that he forsake Masanaga, Katsumoto agreed to do so through fear of becoming an enemy of the shogun in contravention of the oath that binds lord and vassal. Thus he has endured disgrace rather than flout the law, either private or public. But how can you say that his power and strategy are inferior? He is the product of many generations of noted men." In thus praising Katsumoto they even went so far as to speak of his ancestor Hosokawa Yoriyuki.

Yamana Sōzen and Hatakeyama Yoshinari, meanwhile, were totally unaware of Masanaga's escape. With the country already settled down to a state of idleness, they sang of peace and were filled with joy. Seeing little need to retain their military forces longer, they gave all the men leave to return to their provinces. The soldiers, who had endured such hardships in the Capital, felt

[53] *Goryō* can stand for both a place name and a small sum of money. But the chief play in these poems is on the word *hosokawa*, which means, literally, "narrow river."

like white geese released from their cages or like mudfish finding water. Shouting "Banzai!" and singing fanciful ditties of peace, they returned home.

It was announced that Their Imperial Highnesses would return to the palace on the twentieth, and on that date the emperor, his father, the dowager empress, and the royal children set out from the Hana-no-Gosho. Their procession was far different from that of the eighteenth. Since the shogun's brother, Yoshimi, had joined them, there were many daimyo in attendance. With the voices of harbingers clearing the way, the solemn group moved on to the palace.

The Chronicle of Ōnin: *II*

KATSUMOTO'S UPRISING

There was peace in the Capital, and little prospect in the future that any daimyo would be able to raise a hand against the Yamana or the Hatakeyama, who were enjoying the luxuries of life to the fullest. Day and night they spent their time in drinking parties and in the enjoyment of Nō and *dengaku*.[54] They appeared to be utterly unconcerned with the opinions of others, and in fact there were none in the land to speak out against them.

Before long the third day of the third month arrived and the revelers attended the shogun's court in all their finery: Yamana Sōzen and his son Noriyuki; Yamana Katsutoyo; Isshiki Yoshinao; Toki Shigeyori; Sasaki-Rokkaku Takayori, and others—all cohorts of Yamana. After paying their respects at the shogunal palace, they went directly to call on the shogun's brother, Yoshimi. Since the

---

[54] A type of dance-play, originating in agricultural ceremonies, which became fashionable among the aristocracy in the late Kamakura period.

distance was a mere two wards,[55] they left their carriages and went by foot.

They formed a sumptuously adorned procession as they set out in lavish costume amidst strewn blossoms, carrying swords inlaid with gold, silver, pearls, and gems, and looking for all the world like the scattering of peach flowers on Konron Mountain.[56] In all there were three thousand people, both high and low, thus beautifully arrayed in glittering jewels. The expense was so great that it would appear to have exhausted half the wealth of the empire.

But among the Hosokawa and the Kyōgoku there was not one who attended the shogun's court. Day and night they met privately to converse and discuss various plans. Katsumoto's uncle, the Monk Dōgen, fighting to hold back his tears, approached his nephew and said: "The dishonor we suffered in the first month has made us an object of derision before the people. What do you think we should do? It would be unthinkable not to wipe away this shame of Kaikei.[57] Are you resigned to the scorn of heartless people?" Kagawa, Naitō, Yasutomi, Yakushiji, Akiba, and the others voiced their agreement, as Katsumoto himself spoke with tears of sorrow in his eyes: "What a pitiful state of affairs we have arrived at as a result of not aiding Masanaga in the spring. This House has never been an enemy of the shogun for even a single day. Now in this generation we have become alienated from others and it appears that we may even find ourselves unwillingly in opposition to our lord." As for Dōgen, he had pleaded tearfully before the battle that no aid be given Masanaga. This time his tears accompanied a plea for support of the Hatakeyama leader. Thus people dubbed him the "two-faced" monk.

During the course of their conversations they struck upon a

---

[55] A distance of approximately 238 yards.

[56] The reference here is to a mythical mountain in western China, the K'un-lun, which had rich deposits of precious stones.

[57] In 494 B.C. Fu-ch'a of the state of Wu defeated Yüeh at K'uai-chi (Kaikei). Against the advice of his chief minister, Fu-ch'a made peace and allowed the king of Yüeh to rebuild his state and, sixteen years later, return to destroy Fu-ch'a and erase the "shame of K'uai-chi."

plan. Isshiki Yoshinao's mansion was located in front of the four-posted gate of the shogunal palace. If a camp were established from the Hosokawa-Kyōgoku base to the Jissō-in and the Shōjitsubō, Akamatsu Sadamura's position and Hosokawa Shigeyuki's mansion could be joined as one,[58] with the result that Isshiki would be separated from the western camp—an intolerable situation for the enemy. They realized, of course, that the Yamana people might well have the same idea. Would it not be best, first of all, to erect fortifications as quickly as possible? Therefore they dug moats on all sides, built walls, and constructed fortifications. When the townsfolk and the Yamana, who did not know the purpose of these fortifications, saw all the activity, they laughed and said: "What can be the purpose of these moats and walls? These cowards who did not offer assistance even when Masanaga was attacked and killed at Goryō have been scorned by everyone. Why do they now build fortifications to protect against attack by bow 'after the robbers have gone'?"

Since Yamana Sōzen was Hosokawa Katsumoto's father-in-law, the two families had usually stood side by side down to the lowest retainer. But now they had suddenly become alienated, separated by moat and palisade. Someone shot an arrow, with a note affixed, to Yamana:

If one has not the strength to strike, he should stop.
When Yamana Sōzen was hard-pressed, he relied upon the shogun.

Hatakeyama Masanaga, meanwhile, had been hiding in the interior. Raising available troops, he came forth to Katsumoto's camp. At the same time Yusa and Jimbo galloped up from Kokawa Temple. Katsumoto was overjoyed, and in order to determine the extent of his strength he promptly recorded those who had arrived: Katsumoto's retainers from Settsu, Tamba, Tosa, Sanuki, and other provinces, comprising sixty thousand mounted men; eight thousand soldiers from Awa and Mikawa commanded by

[58] It is difficult to reconstruct accurately the strategy described here, since the Isshiki and Hosokawa mansions cannot be precisely located. Akamatsu's dwelling and the Jissō-in, however, were on a line two and three blocks, respectively, due west of the shogunal palace. The subsequent action, therefore, was apparently concentrated in a fairly small area.

Hosokawa Shigeyuki; four thousand soldiers under Hosokawa Katsuhisa; three thousand under Hosokawa Shigeharu; two thousand under Hosokawa Masaari; two thousand under Hosokawa Noriharu; and Hosokawa Dōgen's two thousand troops. From the hosts of the other houses there were five hundred troops led by Shiba Yoshitoshi; five thousand raised by Hatakeyama Masanaga from the provinces of Ise, Kawachi, and Etchū; ten thousand from Izumo, Hida, and Ōmi, commanded by Kyōgoku Mochikiyo; Akamatsu Masanori's force of five hundred from Harima, Bizen, and Mimasaka; five hundred under Togashi Masachika; Takeda Kuninobu's force of three thousand from Aki and Wakasa; and an additional sixty thousand sympathetic vassals comprised of imperial and shogunal troops and men from collateral and outside provinces. In all he recorded more than 161,500 riders.

On the tenth day of the fifth month of the first year of Ōnin, Akamatsu Masanori and his host of Harima adventurers invaded the provinces of Harima and Bizen. Since these were Akamatsu's home provinces, the farmers and natives united in support and Masanori was able to take control without incident. He also wanted to enter Mimasaka where Yamana Masakiyo's uncle, Kamon-no-kami, was firmly entrenched. But when the fighting threatened Kyoto, he halted his advance and went up to the Capital instead.

Meanwhile Sebo Masayasu of the Toki invaded Ise, which was under the protection of Isshiki's retainer, the monk Ishikawa Dōgo, and his son Chikasada. Several years earlier, when the local samurai of Ise and Shima had turned against Isshiki, Ishikawa had restored order and had recruited these warriors as his personal followers. He also quelled and converted an uprising of adventurers at Hatsugasaki in Kaitō-gun, Owari. And before long he drove out Sebo. Thereupon Seki Morimoto of Kameyama in the same province [Ise] [59] took Sebo as his son-in-law, gathered a band of fighters, and attacked Ishikawa. Completely unflustered, this stalwart set about bolstering his fortifications. But just then a messenger arrived imploring Ishikawa to proceed with haste to the Capital. Reluctantly, he abandoned his position and rode off.

Shiba Yoshitoshi's adventurers attacked Owari and Tōtōmi,

[59] In Suzuka-gun.

while Takeda Nobukata advanced into Wakasa, expelling the Isshiki from the Sai and Imadomi estates. It was then decided that, since a leak in the plot might prejudice chances in battle, Takeda should take the Jissō-in before the enemy occupied it. Accordingly, this position was brought into Katsumoto's sphere. The Jissō-in neighbored on Isshiki's camp, while to the west was a small stream[60] with the Shōjitsubō on its opposite bank. This had been part of Isshiki's territory, but on the twenty-fourth day of the fifth month Jōshin'in of Yamato attacked and occupied it. Isshiki was mortified. "Still," he reflected, "since the shogun decreed the other day that he who first commences hostilities will be branded an enemy of the government, it would not be wise to fight with Jōshin'in. I will confer first with Lord Yamana about means for seeking vengeance." But when he went that night to Yamana, Jōshin'in promptly occupied his position.

At daybreak on the twenty-sixth enemy and ally lined up and the battle of arrows began. The Yamana had previously planned to hold the Jissō-in and Shōjitsubō from the Yamana camp and to occupy a position from Isshiki's mansion to the shogunal palace. But now Isshiki had abandoned his mansion and had fled in haste to the western camp. We read in a satirical poem:

> The enlightened one could not hold the Jissō-in,
> And now has suffered ignominious shame.[61]

Yamana Sōzen also sought to determine the number of troops at his command by recording the arrivals: first, Sōzen's own troops, a combined force of thirty thousand retainers from Tajima, Harima, Bingo, and other provinces; Yamana Noriyuki's force of five thousand from Hōki and Bizen; three thousand under Yamana Katsutoyo; and Yamana Masakiyo's three thousand from Mimasaka and Iwami. Among the others were ten thousand riders from Echizen, Owari, and Tōtōmi under Shiba Yoshikado; Hatakeyama Yoshinari's seven thousand recruited from Yamato, Kawachi, and Ku-

---

[60] This stream runs in a north-south direction two blocks west of the shogunal palace.

[61] Isshiki is sarcastically referred to as the "enlightened one." His name, which means "one color," is identical with part of a Buddhist phrase used to describe the mean, or ignominious, nature of this world.

mano; Hatakeyama Yoshitō in charge of three thousand from Noto; Isshiki Yoshinao's force of five thousand from Tango, Ise, and Tosa; eight thousand riders from Mino under Toki Shigeyori; Rokkaku Takayori's five thousand from Ōmi; twenty thousand from Suō, Nagato, Buzen, Chikuzen, Aki, and Iwami under Ōuchi Masahiro; Kōno's two thousand from Iyo; ten thousand riders from other provinces. The grand total came to 116,000.

. . .

THE IMPERIAL PROCESSION TO THE
MUROMACHI PALACE

Meanwhile, on the eighteenth day of the eighth month, Hosokawa Katsumoto summoned Kagawa, Yasutomi, Akiba, and others to the four-posted gate of the shogunal palace. "You may not have heard," he said, "but there are enemy sympathizers among the retainers serving in the palace. I have learned from reliable sources that this league of men is engaged in secret plots and subversive activities. It is therefore imperative that we inform the shogun and have them expelled from the palace. If we do not do so, there may be grave consequences."

The family elders were greatly astonished by this revelation. They agreed that, in view of the urgency of the situation, the league must definitely be driven out without delay. Thereupon they issued a call for troops, and within a short time six thousand splendid warriors rode forth, surrounded the shogunal palace, and placed a tight restriction on the movement of people into and out of the area. The nobles, ladies, wives, and outsiders passing through the portals of the palace wondered with alarm what might be afoot. Katsumoto dispatched Hosokawa Noriharu to inform the shogun, and after a short while Sanjō Kimparu and Kira Yoshinobu brought His Excellency's reply: "If there are people in the palace at this time who harbor special ambitions, you must write down their names and let me know who they are, so that I can issue orders for their expulsion. Otherwise things will be intolerable, what with soldiers constantly inspecting carriages, regardless of whether they belong to high-born guests or ladies, and creating a general commotion."

Katsumoto rsepectfully agreed and set about making a careful investigation, which lasted from the eighteenth until the twenty-third. He wrote down (in no special order) the names of twelve men of the fifth watch and presented them to the shogun: Isshiki, Sasaki, Ueno, Miya the Lord of Shimotsuke, Yūki, Ise, Arao, Mikami Saburō, Saitō, Miya the Lord of Wakasa, Saitō Tōgorō, and Sen'ami. The shogun, in turn, showed the list to the twelve men concerned. "If you left the palace for a while," he said, "it would be a commendable act. For you would both assuage Katsumoto's anger and calm the anxieties of the people."

The twelve men replied respectfully that they would depart the palace in accordance with the shogun's wish. But later they addressed the two messengers, Sanjō and Kira, in the following manner: "We are not the only ones who have favored the Yamana. It is the same throughout the palace. Even the shogun himself has shown preference for them. As a result all of us in his service brighten upon news that the enemy has gained an advantage and are distressed when we hear of an allied victory.[62] Since everyone feels this way, it certainly is bad luck that we alone should be arbitrarily singled out in this manner. But, alas, there is nothing to be done. We will go at once to the four-posted gate and disembowel ourselves before Katsumoto, thereby fulfilling our desire to join in spirit with the Yamana."

When this statement was passed on to the shogun, the retainers and followers of the twelve men began to clamor: "To arms!" If these partisans had made a mad dash into the palace, they would have completely disrupted the peace and thrown everything into turmoil. But since the gate was being carefully guarded and passage into and out of the palace was difficult, there appeared to be little they could do.

On the same day there was a report that the enemy (the western army) was planning to enter the imperial palace and take the

[62] The enemy is Yamana's western army and the ally is Katsumoto's eastern army.

emperor. Word was passed through Katsumoto that Their Majesties, the emperor and the cloistered emperor, would proceed to the Muromachi quarters. Those guarding the imperial palace at that time were the two Kira, Akamatsu the Lord of Izu, and Nagoe Jirō. Hosokawa Noriharu and his brother came to meet the two sovereigns and the procession set forth with the regalia at the head. In the absence of Their Majesties from the palace, the Kira clan, Akamatsu the Lord of Tosa, and Akamatsu Kunaishōyū mounted guard by the gate. The maids and ladies in waiting, who had become alarmed and were in a state of complete distraction, fled to the camps of the Kyōgoku at Nakamikado-Saionjidono and the Takeda at Nijō-Karasumaru.[63]

Because of the uproar at this time surrounding the twelve men accused by Katsumoto, the carriages of the emperor and the cloistered emperor were detained outside the main gate of the shogunal palace. From about midday until ten at night the nobles, courtiers, and maids accompanying Their Majesties huddled in the narrow streets in great distress. A messenger was again dispatched to the twelve men to remind them that they had been repeatedly directed by the shogun to leave the palace and that their delay in so doing was a flagrant breach of conduct. The twelve, however, became angered at this remonstrance and threatened to set fire to the palace, dash out to the four-posted gate, and die in a clash of arms with Katsumoto.

Sanjō and Kira went to the group and said: "First of all, control your tempers and listen. You men are hereditary samurai of the Ashikaga and have served as bodyguards in the shogunal palace since Kamakura times. You cannot simply reject the shogun's order. If you would first consent to leave the palace for a while, dispel Katsumoto's anger, and bide your time, we have received assurances in private that you will definitely be recalled at a later date. What sort of thing is this to go against the shogun's will and defile the palace in such a peremptory manner? What a disgraceful situation! You will not only bring ruin upon yourselves; you will forfeit the loyalty of your ancestors from generations past. And that is not all. If you are given the punishment

[63] Approximately five to six blocks directly south of the shogunal palace.

for disloyalty, your days on this earth will be numbered. Have you thought of these things?"

When Sanjō and Kira had finished speaking, the twelve men realized that what they said was right, and consented to withdraw from the palace. People everywhere were greatly relieved to learn of their decision. But Katsumoto's followers, hoping to intercept the men as they left the palace, rushed down to Ichijō-Muromachi-Karasumaru.[64] When this was discovered, the group, guided by Inō the Lord of Shimōsa, opened a small gate used by the elders of the Rokuon-in in passing to and from the shogunal palace and hurried into the Shōkoku-ji. So extensive was the temple compound, it was impossible to tell which building they had entered or where they had gone.

But one member of the group, Saitō Tōgorō, had called upon a lady in waiting to whom he had pledged his undying love. Time slipped by as he was taking his leave and, unaware that the others had opened the small gate and had entered the temple, he proceeded to Imadegawa, then turned eastward to the south of the Lord of Ise's mansion. When he reached Mushanokōji-Karasumaru,[65] he was surrounded and killed by a force waiting in ambush.

At the hour of the boar on that day, the twenty-third, a reception was finally arranged at the shogunal palace and the emperor proceeded to his new seat. Detainment of the imperial carriage outside the gate until this hour had been part of a scheme of Katsumoto. According to rumor, the shogun had always been in sympathy with the Yamana. Hence Katsumoto was determined that, in the event the shogun should succor the twelve men and allow them to go over to the enemy, he would maintain custody of Their Majesties and fight. But now that the shogun had come to terms with Katsumoto and had expelled the twelve men, the Hosokawa were greatly joyed.

Inō the Lord of Shimōsa was later assassinated in the shogunal

---

[64] Muromachi and Karasumaru run parallel (north-south) to each other and intersect Ichijō (east-west) a short distance south of the shogun's quarters.

[65] He had covered about half the distance (less than two blocks) to the main Hosokawa ambush.

palace by a force of the Hosokawa. It was rumored that this was a result of his having allied himself to the twelve men and having aided them to escape.

ASHIKAGA YOSHIMI GOES
FROM THE CAPITAL TO ISE

Bands of Yamana rowdies roamed the Capital, burning and looting, and no one among friend or foe dared venture forth without adequate protection.

From the twenty-fifth day of the fifth month Lord Yoshimi had stayed with the shogun and his family at their Muromachi quarters. With conditions becoming more and more unsettled, however, he returned around this time to his own residence at Imadegawa. Hosokawa Katsumoto suggested that Yoshimi visit him. But just as the Ashikaga lord was about to set out on the twentieth day of the eighth month, a retainer of Kyōgoku Mochikiyo, Taga Takatada, voiced objection. Isshiki Tanemura was sent to enquire into Taga's reasons for opposing the journey, but Taga would say only that, since the shogun had been patronizing the Yamana, Yoshimi should remain where he was. Thus there was considerable confusion as the day came to an end.[66]

On the twenty-second Lord Yoshimi sent word through Isshiki that his delay had been due to the Kyōgoku protest, which was lodged just as he was about to set out for the Hosokawa mansion. Katsumoto in turn replied that, after all, Yoshimi had best remain in his own mansion in order to avoid any further complications. But Yoshimi was concerned lest there be trouble later, and at the hour of the dog on the following day, the twenty-third, he left his mansion and set out for the camp of Kitabatake Norichika at Nakayama.[67] From there he and his companions proceeded east

---

[66] This passage is exceptionally difficult to interpret, because most of the sentences have no subjects and one cannot be sure just who is talking to whom. The author of the *Chōhen Ōnin-ki* has attempted to unravel the relationships among the various figures involved and I have accepted his interpretations.

[67] To the east of the Kamo River.

of Mushanokōji, and through Takuyakushi crossing to Ichijō, where Togashi Tsurudōmaru's force was holding the Tominokōji defense works. Norichika, attired in ceremonial hat and robe, addressed him: "The Naidaijin Sanjō is ill at Higashiyama and his lordship Yoshimi is now journeying there to call on him. Please open up." Togashi, however, was suspicious and, without opening, replied that he did not have the key. Fortunately, Norichika had prepared in advance and now produced a duplicate key. Opening the gate, he, along with Yoshimi and the remainder of their party, passed quickly through. They went south of Kyōgoku, east of Konoe, and north of Kawara to Sakamoto.[68] The only ones in attendance with Lord Yoshimi at the time were Isshiki Tanemura; Hatakeyama Shikibu-shōyū; Kitabatake Norichika and his brother, Shinjōin; Takakura Hyōe-no-jō; and Dōbō Saiami. But at Sakamoto, Tanemura the Lord of Harima, Isshiki Kūrō, Isshiki Saburō, Yashima, Nasu, and others arrived with a contingent of six hundred. Together they went to the home of Ishikawa Jirō in Sakamoto.

Because of the turmoil in Kyoto, Lord Yoshimi's wife also went secretly to Sakamoto. There she partook of a farewell repast with her husband. At the time of departure Yoshimi was dressed in light green woven silk with a coarse brown and wadded silken garment above and a divided skirt with a red damask silk ground. He wrapped the swords and had Kijin Daibu Kanehira, Tōshirō, Koka-ji, Hatozukuri, and others carry them.

In twelve boats they arrived with the dawn of the twenty-fourth at the Bay of Yamada[69] in Ōmi Province. When a jellyfish of about one foot in length flew into the salon boat, a thoughtless person retrieved it and tossed it back into the sea. Next, a perch jumped into the same boat.

Now, at the time when Wu-Wang of the House of Chou fought with King Chou of the Yin,[70] a fish jumped into Wu-Wang's boat in mid-stream. Wu bowed down and offered the

[68] They journeyed eastward to Sakamoto on the shores of Lake Biwa.
[69] Kurita-gun.
[70] King Chou was the "bad" last ruler of the Yin (Shang) Dynasty.

fish to heaven, and later he struck down King Chou. Furthermore, when Taira Kiyomori of this land went to worship at Kumano, a perch flew into his boat and he too offered it to heaven. Afterwards Kiyomori reached the exalted rank of chancellor and ruled the country with his power. In view of its being such a good omen, therefore, Yoshimi and his companions prepared the fish for feasting.

Passing from Yamada to Setagoe and then through Nakayama and Tanoue to Kurotsu, they were joined by one of Kitabatake's retainers, Kaizugaani, at the Fukujuji and enjoyed a repast together with him at the sanctuary of the Kasuga Shrine in the mountains. When they approached Nojiri on the twenty-fifth, Tarao came forth to greet them, and that evening they arrived at the Araki Bodai-ji at Hattori[71] in Iga. The following night, as the wind blew violently:

We pass a stormy night on our journey at this ancient temple.
While we are not the leaves of the *bashō* tree, still our dreams are
     broken.
The longing now that the hallowed city is so distant;
Dreams vanish in the nighttime storm.[72]

On the twenty-ninth day of the same month they arrived at the Jōkō-ji[73] of Kowa estate in Ise Province. To their backs were mountains and before them waving stalks of rice in fields outside the gates. They listened to the cry of the deer, their faces reflecting awareness of the season. And the sound of the woodcutter's song and the herdsman's pipes filled their ears, while the hue of bamboo smoke and pine mist obscured their view. All these experiences served only to evoke memories of the Capital.

They turned for hospitality to the provincial governor, who, in view of their journey down from the Capital, graciously agreed to assume responsibility for his guests. On the third day of the ninth month the governor joined them at the Jōkō-ji, and together

---

[71] Araki is part of Hattori-gō in Ayama-gun.
[72] The *bashō* tree is commonly translated as banana tree. It has long leaves that are easily broken in stormy weather.
[73] Suzuka-gun.

they went to the Hasedera[74] on the sixth. Yoshimi and his companions were assured that before long a new residence would be built for them.

.   .   .

[74] Ano-gun.

The Chronicle of Ōnin: *III*

THE TRADITION OF THE AKAMATSU FAMILY
AND THE
PROBLEM OF THE IMPERIAL JEWELS

There was among the Akamatsu a man called Nakamura Gorō, who, although he had but a small force, yearned both day and night to surpass others in the performance of great deeds. He discussed matters with some ten of his comrades and, on the third day of the tenth month, they entered the province of Mimasaka and established themselves at the In estate. While Nakamura and his men were generally successful in a number of encounters, the enemy were still able to move into Higashi-gun and there to ensconce themselves in Myōken Castle, the Bodai-ji and Mount Wasuke. Accordingly, Akamatsu Masanori dispatched additional troops to Nakamura under a clansman, Hirooka Suketaka, and the battling continued without pause for three years.

. . .

It would be impossible to write of all the places where Naka-mura fought, but from this time forth his masters, the Akamatsu, enjoyed control over three provinces.[75] The important thing to note is how this trio of provinces, which now comprised the Akamatsu home territory, was once bestowed on the Yamana. .Let us begin with the time of Ashikaga Takauji's rise to power.

In Kamakura, Suwa Saburō championed the cause of Hōjō Takatoki's son, Tokiyuki, and from the eight eastern provinces to the Tōsandō the imperial influence waned. Ashikaga Takauji was given appointment over these lands of the Kantō for the pur-pose of subduing and bringing them under control, and on the eve of his departure for the Kantō he went to speak to Akamatsu Enshin: "I am leaving once again for Kamakura to destroy the enemies of the throne. This is the most important of assignments as far as I am concerned and I would like one of your sons to join me." After Takauji had repeated this request several times, Enshin brought forth his second son, Sadanori, who went with the Ashikaga chieftain to the east, and there achieved great merit in the battles of Sagami River and the Mizunomi Pass in Hakone. Sadanori also contributed to the downfall of Hōjō Tokiyuki.

As Takauji brought the Kantō under control, Nitta Yoshisada in the Capital issued a steady stream of slanderous charges, which finally resulted in his receiving an imperial order to chastise the Ashikaga leader. When Nitta went down to the Kantō, Akamatsu Sadanori fought with peerless loyalty at the battle of Takenoshita[76] and, on the twelfth day of the twelfth month of the second year of Kemmu, received a grant rewarding him with the Kasugabe estate in Harima and Tamba Provinces. Meanwhile Sadanori's father Enshin, Enshin's eldest son Norisuke, and his third son the Priest Sokuyū proceeded together to Suzumi no Matsubara in Settsu Province under orders from the Emperor Go-Daigo. But when word reached them that Yoshisada, defeated during the fighting in the east, had fled to the province of Owari and that the victorious Takauji would soon proceed to the Capital, Akamatsu Enshin and his sons, in possession of an edict rewarding them

[75] Harima, Mimasaka, and Bizen.
[76] Near Ashigara Village in Suruga Province.

with the province of Harima, returned from Suzume no Matsubara to Harima and unfurled the flag of allegiance to the shogunal
(Ashikaga) house.

Because Sadanori was filial toward his father and was deeply
devoted to his brothers, he succeeded Enshin to the headship of
the Akamatsu. An edict awarding him the provinces of Harima
and Mimasaka was carefully recorded. Sadanori's brother Sokuyū,
who performed meritorious service in the Capital, came to control the provinces of Bizen and Inaba, while Norisuke and his
son Mitsunori held the office of constable in Settsu Province for
two generations.

Then, during the time of Ashikaga Yoshimochi, three provinces
were bestowed on Akamatsu Mochisada, the seventh and youngest
son of Sadanori's son, Akinori. This was when it started, was
it not? For Mochisada, taking advantage of the shogun's favor,
behaved in a most improper manner. As a result his kinsman,
Akamatsu Mitsusuke, in conference with other daimyo, petitioned the Bakufu and at length forced the shogun to issue an
edict calling on Mochisada to disembowel himself.

Yoshimochi's brother and successor, Ashikaga Yoshinori, talked
of this matter in private: "My brother did not order the family
of Akamatsu Sadamura according to the proper succession. Without justification he selected the seventh and youngest son and
bestowed the shogunal favor on him." And so Yoshinori secretly
dispatched an edict to Sadamura. Akamatsu Mitsusuke and his
son Norisuke heard rumors of this transmission and, on the twenty-
fourth day of the sixth month of 1441, invited the shogun to view
some ducklings and struck him down. It was a terrible thing, un-
heard of in former ages. It is written:

Because Harima was taken by Izu,
Akamatsu has cut off the shogun's head in this first year of Kakitsu.[77]

Akamatsu and his followers went down to Harima, constructed
a mountain fortress at Shirahata,[78] and awaited arrival of the
punitive force. The attackers, led by Hosokawa Shigeyuki, Aka-

[77] Izu refers to Akamatsu Mochisada, the Lord of Izu.
[78] Akaho-gun, in the western part of Harima.

matsu Sadamura, and Takeda Nobushige, pitched camp at Akashi in Suma. But Hosokawa Shigeyuki, the leader of the advance group, secretly favored the Akamatsu and would not allow a single warrior to enter the heart of the province. Takeda and Akamatsu Sadamura argued hotly, but to no avail.

The leaders of the rearguard were Yamana Sōzen, Yamana Norikazu, and Yamana Masatoyo. Sōzen was the type of person who yearned to win over others and to perform great deeds. Like Terutaka,[79] he would seek to take the jewels from under the chin of the black dragon. He could hardly have been expected to hesitate. Cutting into the center of the province from the entrance at Oyama,[80] Sōzen made his camp above the Saifuku-ji, opposite the Akamatsu fortress and separated from it by the Hashizaki River. When the Inaba and Hōki forces of Norikazu and Masatoyo circled around to the rearguard, he crossed the river, pitched camp at the base of the mountain fortress, and surrounded it ten and twenty deep.

On the tenth day of the ninth month Akamatsu Mitsusuke committed suicide. The number of others who died in battle or disemboweled themselves is not known, but Mitsusuke's son Norisuke also perished. Their heads were sent to the Capital and Mitsusuke's was hung from the prison gate.

Ashikaga Yoshinori was given the posthumous rank of minister of the left and the Buddhist name of Fukō-in. In reward for their meritorious service, the Yamana—Sōzen, Norikazu, and Masatoyo —received, respectively, the provinces of Harima, Mimasaka, and Bizen. The only grant made to Akamatsu Sadamura, who had been checked by Hosokawa Shigeyuki and missed the fighting, was the seal of daimyo authority in his home territory. While this carried much formal, ceremonial prestige and entitled Sadamura to participate in the shogunal fete on the seventh day of the first month, it brought no power whatsoever.

Meanwhile Yoshinori's son, Yoshikatsu, succeeded to the sho-

---

[79] The *Chōhen Ōnin-ki* suggests that this may have been one of Sōzen's sons.

[80] Oyama is in Taki-gun, Tamba Province, on the border of Harima. Sōzen, therefore, invaded from his own province, Tanba.

gunacy. When he died at an early age, his younger brother, Yoshimasa, assumed the office.

The Yamana, recipients of three provinces, were overjoyed.

Akamatsu Saburō was a son of Akamatsu Sokuyū and a descendant of Akamatsu Mitsunori, who was killed at the battle of Uchino.[81] In recognition of past deeds, Saburō was pardoned; but in 1443 he gathered the adventurers of Harima and rose up in that province. Saburō's efforts, however, were to no avail, and in the end he disemboweled himself at Arima-gun.

In 1454 bad relations between the Yamana—Masatoyo and Sōzen—and the shogun permitted the Akamatsu to return to the shogunal fold. Specifically, when Yamana Sōzen went against the shogun's wishes, Akamatsu Sukeyuki and Akamatsu Norinao secretly gained pardon through the good offices of Hosokawa Shigeyuki. Shortly thereafter, on the second night of the eleventh month, troops were summoned to the shogun's quarters and the decision was made to attack Yamana Sōzen at the signal of the Shōkoku-ji bell. But Katsumoto, as Sōzen's son-in-law, privately favored the Yamana, and, despite his agreement to abide by the shogunal order, absconded around midnight on the second day. Those gathered at the shogun's quarters, upon learning of this development, were forced to postpone their raid. And when word reached the men of Katsumoto's house that their master was at Godaidō in Higashiyama, they flocked to his side. Thus, plans to subjugate the Yamana were canceled. Sōzen himself was told that he had best go to Tamba; and, leaving his heir Noritoyo in the Capital, he went down to that province.

In the meantime, Akamatsu Hikojirō and Akamatsu Hikogorō entered Harima and started an uprising. During the fifth month of the following year, Yamana Sōzen also entered and established his camp at Mount Futō. He attacked the enemy position at Dantoku Mountain, but was not successful. Abandoning this effort, Sōzen made his way toward Sakamoto. According to report, his son Koretoyo and a Bingo group were in difficulty, bottled up at

---

[81] Uchino, the scene of a number of famous battles, was the site of the old imperial palace, which was destroyed by fire and never completely restored.

Muroyama[82] under attack by Hikojirō and Hikogorō. Yet when Sōzen went behind the enemy position and passed through to Sakamoto, the enemy, as expected, abandoned their attack on Muroyama and scattered. News of this disaster also brought collapse of the enemy force at Dantoku Mountain. Hikogorō committed suicide at Kakuijima[83] in Bizen Province, while Hikojirō requested asylum from his relative Kitabatake the governor of Ise. Hikojirō's request was denied and he later disemboweled himself in Ise.

Thereafter, from 1455 until the first year of Ōnin, 1467, there were few in the land who could rank with Yamana Sōzen. If one attempted to record all the disturbances that occurred in the various provinces during this time, he would exhaust an ocean of ink with his pen and still not complete the task. Let us turn instead to the details of Akamatsu Masanori's pardon.

Among the Akamatsu clan was a man named Iwami Tarō, who began work in the service of the minister of the center, Sanjō Sanekazu. By exhausting all his efforts in palace duty, Iwami earned Sanjō's admiration, and occasionally the two would talk about the affairs of the Akamatsu family. They discussed at length such matters as the details of the imperial edict, the seven pledges from Takauji to Akamatsu Enshin, Takauji's letter in which he referred to the Hosokawa as "the father" and the Akamatsu as "the mother," and the presentation of the silk brocade robe.[84] In this way Sanjō learned the entire story of the Akamatsu, point by point, and on one occasion he suggested to Iwami the possibility of some act significant enough to bury the Kakitsu treachery.

Iwami mulled over this suggestion day and night. "Of Japan's treasures, the sword is in the Naishidokoro,[85] while the jewels are

---

[82] The two Akamatsu positions, Dantoku Mountain and Muroyama, are in Ibo-gun, whereas Sakamoto is in neighboring Shikama-gun.

[83] Wake-gun.

[84] This was presumably a gift from the Akamatsu to the shogun. Details, however, are few on this and the other events that were so important to the prestige of the House of Akamatsu.

[85] A special name for the Ummei-den in the compound of the imperial palace. The Naishidokoro was the traditional repository for the sword.

held by the southern court," he said. "How would it be if we were to retrieve the jewels and return them to the Capital?" Sanjō thought to himself at the time that this was a reasonable proposal, and spoke confidentially about it to the shogun. A messenger was then sent to inquire whether there might be an imperial edict granting pardon to the Akamatsu, and His Majesty replied that there would be no difficulty if the dynastic jewels were returned to the Capital. Iwami was delighted with this news, and directed a clansman, Majima, and a vassal, Nakamura Taroshirō, to discuss plans with some ten sympathizers.

These men then requested service with the southern pretender. Officials of the pretender's court, recalling innocently that the petitioners were among the enemies of the Bakufu who had slain the Shogun Yoshinori, accepted their request and assigned them to night service near the imperial dwelling. One evening the men of Akamatsu stole into the pretender's quarters, slew him without difficulty, and slipped away with the jewels.

Men of the eighteen districts of Yoshino rose up and gave pursuit. They succeeded in killing Nakamura, who had possession of the pretender's head, but Majima and the others took the jewels back to the Capital. Sanjō went quickly to report the news to the shogun, who then informed the emperor. His Majesty was highly pleased, and the jewels were duly transferred to the Shishiden.[86]

Punishment had formerly been meted out to the Akamatsu during the Kakitsu period, but now a statement was sent to them granting forgiveness. The official pardon was issued through imperial edict and shogunal endorsement in 1459, when Masanori was five years old. Soon thereafter another edict and endorsement were passed down bestowing on the Akamatsu half the province of Kaga, which was without a constable. Yamana Sōzen was displeased with these developments. And one time after Iwami Tarō had attended a *kōwakamai*[87] at Sanjō's residence, he was struck

[86] A principal building at the imperial palace that was used for great state functions.
[87] A type of dance-play popular during this period.

down in the manner of a street-murder by Yamana's men, who had mingled with the crowd returning home.

Yamana's resentment stemmed from the pardon of Akamatsu Masanori. In the end things progressed from the Shiba struggle to the beginning of national conflict. As a result of the clash of arms between the two branches of the Hatakeyama, the Houses of Hosokawa, Hatakeyama, and Yamana came to harbor ill will towards each other.

When this disturbance occurred, the home territory of the Akamatsu was confirmed.

· · ·

YOSHIMI GOES TO THE WESTERN CAMP

There was at that time a strange rumor. Someone told the shogun in confidence that Katsumoto was planning to champion the cause of Yoshimi, and urged His Lordship to make ready for secret passage to Yamana's camp.

When Katsumoto learned of this, he was aghast. After pondering the problem day and night, he decided: "I must try to make the shogun's position secure by arranging for Lord Yoshimi to go to the enemy camp." He spoke to Takeda Nobukata and had Yoshimi escorted from the Seizōguchi directly to Mount Hiei. They left in a driving rainstorm during the night of the thirteenth of the eleventh month, and the hardships of their journey were truly beyond the power of words to describe.

Just as Katsumoto had planned, news of Lord Yoshimi's presence on the mountain reached Yamana Sōzen, and on the twenty-fifth day of the same month Yoshimi was escorted to Shiba Yoshikado's mansion at Kadenokōji. It was astonishing to see how Yamana and his allied daimyo all vied with one another to present horses and swords to the new arrival.

On the following day, the twenty-sixth, Lord Yoshimi's wife was brought from the Tsugen-ji to join her husband. Their young child (the future Shogun Yoshitane) had been placed in the care of Takeda Nobukata, but on the twenty-ninth Nobukata secretly sent the lad to his parents. Yamana Sōzen and the daimyo in league with him again presented horses and swords.

. . .

The Final Moments of Ichijō Masafusa

A most lamentable thing occurred at this time. Ichijō Masafusa, grandson of the retired regent, was sojourning in Hyōgo, where he had his estates. Wearing his normal attire, which included court robe and hunting habit, Masafusa cut a splendid figure. Any crude barbarian should have recognized him as an exalted personage. Yet on the seventh day of the tenth month of 1469 some warrior, without pausing to think, assumed that Masafusa was an enemy and ran a long spear through his breast.

Not wavering in the slightest, Masafusa chanted: "Hail Amida Buddha of the paradise world in the west." Thus he perished with the morning dew. Few are the regents or other high personages who have come to such an end.

The retired regent learned of his grandson's fate later in Nara. Although one might wish to write movingly of the older man's grief, even the phoenix could not soar to such heights, and even the tongue of the parrot would be unable to find expression. He himself wrote of the overwhelming tragedy in the following manner:

How regrettable for one who was not born into a military house to die
   in this manner.

. . .

The Death of Yamana Sōzen

On the nineteenth day of the third month of 1473 Yamana Sōzen died in his seventieth year. He had been an unparalleled leader and there was no end to the grief in the western camp. Before long, on the eleventh day of the fifth month of the same year, Hosokawa Katsumoto, who was then forty-four, also died unexpectedly.

These two stalwarts had fought without let-up for years, during which time the Capital, its temples, and its shrines, had all been reduced to ashes. The people suffered from starvation and cold, and both sides, their strength exhausted, made mutual peace overtures.

When Yamana's forces had all left for the provinces, Katsumoto had had things his own way. Shogunal retainers and other samurai from the home provinces had called at his door.

Because Yamana was seventy years of age, his strength was gone, and in the end he simply passed away. He was given the posthumous name of Empeki-in. But that Katsumoto died thus at the age of forty-four and still in possession of his energies is not the sole instance when, on the death of one antagonist who had fought with pride in his brute spirit, the other one has invariably also died.

Fighting in the Provinces and Peasant Uprisings

The first and most obvious result of the spread of fighting to the provinces after 1477 was the exposure of a far wider range of people to the ravages and hardships of war. While there had been scattered outbursts and strategical forays in the provinces from the outset of hostilities in 1467, the Ōnin War was perhaps unique in Japanese history for its concentration over such a long period within an extremely limited area (the city of Kyoto and its adjacent districts). But once certain major phases of the war, such as the Hatakeyama dispute, had been transferred to regions outside the vicinity of the Capital, the war itself became inextricably bound up with the endemic unrest and ferment of the countryside.

The word countryside, for the purpose of the present discussion, refers to the rural areas of central Japan, and, more specifically, to the two provinces of Yamashiro and Yamato. For it was in these lands that, during the preceding half-century, agrarian unrest had manifested itself in the form of peasant uprisings of such size, organization, and frequency that they must be re-

garded as part of a distinct and significant social movement. There
are a number of reasons, some of which I have already noted, why
this particular section of the country came to be the spawning
ground for armed revolts that were soon to challenge large armies
and to intimidate nearly all quarters of the ruling classes.

As the power of the Bakufu waned, its sphere of activities became restricted to an increasingly small area. The province of
Yamashiro, in particular, came to occupy a disproportionately important role in the efforts of the Ashikaga government to maintain
its financial solvency; and Bakufu leaders were forced to impose
a heavy burden of taxation on the farmers of Yamashiro and its
neighboring lands. These leaders also tended to disrupt the state
of affairs in Yamashiro by their handling of the local post of constable. While most of the constable appointments in the central
and western provinces were monopolized by great daimyo families,
the same office in Yamashiro had a high turnover in occupancy.
Appointment as Yamashiro constable was usually held on a concurrent basis by the head of the board of retainers, although the
Bakufu also used the position on occasion for political patronage.
In any event, this insecurity of office, coupled with the Bakufu's
further policy of establishing direct relationships with neighboring
warriors, made difficult the development of an organized constable-
daimyo domain in Yamashiro.

Another factor contributing to unrest in the central provinces
during these years was the increasing pressure of the great estate
holders on their remaining tribute-paying lands. As the estate system continued to disintegrate at a rapid rate throughout the country, the important religious institutions attempted desperately to
retain, at all costs, their holdings near home. But the traditional
estate as an economic and political unit had already become an
anachronism. The estate holder had no special power of his own to
retain lands even in the central provinces. He survived, as it were,
partly because of Bakufu policy, which favored the estate system,
and partly because of the competitive conditions in provinces like
Yamato and Yamashiro, where no single local samurai or other
warrior was able to exert his hegemony over the others. If one stalwart sought to dominate the province, for example, another could

always, for tactical reasons, raise the banner of support for the estate holder. As we shall see, this was what occurred during the Yamashiro Uprising of 1485.

This relationship between great religious institutions and contending samurai is best observed in the province of Yamato, where the Kōfuku-ji of Nara was the traditionally dominant land-holding power. The Kōfuku-ji, however, could no longer mount an effective defense against such dynamic warriors as Furuichi, Ochi, Tsutsui, and Tōichi.[1] Nevertheless, as the result of Bakufu policy and the entanglement of these chieftains in the Hatakeyama succession dispute, the temple remained the foremost titular institution in the province. Leaders of the Kōfuku-ji even continued to discharge the duties of Yamato constable, as they had done throughout the first century and more of Muromachi rule.

The final, and in many ways the most significant, factor that must be discussed in regard to agrarian distress in Yamashiro and Yamato is the high degree of commercial development that was characteristic of these provinces. In the previous discussion of the sake brewers and pawnbrokers of Kyoto we noted the rapid growth during Muromachi of a class of affluent brewer-brokers who, with Bakufu protection, were able to accumulate great sums of capital and to enter the field of usury on a large scale. The moneylender soon became an indispensable agent, not only for the luxury-loving warrior and aristocrat of the Capital, but for the nearby peasant as well.

The picture of the heavily taxed peasant confronted by the rapidly expanding and officially favored capitalist is a familiar one in Japanese history. Pressed to meet the exacting demands of the payments collector and helpless in the face of natural disaster, the peasant was also a frequent victim of price fluctuations to which he could not effectively adjust because of the nature of his planting and harvesting cycle. Thus he often had no recourse but to approach the moneylender for funds he hoped would tide over until better times. Since the average peasant had little in the way of

---

[1] See section in Chapter V on the Hatakeyama succession dispute for information about the activities of these Yamato warriors in the struggle between the two Hatakeyama.

personal possessions to offer, he was usually obliged to put up as collateral whatever interest he might have in land. In this way many small holdings throughout the central provinces came to be mortgaged to the moneylender and, upon failure of payment, fell permanently into his hands. The gravity of this problem can be seen in the fact that virtually every uprising around the years of the Ōnin War had as its sole, or at least partial, aim destruction of the pawnshops and demands for cancellation of debts, or acts of grace.

These conditions of rural unrest and the resulting course of peasant uprisings in the central provinces during the fifteenth century have become the focal point for important research into this period, and, indeed, have become a means for interpreting the Ōnin War itself. The most influential figure in this field of research has been Professor Suzuki Ryōichi, whose work over the past twenty-five or more years has produced certain general premises about the nature of peasant uprisings that are almost universally accepted in Japanese academic circles today.[2] Whatever one's personal opinions of Professor Suzuki's ideological convictions, it is impossible to understand modern trends in scholarship on the Muromachi period without at least a partial grasp of his interpretations.

Professor Suzuki has chosen to view this period largely in terms of class struggle, with the result that he pays slight attention to certain political developments that have been stressed in the present study. The most serious objection that must be directed toward Suzuki's work concerns his attempts to oversimplify the motive force behind these peasant movements by asserting that, no matter what their outward form, all uprisings at this time were reactions by the peasantry against an excessive feudal levy.[3] As we shall see, the uprisings had a variety of targets, and were not directed solely against the tax collector or the tribute assessor. Suzuki's statement,

---

[2] Typical of Professor Suzuki's works are: *Junsui Hōken-sei Seiritsu ni Okeru Nōmin Tōsō; Doikki Ron*, in Chūō Kōron Sha, *Shin-Nihon Shi Kōza; Nihon Chūsei no Nōmin Mondai.*

[3] Suzuki, "Bummei Jūni Nen no Tokusei ni Tsuite," in *Nihon Chūsei no Nōmin Mondai*, p. 113.

therefore, is tantamount to saying: a) the peasant masses suffered under unbearable taxes and levies; b) as a result they struck out blindly until they gained relief from these taxes and levies. In a very general sense this was probably true; but to form a simple, set conclusion like this seems to risk losing sight of many other political, social, and economic factors that contributed to this phenomenon of the peasant uprising.

Suzuki and his colleagues divide early Muromachi society into two basic classes, the exploiters and the exploited. They list as exploiters the Bakufu, the estate holder, the military representative and the usurer-capitalist, and as the exploited, the peasantry. The composition of the peasantry, which Suzuki terms *hyakushō*, is important. There were originally three grades of peasant: the holder of name-lands (*myōshu*); the producer (*sakunin*); and the lower-level producer (*gesakunin*). By the time of the peasant uprisings in the fifteenth century the producer, for all practical purposes, had merged with the holder, and the principal division within the peasantry was between this holder, as an incipient landlord, and the basic agricultural producer (now called *nōmin*).[4]

The key figure in this interpretation is the holder of name-lands, whose many facets can best be described in the phraseology or jargon favored by the Suzuki school of scholars: landholder in residence (*zaichi ryōshu*), who was in the process of destroying the last remaining interests of the estate holder, even while he himself was engaged as an estate functionary; collector of estate tribute; commercialist in charge of estate markets; warrior and retainer of a more powerful military man. As we can see, the holder of name-lands tended to merge with the exploiter class; yet he still remained very much a part of the peasantry and could join with and lead the peasants in their struggle against the principal exploiters. In fact it was this assumption of leadership by the holder of name-lands, according to Suzuki, that gave form and scope to the peasant uprisings around the time of the Ōnin War, and that made possible the great success of the 1485 Yamashiro Uprising.

The ranking of these upper-grade peasants varied considerably, from the small holder whose influence did not extend beyond his

[4] *Ibid.*, pp. 136–38.

own estate to the powerful samurai-level warrior. As we shall see, the name-land holder's relations with the basic producer were complex, differing according to time, place, and his own size. On occasion, especially during the early years of Muromachi, the holder of name-lands even found himself the target of peasant unrest.

Professor Suzuki divides the years of peasant unrest and struggle from the beginning of Ashikaga rule to the end of the Ōnin War into four stages:[5]

1. The early years of confusion during the war between the courts, when discontented peasants turned against their immediate oppressors, the estate functionaries, and sought to obtain their removal by submitting informal petitions (sosho) to the estate holder. As a form of protest, certain peasants abandoned their fields and fled the estate (chōsan). This was a time, as we have noted, of turmoil and competition among the functionaries, the local samurai, and other small-scale warriors after the breakdown of Kamakura and before the full establishment of Muromachi.

2. The later years of the war, when peasant activities within the estate took the form of joint grievances (gōso) presented to the estate holder, and organized field abandonment.

3. Beginning in 1428, the period of the true peasant uprising, which was characterized by leadership of the peasantry by the holders of name-lands and the expansion of activities beyond estate boundaries.

4. The province-wide uprisings (kuni-ikki) after the Ōnin War. With the failure of central and even provincial control, certain powerful warrior-peasants took over leadership of the general peasantry and posed an organized threat to the highest provincial authorities.

During the first two of the above stages, peasant activities were confined to the various estates and were aimed primarily at the abuses of the estate functionary and the excessive levies of the estate holder. On the whole, according to the Suzuki interpretation, there was no marked participation by these name-land holders

[5] These are conveniently classified in Inagaki Yasuhiko, "Ōnin-Bummei no Ran," in Iwanami Shoten, *Iwanami Kōza Nihon Rekishi*, VII, 176–77.

at this time in peasant activities, which were limited both in size and scope. It was only when leadership of the peasant movement was grasped by the holders of name-lands during the fifteenth century that the first genuine uprisings occurred. For the local holder, with his wider range of contacts as warrior and as small-scale commercialist responsible for the transport of produce and goods, was able to form pacts with name-land holders in other estates and to contribute a degree of organization previously unknown in peasant activities.

Once estate boundaries had been breached, the peasants could direct their discontent against other members of the "exploiter" class and not simply the estate holder. New targets included the constable, the Bakufu and, above all, the usurer.

Thus both the composition and the targets of the peasant movement changed radically with the commencement of full-scale uprisings. Even so, the motive force for these uprisings, in Suzuki's abstract language, was still the energy of the peasants (*nōmin,* exclusive of name-land holders), and the fundamental goal remained the lessening or removal of excessive levies. The usurer became a favorite target simply because he was the villain immediately responsible for the peasant's loss of land.[6] Had it not been for exploitation of the peasant through exorbitant levy and taxation in the first place, however, the usurer would not have been able to administer the final foreclosure.

While it would be impossible to describe all aspects and phases of these violent social protests that occurred with such frequency (sometimes two or three a year) during the decades before and after the Ōnin War, we can nevertheless make certain general observations that will help us understand their basic nature and trend. First, although uprisings occurred in many widely separated places, such as Harima, Bitchū, Wakasa, Kawachi, Ise, and even Kyushu, the great majority were centered in or near the cities of Kyoto and Nara. Second, although the insurgent peasants put forth a variety of demands over the years, including reduction of estate levies, removal of constables, and destruction of commercial bar-

[6] Suzuki, "Bummei Jūni Nen no Tokusei ni Tsuite," p. 115.

riers (*sekisho*),[7] again the great majority called for a cancellation of debts in the form of acts of grace. Those outbursts that did,
in fact, specifically demand debt cancellation are known by the
special term "act of grace uprisings" (*tokusei ikki*). Third, the
most violent uprisings seem to have taken place during years of
exceptional political unrest. Two of the three largest pre-Ōnin ris-
ings, for example, occurred in 1428 (this was also the first recognized peasant uprising) and in 1441. The year 1428 was the year
of Yoshimochi's death and of subsequent agitation within the
Bakufu over the selection of a successor,[8] and 1441 witnessed the
assassination of Yoshinori.

A typical uprising might occur in the following manner. Some-
time during the harvest season, between the seventh and eleventh
months, a group of peasants in estates near Kyoto or Nara would
rise up, form into a body, and spread to the city. There they would
receive the support of a number of townspeople, as well as that of
certain undersirable elements who would commence burning and
looting. If the insurgents were well organized, they might establish headquarters in a great monastery, such as the Tō-ji or the
Tōfuku-ji. After making preliminary attacks on the brokerage
houses and destroying some pawn receipts, they would demand
issuance of a general cancellation of debts. The Bakufu might try
to deal with the rioters by despatching troops, but on most occasions the military found themselves singularly unsuccessful in restoring order without yielding to at least part of the peasant demands.[9] On the contrary, Bakufu leaders, for reasons which we
will see, soon showed themselves to be suspiciously agreeable to
the issuance of acts of grace.

The act of grace, a seemingly simple decree proclaiming the
cancellation of debts, was to have endless ramifications among the

[7] Commercial barriers were erected by the Bakufu and other parties at strategic
points to collect tolls from travelers or those transporting goods.
[8] The Kantō deputy, Ashikaga Mochiuji, expected to receive the call, but
Bakufu leaders decided upon Yoshimochi's brother, Yoshinori. As a result,
Mochiuji harbored great ill will toward the new administration.
[9] This summary of a typical uprising is based largely on Suzuki, "Bummei
Jūni Nen no Tokusei ni Tsuite," p. 114.

various parties it affected. Before long it even came to occupy an important position in the Bakufu's own scheme of revenue devices.

Ostensibly the first acts of grace were a great boon to the debtor and a disaster to the creditor. But the disaster was not as great as it may have seemed, for the creditor had several means at hand to soften the blow. He could, for example, tighten his lending policy, raise rates, or limit the duration of loans. Since many of those who availed themselves most freely of the moneylender could ill afford to forsake his services or to be penalized in the future, the lender was eventually able to transfer much of his initial loss back to the debtor.[10]

In fact the party that probably suffered most severely from these early acts of grace was the Bakufu itself. We have seen how Bakufu leaders reserved the sole right to tax the brewer-brokers of the Capital and its environs, and, in addition to extraordinary levies, received regular monthly income from these establishments. Although we do not know the exact nature and extent of all Bakufu revenues, it seems certain that this commercial income came to occupy an increasingly important part. Now, however, the peasant uprisings and the acts of grace were causing interruption of its inflow, for the broker was obliged to pay taxes only on his inventory of pawns and notes. If these collaterals were destroyed or rendered void, there would obviously be no basis for taxation. Thus a major uprising and issuance of a general act of grace could result in a grievous financial loss for the Bakufu. Records indicate, in fact, that income from the brokers might cease for several months and perhaps even for a year after an uprising.[11]

Bakufu leaders attempted at first to recover some of their losses through an increase in emergency levies. Then, in 1454, they took a more direct approach to the problem. During the sixth month of that year a group of peasants had risen in the Yamashiro-Daigo district southeast of the Capital in protest against the erection of barriers, and in the ninth month had entered Kyoto to demand an act of grace. Even before the Bakufu could act, harried brokers

[10] Kuwayama Kōnen, "Muromachi Jidai no Tokusei," in Inagaki Yasuhiko and Nagahara Keiji, *Chūsei no Shakai to Keizai*, p. 500.
[11] *Ibid.*, p. 501.

agreed voluntarily to return certain notes of indebtedness. A few weeks later (on the twenty-ninth day of the ninth month) Bakufu leaders, far from endorsing these *de facto* or private acts of grace, issued an order prohibiting their application (*tokusei kinsei*).

Having taken this step to restore some degree of order and control, the Bakufu, on the twenty-ninth day of the tenth month, issued what has come to be known as a "percentage" act of grace (*buichi tokusei*). Any debtor who wished to enjoy the benefits of an act of grace could do so by paying to the Bakufu an amount equal to 10 per cent of the total owed. In this manner Bakufu leaders attempted to salvage some profit from the cancellation of debts. But, in fact, the income that accrued therefrom did not at all meet their expectations. For many of the same reasons that the debtor had been unable to take full advantage of the first acts of grace, those who had borrowed heavily again hesitated to come forth and do away with their debts. The relationship between certain debtors and their creditors could not be so easily destroyed.[12]

In the following year, 1455, the Bakufu issued another combination prohibition and percentage act of grace, this time giving the *creditor* the option to pay 10 percent (later increased to 20 percent) of the debt to the Bakufu in return for confirmation of his right to collect. According to a similar edict in 1457, if the creditor failed to take advantage of this option within sixteen days, the debtor could then pay the same amount and have the debt canceled. In this way, by playing one end against the other, Bakufu leaders finally achieved the results they desired.

The aim now was not to meet the demands of the debtor at all, but to extort more money from the creditor. In effect the Bakufu was suggesting that the broker-creditor invest in a form of insurance to protect his larger outlay in pawn receipts.[13] The creditor, after all, was the party who could best afford this additional cost. The sixteen-day option period, which the Bakufu added, was not designed to give the debtor his chance later, but to pressure the creditor into quicker action. Unlike the original percentage act of grace, whose goal had been to alter unrealistically the intimate

[12] *Ibid.*, p. 506.
[13] *Ibid.*, p. 511.

relationship between debtor and creditor by giving the former the opportunity to avoid his debt, this creditor option had no effect whatsoever on that relationship.

By the time of the Ōnin War, therefore, the act of grace had assumed a far different form from that envisioned by the peasants in their early revolts against "excessive feudal exaction." The question we must ask is precisely what effect did this distortion of the act of grace have on peasant aspirations? Data compiled on a percentage act of grace in 1480 reveals that not a single peasant applied either for confirmation or for cancellation of debt. The only peasant names that appear are those listed as defendants in applications by others for confirmation of debts.[14] In other words the later acts of grace were restricted almost exclusively in their effect to relationships between members of the ruling classes, and, in the opinion of Suzuki, had nothing whatsoever to do with the fundamental class struggle.[15] Even though it had been the efforts of the peasants that had brought about issuance of the act of grace, they ironically did not share in its benefits. The desperate peasant in revolt undoubtedly had little in the way of funds to pay even the ten or twenty percent necessary to receive cancellation of debt from the Bakufu.

Why, then, did the peasants continue their uprisings in quest of acts of grace? We can only speculate that they were able to acquire some relief through the destruction of pawn slips and through private arrangements with the brokers under duress. Meanwhile the Bakufu took advantage of these chaotic conditions to extort additional revenue from the usurer-capitalist, warrior, aristocrat, and other members of the ruling classes who were deeply involved in mutual lending relations.

It was during these conditions of peasant unrest and organized protest that major fighting was transferred to the provinces in the late 1470s. Again it would be impossible to generalize about each phase of this fighting as it unfolded in various parts of the country; but probably the most significant, and by far the best

[14] Suzuki, "Bummei Jūni Nen no Tokusei ni Tsuite," p. 126.
[15] *Ibid.*, p. 129.

documented, aspect was the continuation of the Hatakeyama succession dispute in southern Yamashiro and Yamato. This intra-family struggle had begun nearly thirty years before, and had been one of the principal sparks to ignite the conflagration that became the Ōnin War. Both Hatakeyama contenders had fought at the forefront in the Capital, Masanaga for the Hosokawa and Yoshinari for the Yamana. Now, after the end of hostilities in Kyoto, they were again locked in struggle in the provinces.

The relationships between the various participants in this fighting—the respective Hatakeyama leaders, the powerful warriors of Yamato, such as Furuichi and Tsutsui, who had fought for both sides through the years, and the Kōfuku-ji as a great estate holder in both Yamato and Yamashiro—were complex indeed. While there is no need to trace here their endless struggles, we can be certain that the suffering and devastation they brought upon the people and the land were considerable. Finally, in the twelfth month of 1485, the peasants of southern Yamashiro, their patience exhausted, rose up to expel both armies; and such was the force of their rebellion that the fighting between the Hatakeyama was brought to a speedy conclusion.[16] The insurgents immediately issued three demands: 1) that both Hatakeyama armies withdraw from Yamashiro; 2) that all estates seized by the military be returned to their original holders; 3) that all barriers within the province be removed, and that no new ones be erected. On the thirteenth day of the second month of 1486 a group of thirty-six, representing the peasants, convened at the Byōdō-in in Uji to establish the administration by means of which they were to conduct the affairs of southern Yamashiro for nearly eight years.

This extremely successful action in Yamashiro was a genuine province-wide uprising, and the thirty-six who took command were local samurai. Their first aim was to bring an end to the fighting and to eject the "foreign" military from Yamashiro. Second, they called for a return of lands to the estate holders, thereby granting what appeared to be a great boon to the Kōfuku-ji and others.

[16] Not too much is really known about the early days of this uprising and the extraordinary military success of the peasants. See Nakamura Kichiji, *Tokusei to Doikki*, pp. 118–19.

Some temple officials were apparently naïve enough to suppose that the clock could really be turned back. As we shall see, the terms under which these holders regained their lands were not at all what they had expected. For, although both Hatakeyama leaders had been driven from the province, the Yamashiro Uprising was still a victory for the Masanaga side, if not for Masanaga himself.

Not only the two Hatakeyama, but also the Hosokawa and Yamana camps they represented, differed in their attitudes toward the estates. This was not a fundamental ideological rift, but a variance in the respective tactical approaches of the two forces to the confiscation of estate lands. While the Hosokawa were, in general, the political "ins," the Yamana were the political "outs"; consequently, while the former were able to cloak their actions by outwardly espousing the Bakufu's policy of preference for the estate holder, the latter were forced to take whatever measures they could in dealing with the holder and his lands.

In areas like Yamato and southern Yamashiro, where there was continuous fighting between the Masanaga and the Yoshinari forces, this tactical alignment had real significance, even down to warriors in the individual estates. No one could afford to remain neutral. In Kōfuku-ji's Komano estate in southern Yamashiro, for example, the two principal contenders for control, Koma and Tsubai, both had ties with the Hatakeyama leaders. Koma was allied to the Masanaga forces and held the estate posts of *kumon* and *geshi*, while Tsubai enjoyed the backing of the Yoshinari side and aimed at establishing direct jurisdiction over the land through receipt as military representative (*daikan ukeoi*).[17] Here, then, we see one warrior working through the established order and the other attempting to destroy it. Shortly after the council of thirty-six directed the return of lands to the estate holder, both Koma and Tsubai petitioned the Kōfuku-ji for recognition of their positions in the estate. The Kōfuku-ji elders, needless to say, bestowed their blessing on Koma, who they hoped would become an obedient representative. But Koma had no more intention of allowing the

---

[17] Suzuki, "Yamashiro Kuni-ikki to Ōnin no Ran," in *Nihon Chūsei no Nōmin Mondai*, pp. 165–66.

Kōfuku-ji to resume direct control over estate affairs than did Tsubai. And when temple officials tried to assess the holding at Komano, Koma blocked their entrance.[18]

Thus the return of lands to the direct rule of the estate holder was largely an illusion. Certain local samurai had risen at the head of the peasants of southern Yamashiro to drive out the foreign military, including Masanaga and Yoshinari. But the Masanaga and Yoshinari tactical alignments still persisted. In fact it was the Masanaga side that had gained the upper hand in this instance, for the council of thirty-six, by ordering the return of lands, revealed that they were willing to work through the existing order in the Hosokawa-Hatakeyama Masanaga manner.[19] They maintained their interest in Komano estate through the warrior-functionary Koma, who, despite the sham of Kōfuku-ji overlordship, was attempting to establish just as firm personal control as had Tsubai.

Professor Suzuki interprets this period of the later fifteenth century as a time that witnessed the establishment of a "pure" feudal system.[20] By this he means the elimination or emasculation of outmoded institutions, such as the estate, the Bakufu, and the constable-daimyo, and the formation of pure feudal relations between the holder of name-lands and the lesser peasantry. It seems however that we should, in evaluating this post-Ōnin period, seek to gain a wider perspective politically, as well as economically and socially. Throughout this study the growth and development of the constable-daimyo have been used as points of departure from which to examine the course of affairs leading to the Ōnin War. The war and its aftermath, for the many reasons already cited, are generally regarded as the terminal period of the constable-daimyo as an historical figure. It was at this time that he gave way to the *sengoku-daimyō* (daimyo of the period of war in the provinces), a smaller and more locally oriented warrior chieftain. As a means of recapitulating some of the major characteristics of the constable-daimyo and of suggesting the nature of his successor, the provincial

[18] *Ibid.*

[19] *Ibid.*, p. 170.

[20] This is the subject of *Junsui Hōken-sei Seiritsu ni Okeru Nōmin Tōsō.*

wars-daimyo, the following five-point comparison will be useful:[21]

1. The provincial wars-daimyo did not, by and large, emerge from the ranks of the constable-daimyo. Rather he came from the class of deputy constables and local samurai warriors who served within the various constable-daimyo domains.

2. While the constable-daimyo was responsible for the destruction of the estate system, this was not his conscious aim. He sought instead to use the estate structure to increase his own power. The provincial wars-daimyo, on the other hand, rejected entirely the concept of estate lands.

3. The public authority and prestige of the Bakufu were essential elements in the growth of the constable-daimyo. Without the Bakufu as an effective central government, the provincial wars-daimyo relied only upon his own strength and authority, and ruled in accordance with his personal House laws (*kahō*).

4. The constable-daimyo had depended to a large extent upon the recruitment of local samurai, who were associated regionally in clan-centered groups (e.g., *akutō*, or "bands"). While retaining his own clan structure as a nucleus, the provincial wars-daimyo recruited individual vassals on the basis of a more intimate feudal relationship.

5. Unlike the constable-daimyo, whose only contact with the peasant had been through the estate structure, the provincial wars-daimyo sought to establish direct feudal relations with the peasantry.

[21] What follows is paraphrased from Sugiyama Hiroshi, "Shugo Ryōkoku-sei no Tenkai," in Iwanami Shoten, *Iwanami Kōza Nihon Rekishi*, VII, 84–85.

A Note on Primary Sources

Apart from documents and records relating directly to the government, there are three principal classes of source materials available for the study of Japanese history during the mid-fifteenth century: 1) public and private papers, usually in the form of correspondence between persons or organizations, and known in Japanese under the general term *komonjo*; 2) personal or semiofficial journals compiled by members of the aristocracy, officers of the Bakufu and imperial court, and by Buddhist prelates; 3) accounts or histories of the times, frequently bearing titles based on the year periods they cover, and almost without exception of anonymous authorship and unknown date of composition.

In many ways the first category of public and private papers is the richest source for the study of fifteenth-century Japan. It is also the most difficult to exploit. Private papers are widely scattered and often hard to obtain; moreover, they are linguistically complex, requiring in some cases a technique bordering on decipherment. Yet these papers are of such great value for an understanding of the economic and social growth of Muromachi Japan that they have become the object of intense and widespread study among interested scholars. In addition to detailed information on economic matters, such as the day-to-day transactions of great estate holders and their distant managers, *komonjo* contain intimate glimpses into the social relationships of the period, as reflected in choice of vocabulary, salutation, and form of address.

But it has been the second class of materials that has provided the foundation for traditional studies in the past. This was the golden age of the journal as a primary historical source, a development that can be attributed to the concentration of both military government and imperial court in the city of Kyoto, where any person of high connections could have ready access to the latest news of the day; and the intimate relationship between successive Ashikaga shoguns and certain journal-keeping Buddhist prelates, especially those of the Zen sects, who enjoyed a greater degree of participation in government than at any other time in Japanese history. When the Ōnin War caused disintegration of the central government and brought an end to Kyoto's unique role as the spiritual and administrative heart of the country, the journal as a historical record began to decline.[1] Buddhist prelates no longer had the same degree of privilege as before, while many of the aristocrats, impoverished and neglected, were forced to depart the Capital in search of new means of livelihood. Even those who remained found that the events of Kyoto held little of their former significance.

Most of the Muromachi journals as well as the *komonjo* are written in a linguistic style called *wa-yō kambun,* or Chinese-type composition, heavily weighted with Japanese vocabulary, honorifics, compound verbs, and the like. This style of writing is not conducive to literary excellence, and the journals, despite their factual value, are artistically limited.

Two of the most important journals for the early years of the fifteenth century are the *Manzai Jugō Nikki* and the *Kammon Gyoki.* Manzai, a Shingon priest of the Daigo-ji, was a confidant of successive shoguns, and his journal, which spans the years 1411–35, is indispensable to those interested in the period of Yoshimochi and Yoshinori. The *Kammon Gyoki* (covering selected years from 1416 until 1448), on the other hand, was compiled by Go-Sukōin, a member of the imperial family and father of the Emperor Go-Hanazono. It is interesting to compare Go-Sukōin's journal with Manzai's account in order to gain the perspective of both the aristocrat and the cleric. A third journal of major importance that should be mentioned with these two is the

[1] This is not to say that journal-keeping ceased; but the post-Ōnin journals do not have the same value for the study of political history as do those compiled before the war.

Kennai-ki, a record kept by the aristocrat Madenokōji Tokifusa (1394–1457). It is now in the process of publication and should be of immense value to the general student as successive volumes are made available.

Among those journals compiled by officials of the Bakufu and the imperial court, there are the records of Saitō Mototsune (1394–1471) and his son Chikamoto, entitled *Saitō Mototsune Nikki* (covering 1440–56) and *Saitō Chikamoto Nikki* (covering 1465–67), and the *Yasutomi-ki* (covering 1401–55) of Nakahara Yasutomi (1399–1457). The two Saitō were officials of the Bakufu's administrative board, whereas Nakahara was in the records department of the chancellor's office at court.

Three journals that I have found especially valuable for the purposes of this study are the *Inryōken Nichiroku,* the *Hekizan Nichiroku,* and the *Daijō-in Jisha Zōjiki.* We have already noted the first of these, which was a product of the office of Inryōken at the Shōkoku-ji. Owing to the close relationship between its chief pre-Ōnin author, Kikei Shinzui, and the Shogun Yoshimasa, the *Inryōken Nichiroku* is an exceptionally intimate record of affairs in the Capital during these years. The *Hekizan Nichiroku* (covering 1459–63 and 1465–68) was also recorded by a Zen priest, Taikyoku Zōsu of the Tōfuku-ji. It differs from the other journals in style, being more nearly related to pure Chinese (*kambun*). Perhaps because of this greater stylistic freedom, the *Hekizan Nichiroku* comes closer to capturing the true spirit of the age than do those journals burdened with the stereotyped language of *wa-yō kambun.* Indeed some passages of Taikyoku's record are almost literary in quality.

The *Daijō-in Jisha Zōjiki* is a journal kept by the abbots of the Daijō-in of the Kōfuku-ji in Nara between the years 1450 and 1527. It is one of the most important sources for the study of the late fifteenth and early sixteenth centuries. Not only do its voluminous pages contain invaluable economic information relating to the affairs of both the Kōfuku-ji and the Kasuga Shrine, but, owing to the exalted connections of one of the chief compilers, Jinson (1430–1508),[2] they also provided many entries dealing with the latest politics of the day. From the standpoint of the present study, the *Daijō-in Jisha Zōjiki* was especially useful for references to the independent warriors of Yamato Province, whose activities we can observe throughout the Hatakeyama succession dispute.

The third class of source materials—accounts and histories—is generally known as war tales (*gunki monogatari*) and is fully within the

[2] Jinson was the son of the celebrated courtier Ichijō Kanera (1402–81).

mainstream of Japanese linguistic development stemming from the
Heike Monogatari and the *Taihei-ki*. After the *Taihei-ki*, which deals
with the war between the courts, the quality, but not the number, of
these war tales declines, and it is difficult to assess their historical re-
liability. Nevertheless, although none have been extensively studied
or annotated until now, the later war tales must, apart from those
passages that are obviously hyperbolic, be accepted as fairly accurate
records of the times.

The *Chronicle of Ōnin* and two other tales, the *Jōkyū-ki*[3] and the
Meitoku-ki, comprise what are sometimes called the *sandaiki,* or "records of three periods," which span nearly two and a half centuries of
history from Kamakura to mid-Muromachi. Further, *The Chronicle of
Ōnin* itself encompasses several separate tales, such as the *Kakitsu-ki,*
which deals with the assassination of Yoshinori, and the *Chōroku-
Kanshō-ki,* based on the Hatakeyama succession dispute. Thus *The
Chronicle of Ōnin* is the final work of one tradition and the focal point
of another. As such it occupies a position among the most important
records of its kind within the century or more before and after the
Ōnin War.

The *Chronicle of Ōnin* is divided into three parts. The first describes
the extravagance of Yoshimasa and the origins of dispute within the
Shiba, the Hatakeyama, and the shogunal house itself. It concludes
with the battle of Goryō between the two Hatakeyama in the first
month of 1467. The outbreak of hostilities between Yamana and Hosokawa, the flight of the shogun's brother to the provinces, and the early
battling in the Capital are recorded in Part Two; and in Part Three
there are a condensed version of the *Kakitsu-ki* and accounts of various
battles, interspersed with anecdotes and descriptions of other events,
until the deaths of Yamana Sōzen and Hosokawa Katsumoto in 1473.
The last four years of the war are not covered by *The Chronicle of
Ōnin.*

Two companion works that are usually associated with *The Chronicle
of Ōnin* are the *Ōnin Bekki* and the *Ōnin Ryakki.* Apart from a variant introduction and a shorter text, the *Ōnin Bekki* is almost identical,
word for word, with *The Chronicle of Ōnin.* The *Ōnin Ryakki,* on the
other hand, is an entirely separate work, at least stylistically. It covers
roughly the same material as *The Chronicle of Ōnin,* but is heavily
laden with Buddhist moralisms and possesses a vocabulary and style
unlike that of the usual war tale.

[3] Dealing with the Jōkyū Incident of 1221.

A final work that I found indispensable as an aid in translating *The Chronicle of Ōnin* is the *Chōhen Ōnin-ki.* It was written at a much later date, probably during the Tokugawa period, and brings together a number of accounts that are within what we might call the "Ōnin tradition." The opening section is entitled the *Ōnin Zenki,* and deals with the same material as the *Chōroku-Kanshō-ki.* This is followed by the *Ōnin Kōki* (Broad Chronicle of Ōnin), derived from *The Chronicle of Ōnin* itself, and two final sections, the *Ōnin Kōki* (Later Chronicle of Ōnin) and the *Zoku-Ōnin Kōki* (*Later Chronicle of Ōnin, Continued*), that trace the narrative of events for the century following the Ōnin War until the rise of Oda Nobunaga. The great merit of the *Chōhen Ōnin-ki* lies in its clarity of style and grammar. It is, in effect, a "revised edition" of *The Chronicle of Ōnin* and other earlier works.

Akutō 悪党

Bands, or groups, formed for joint action by local warriors, especially in the home provinces, at the end of the Kamakura period.

Ando 安堵

Shogunal confirmation of landholding.

Ashigaru 足軽

Low-ranking foot soldiers engaged by armies on a large scale from the fourteenth century. *Ashigaru* were particularly notorious for their destructiveness in street-fighting during the Ōnin War.

Bugyō–nin 奉行人

Administrator.

Buichi tokusei 分一徳政

"Percentage" act of grace.

Chōsan 逃散

Absconding, a practice engaged in by discontented peasants of the early Muromachi period, who abandoned their fields as a means of protest against oppressive landholders.

Daijōe 大嘗会

Great Thanksgiving ceremony at the time of an emperor's accession.

Daikan 代官

Representative.

Daikan ukeoi 代官請負

Receipt as military representative.

Daimyō 大名

A baron or overlord in control of an extensive domain.

Dajō daijin 太政大臣

Chancellor of the imperial government.

Doikki 土一揆

Peasant uprising.

Dorei 奴隷

Slave.

Dosō 土倉

Pawnbrokerage.

Gekokujō 下剋上

"Those below overthrow those above," a term used to characterize social upheaval at various levels during the medieval period.

Gesakunin 下作人

Lower-level peasant producer.

Geshi 下司

An administrative office in the estate.

Go-kenin 御家人

Houseman, or direct vassal, of the shogun.

Go-kōnōyaku 御公納役

Regular payment, or tax, due the Ashikaga Bakufu from the constable.

Goryōsho 御領所

The holdings and rights of the shogunal branch of the Ashikaga family.

Gosan 五山

Five (famous Zen) temples. During the Muromachi period there were five in Kyoto and five in Kamakura.

Go-seibai Shikimoku   御成敗式目

Official title of the Jōei Code of 1232, which became the model for military law in succeeding centuries.

Gōso   嗷訴

Protest petition.

Gōson   郷村

Village during the Muromachi period.

Gōzoku   豪族

A powerful, locally based warrior family.

Hanzei   半済

Equal division system, in which the Muromachi constable was allowed to assign half the income of certain estates to warriors under his jurisdiction.

Hi-gokenin   非御家人

Warriors who were not housemen of the shogun.

Hikitsuke-shū   引付衆

Board of coadjutors.

Honjo ichien shoryō   本所一円所領

Lands controlled entirely by religious institutions (i.e., to which no steward or other military officer had been appointed).

Honjo-ka   本所化

Process by which the constable took over the functions of the estate holder.

Honryō ando jitō   本料安堵地頭

Steward confirmed in his holdings. See *Shin'on jitō.*

Horikoshi kubō   堀越公方

Informal title held by Ashikaga Masatomo and his successors, who contended for control of the eastern provinces from their base at Horikoshi in Izu Province after the break-up of Ashikaga hegemony in that region during the mid-fifteenth century. See *Koga kubō*.

Hyakushō 百姓

Peasant.

Hyōjōshū 評定衆

Council of state.

Hyōrōmai 兵粮米

Commissariat rice.

Hyōrō ryōsho 兵粮料所

Estate funds granted to warriors in the early Muromachi period.

Ichimon 一門

Clan, or extended family.

Ikki 一揆

A league and, by extension, the action of such a league.

Jidai 地代

Feudal rent.

Jinushi 地主

Landlord.

Ji-samurai 地侍

Local samurai warrior. See *Kokujin*.

Jisha honjoryō 寺社本所領

Literally, estate lands held by religious institutions; but during the Muromachi period this term was loosely used to refer to all estate lands that had not yet been confiscated by the military.

Jitō 地頭

Steward.

Jitō-uke　地頭請

Receipt and administration of estate income by the steward.

Kagariya banyaku　篝屋番役

Guard duty in the streets of Kyoto.

Kahō　家法

House law.

Kamakura ōban yaku　鎌倉大番役

Guard duty at Kamakura.

Kampaku　関白

Imperial regent.

Kanrei　官領

Shogunal deputy.

Kantō goryō　関東御領

Eastern domains of the Kamakura Bakufu.

Kantō kanrei　関東官領

Deputy to the Kantō *kubō;* an office traditionally occupied by the Uesugi family.

Kantō kubō　関東公方

The highest ranking officer of the Ashikaga in Kamakura. The government of the Kantō *kubō* mirrored in miniature the Bakufu in Kyoto.

Karita rōzeki　苅田狼藉

Power granted the Muromachi constable to deal with harvest disorders and the cutting and theft of crops.

Kendan-ken　検断権

Authority in criminal and punitive cases.

Kessho 闕所

A confiscated holding.

Koga kubō 古河公方

Descendants of the last Kantō *kubō*, Ashikaga Mochiuji, who held out at Koga in the province of Shimōsa in opposition to the Horikoshi *kubō*. See *Horikoshi kubō*.

Kokuga 国衙

Old provincial administration of the *ritsu-ryō* system.

Kokujin 国人

Local samurai warrior. See *Ji-samurai*.

Kokushi 国司

Provincial governor.

Komonjo 古文書

Ancient document.

Kōshitsu-ryō 皇室領

Estate lands held by the imperial family.

Kubō 公方

Signified title for shogun during the Muromachi period; used also by the ranking Ashikaga officer in the east.

Kumon 公文

An administrative office in the estate.

Kuni-ikki 国一揆

Province-wide uprising.

Kura bugyō 倉奉行

A Bakufu administrator whose function was to collect tax payments in kind. See *Nōsen kata*.

Kyōto ōban yaku 京都大番役

Guard duty at the imperial palace.

Mandokoro 政所

Administrative board.

Mishin 未進

Unremitted rice income from the estates.

Misoya 味噌屋

Dealer in *miso* sauce.

Miuchi 御内

Special term for direct vassals of the Hōjō family.

Monchūjo 問注所

Board of inquiry.

Munebetsu-sen 棟別銭

Tax on households.

Myōden 名田

Rice lands, or name-fields.

Nengu 年貢

Annual rice income from estates.

Nōdosei 農奴制

Term used by certain Japanese scholars to describe the transition in rural society during the early Muromachi period from so-called slave labor to landlord-peasant relations. System of serfdom.

Nōmin 農民

Farmer.

Nōsen kata 納銭方

Bakufu official authorized to collect tax payments in cash. See *Kura bugyō*.

Onshō 恩賞

Grants in award.

Ōshū tandai 奥州探題

Representative of the Bakufu dispatched to the northern provinces of Mutsu and Dewa.

Ōtabumi 大田文

Land registers.

Rensho 連署

Co-signer, an office instituted by the Hōjō regents.

Rimu 吏務

An official.

Ritsu-ryō 律令

Legal system established by the Taika Reform of 645.

Ryōkoku 領国

A term used in this study to designate the constable-daimyo domain.

Sakaya 酒屋

Sake brewer.

Sakunin 作人

Peasant producer.

Samurai-dokoro 侍所

Board of retainers.

Sandaiki 三代記

Literally, "records of three periods": *Jōkyū-ki, Meitoku-ki, The Chronicle of Ōnin.*

Sankan-shishiki 三管四職

The three shogunal deputy families and the four families qualified to head the board of retainers.

Sanmi ittai 三位一体

Literally, the trio or trinity; used in this study to designate the estate holder, the Bakufu, and the usurer.

Sekisho 関所

Commercial barrier.

Sekkan-ke watari-ryō 摂関家渡領

Estate lands belonging to the aristocratic Sekkan (imperial regent) families.

Sengoku jidai 戦国時代

Literally, the period of warring states; but more accurately, in the case of Japanese history, the period of war in the provinces or the period of warring barons, which extended roughly from the Ōnin War to the demise of the Ashikaga Bakufu in 1573.

Sensei taisei 専制体制

Authoritarian structure or authoritarianism.

Shiki 職

A right (e.g., in land).

Shikken 執権

Shogunal regent, an office held by the Hōjō under the Kamakura Bakufu.

Shin'on jitō 新恩地頭

Steward who received a new benefice in the form of land or interest in land during the early Kamakura period. See *Honryō ando jitō.*

Shisetsu jungyō 使節遵行

Power granted the constable by the Muromachi Bakufu to enforce judicial decisions and to ensure the transfer of confiscated lands to the winning claimant.

Shitaji chūbun 下地中分

A judicial decision whereby estate lands were divided between the holder and the steward.

Shitsuji　執事

Assistant (e.g., to the shogun).

Shōen　荘園

Estate.

Shōen ryōshu　荘園領主

Estate holder.

Shōgun gosho naiban yaku　将軍御所内番役

Guard duty at the shogunal palace.

Shōkan　荘官

Estate functionary.

Shōmyō　小名

Holder of name-lands which were not extensive enough to qualify him as a daimyo.

Shoryō　所領

Lands under the control of an individual.

Shoshi　所司

Head of the board of retainers.

Shoshi　庶子

Member of a branch family.

Shugo　守護

Constable.

Shugo-bito hihō jōjō　守護人非法条々

Prohibitions against constable activities.

Shugo buyaku　守護夫役

Corvée levies made by the constable.

Shugo-dai 守護代

Deputy constable.

Shugo daimyō 守護大名

Constable-daimyo.

Shugo ryōkoku-ka 守護領国化

Transition to the constable domain, a phrase used to describe establishment of the constable-daimyo domain in early Muromachi.

Shugo-uke 守護請

An arrangement whereby the collection of rice income and the administration of estate affairs were placed in the hands of the constable.

Sōryō 惣領

Family head.

Soshō 訴訟

Informal petition.

Sō-tsuibushi 総追捕使

A constabulary or police official from the Heian period, who was the forerunner of the Kamakura constable.

Taihon sankajō 大犯三ケ条

The powers granted the early Kamakura constable, which were codified in the Jōei Code.

Taishō 大将

General, or military commander.

Tandai 探題

Deputy.

Tansen 段銭

A land tax.

Tō 党

Party, or group.

Tokusei 徳政

A decree authorizing cancellation of debt and translated as "act of grace."

Tokusei kinsei 徳政禁制

Prohibition of act of grace.

Tokusō 得宗

An alternate name of Hōjō Yoshitoki, which was used to designate the head of the Hōjō family during Kamakura times.

Tōryō 棟梁

Military leader.

Tozama 外様

Non-hereditary (e.g., daimyo).

Ukon'e-taishō 右近衛大将

Captain of the Inner Palace Guards, Right Division.

Wa-yō kambun 和様漢文

Chinese-style writing overlaid with strongly Japanese idiom.

Yoriai 寄合

Hōjō family council.

Za 座

Trade guild.

Zaichi ryōshu-ka 在地領主化

Landholder in residence. Certain Japanese scholars envision a steady process during the Muromachi period of local warriors gaining control of land at the expense of absentee estate holders.

BIBLIOGRAPHY

Arai Hakuseki. *Dokushi Yoron*. In *Jinnō Shōtōki*, etc., in *Nihon Bungaku Sōsho*, Vol. X. Tokyo, 1923.

Brown, Delmer M. *Money Economy in Medieval Japan*. New Haven, 1951.

Daijō-in Jisha Zōjiki. Edited by Tsuji Zennosuke *et al.* 12 vols. Tokyo, 1931-37.

Go-Hōkōin-ki. Edited by Hiraizumi Kiyoshi *et al.* 2 vols. Tokyo, 1930.

Gotō Tanji and Okami Masao, eds. *Taihei-ki*. 3 vols. Tokyo, 1962.

Hanawa Hokiichi, ed. *Gunsho Ruijū*. 30 vols. Tokyo, 1928-33.

  Bunshō-ki. Vol. XX, pp. 347-54.

  Chōroku-Kanshō-ki. Vol. XX, pp. 327-47.

  Kaei Sandai-ki. Vol. XXVI, pp. 66-142.

  Kakitsu-ki. Vol. XX, pp. 317-26.

  Meitoku-ki. Vol. XX, pp. 232-301.

  Ōnin Bekki. Vol. XX, pp. 471-507.

  Ōnin-ki. Vol. XX, pp. 355-419.

  Ōnin Ryakki. Vol. XX, pp. 420-70.

Hattori Kentarō. "Ashikaga Yoshimitsu." In Kawade Shobō, *Nihon Rekishi Kōza*, Vol. III. Tokyo, 1951.

Hekizan Nichiroku. In Kondō Keizō, *Kaitei Shiseki Shūran*, Vol. XXV. Tokyo, 1902.

Inagaki Yasuhiko. "Ōnin-Bummei no Ran." In Iwanami Shoten, *Iwanami Kōza Nihon Rekishi*, Vol. VII. Tokyo, 1963.

Inryōken Nichiroku. In Bussho Kankōkai, *Dai-Nihon Bukkyō Zensho*, Vols. CXXXIII-CXXXVII. Tokyo, 1912-13.

Ishii Susumu. "Kamakura Bakufu Ron." In Iwanami Shoten, *Iwanami Kōza Nihon Rekishi*, Vol. V. Tokyo, 1962.

Kammon Gyoki. Edited by Ōta Tōshirō. 2 vols. Tokyo, 1930.

Kasamatsu Hiroshi. "Chūsei Kessho-chi Kyūyo ni Kan Suru Ichi Kōsatsu." In Ishimoda Shō and Satō Shin'ichi, eds., *Chūsei no Hō to Kokka*. Tokyo, 1960.

"Kemmu Irai Tsuika Hō." In Satō Shin'ichi and Ikeuchi Yoshisuke, *Chūsei Hōsei Shiryō-shū*, Vol. II. Tokyo, 1957.

"Kemmu Shikimoku." In Satō Shin'ichi and Ikeuchi Yoshisuke, *Chūsei Hōsei Shiryō-shū*, Vol. II. Tokyo, 1957.

Kurokawa Tadanori. "Shugo Ryōkoku-sei to Shōen Taisei." In *Nihonshi Kenkyū*, No. 57 (1961), pp. 1-19.

Kuwayama Kōnen. "Muromachi Jidai no Tokusei." In Inagaki Yasuhiko and Nagahara Keiji, *Chūsei no Shakai to Keizai*. Tokyo, 1962.

Matsumoto Shimpachirō. "Namboku Chō Nairan no Sho-zentai." In *Chūsei Shakai no Kenkyū*. Tokyo, 1956.

Miura Hiroyuki. "Hino Tomiko." In *Rekishi to Jinbutsu*. Tokyo, 1916.

―――― "Shugo to Daimyō." In *Zoku Hōsei-shi no Kenkyū*. Tokyo. 1925.

"Muromachi Seiken e no Gimon." In Yūzankaku, *Shinsetsu Nihon Rekishi*, Vol. V. Tokyo, 1960.

Nagahara Keiji. "Namboku Chō Nairan." In Iwanami Shoten, *Iwanami Kōza Nihon Rekishi*, Vol. VI. Tokyo, 1963.

―――― "Namboku Chō no Nairan." In Tōkyō Daigaku Shuppan Kai, *Nihon Rekishi Kōza*, Vol. III. Tokyo, 1962.

―――― "Shugo Ryōkoku-sei no Tenkai." In *Nihon Hōken-sei Seiritsu Katei no Kenkyū*. Tokyo, 1961.

Nakada Kaoru. "Kamakura-Muromachi Ryō-Bakufu no Kansei ni Tsuite." In *Hōsei-shi Ronshū*, Vol. III. Tokyo, 1943.

Nakamura Kichiji. *Tokusei to Doikki*. Tokyo, 1959.

Nitta Eiji. "Kamakura Bakufu no Go-kenin Seido." In Tōkyō Daigaku Shuppan Kai, *Nihon Rekishi Kōza*, Vol. II. Tokyo, 1962.

Ōkubo Toshinori, *et al*. *Shiryō ni Yoru Nihon no Ayumi, Chūsei-hen*. Tokyo, 1958.

Ono Akitsugu. "Muromachi Bakufu no Sakaya Tōsei." In *Nihon Sangyō Hattatsu Shi no Kenkyū*. Tokyo, 1941.

Ōta Akira. *Seishi Kakei Dai-jiten*. 3 vols. Tokyo, 1934–36.

Satō Shin'ichi. "Bakufu Ron." In Chūō Kōron Sha, *Shin Nihon-shi Kōza*. Tokyo, 1949.

―――― "Kamakura Bakufu Seiji no Sensei-ka ni Tsuite." In Takeuchi Rizō, ed., *Nihon Hōken-sei Seiritsu no Kenkyū*. 2d ed. Tokyo, 1948.

―――― "Muromachi Bakufu Ron." In Iwanami Shoten, *Iwanami Kōza Nihon Rekishi*, Vol. VII. Tokyo, 1963.

―――― "Shugo Ryōkoku-sei no Tenkai." In Toyoda Takeshi, ed., *Chūsei Shakai*, in *Shin Nihon-shi Taikei*. 5th ed. Tokyo, 1956.

Shinoda, Minoru. *The Founding of the Kamakura Shogunate, 1180–1185*. New York, 1960.

Sugiyama Hiroshi. "Muromachi Bakufu." In Tōkyō Daigaku Shuppan Kai, *Nihon Rekishi Kōza*, Vol. III. Tokyo, 1962.

―――― "Shugo Ryōkoku-sei no Tenkai." In Iwanami Shoten, *Iwanami Kōza Nihon Rekishi*, Vol. VII. Tokyo, 1963.

Suzuki Ryōichi. "Bummei Jūni Nen no Tokusei ni Tsuite." In *Nihon Chūsei no Nōmin Mondai*. Kyoto, 1948.

———— "Doikki Ron." In Chūō Kōron Sha, *Shin Nihon-shi Kōza.* Tokyo, 1948.

———— *Junsui Hōken-sei Seiritsu ni Okeru Nōmin Tōsō.* Tokyo, 1949.

———— "Sengoku no Sōran." In Iwanami Shoten, *Iwanami Kōza Nihon Rekishi,* Vol. VIII. Tokyo, 1963.

———— "Yamashiro Kuni-ikki to Ōnin no Ran." In *Nihon Chūsei no Nōmin Mondai.* Kyoto, 1948.

Tanaka Yoshishige. *Ashikaga Jidai Shi.* Tokyo, 1923.

Tōkyō Teikoku Daigaku. *Dai Nihon Shiryō,* part 8, Vols. I–X. Tokyo, 1913–24.

Tōkyō Teikoku Daigaku Bungaku-bu. *Shiryō Sōran,* Vols. VII–VIII. Tokyo, 1932–33.

Tōyama Shigeki and Satō Shin'ichi. *Nihon-shi Kenkyū Nyūmon.* 2 vols. Tokyo, 1962.

Usui Nobuyoshi. *Ashikaga Yoshimitsu.* Tokyo, 1960.

Watanabe Yosuke. *Muromachi Jidai Shi.* Osaka, 1948.

Yasuda Motohisa. *Nihon Shōen-shi Gaisetsu.* Tokyo, 1957.

———— *Nihon Zenshi,* Vol. IV. Tokyo, 1958.

Yomiuri Shimbun Sha. *Nihon no Rekishi.* 12 vols. Tokyo, 1959–60.

INDEX